THE WORLD OF THE
AUTOMOBILE

THE WORLD OF THE AUTOMOBILE

By RALPH STEIN

with special photography by the author

A Ridge Press Book | Random House, New York

Editor-in-Chief: Jerry Mason
Editor: Adolph Suehsdorf
Art Director: Albert Squillace
Associate Editor: Moira Duggan
Associate Editor: Barbara Hoffbeck
Associate Editor: Jean Walker
Art Associate: Mark Liebergall
Art Associate: David Namias
Art Production: Doris Mullane

First printing. All rights reserved. Published
in the United States by Random House, Inc.,
New York, and simultaneously in Canada by
Random House of Canada, Limited, Toronto.
Prepared and produced by The Ridge Press, Inc.

Library of Congress Cataloging in Publication Data
Stein, Ralph, 1909-
        The world of the automobile.
        "A Ridge Press book."
        1. Automobiles. I. Title.
GV1021.S73   796.7   73-4729
ISBN 0-394-47964-5
Printed in Italy by Mondadori Editore, Verona.

CONTENTS

ACKNOWLEDGEMENTS

The automobile is the phenomenon of our time. At no other period in history was any object or device so important to the culture within which it existed. The car is a remarkable artifact which can be enjoyed as a work of art even while not in motion. It can display the results of all the skills which the human mind and hand have learned since a man first cut a log into slices to make himself wheels. But besides being a beautiful, stationary object whose shape and mechanical perfection please our eyes, this sculptured entity has another life—its life on the road, its only real reason for being. Both of these facets of its existence are important to the lover of the automobile. Further, the car does not dwell in a vacuum. It runs on roads, it is raced, it is displayed at exhibitions, it is collected, people inhabit it while it runs.

This is a rather personal book and I have tried to relate these varied aspects of automobilism to my own experiences—the joys, troubles, and frequent embarrassments I have known during my life in the world of the automobile.

I am deeply indebted to the many people and institutions who gave me such great assistance. William Harrah and his associates at the Harrah Automobile Collection in Reno, Nevada, went to great lengths to help me photograph some of the superb cars in the collection. Lord Montagu of Beaulieu and his notable staff at Britain's National Motor Museum not only gave me unstinting assistance in photographing the fine automobiles at Beaulieu, but they also helped me delve into the Museum's great photographic collection. Josiah K. Lilly III, whose museum, the Heritage Plantation of Sandwich, Massachusetts, displays a magnificent collection of cars, also graciously aided me in photographing some of them.

My friend, Tony Dawson of the British Leyland Motor Corporation, went to an unparalleled amount of trouble to help me, as did his son, Peter Dawson. Peter Garnier, editor of England's *Autocar*, very kindly gave me access to that venerable periodical's huge photographic files. Ronald Barker, Geoffrey Seaton, Gordon Cussens, D. E. A. Miller-Williams of Rolls-Royce, Patrick Fitz-Gibbon of Smith's Industries Ltd.—all in England—and James A. Bradley of the Detroit Public Library, Ed Bond, Luigi Chinetti, and Bob Grossman in America all get my sincere thanks for their aid. In France my friend Jacques Rousseau helped me greatly.

—R.S.

Tumbril's End, Westbrook, Connecticut

1.

RECOLLECTIONS

None of the cars in this book is an "ordinary" automobile. I would no more enjoy writing about or photographing a Ford Galaxie or a Chevrolet Impala or, say, a Hillman Minx or a Simca than the reader would be in hearing about such common fare. He would not, I think, have picked up this volume if he did not have an educated taste in motor cars.

But how and why do some of us acquire this special taste in cars? I cannot speak for anyone but myself, although I have, of course, read of many other people's adventures with automobiles. In almost every instance these men have written about their intimate affairs with cars from infancy onward. They talk about having taken apart Model T Ford transmissions when they were eleven years old. I am almost ashamed to say that I didn't get behind the wheel of a car until I was twenty-one.

My parents never owned an automobile. They went places in trolley cars or aboard New York's Third Avenue "el." For state occasions like weddings or funerals they negotiated with one of a group of hire-car roughnecks who parked several vast Twin-Six Packard touring cars on a corner a few blocks from where we lived. For two dollars (this was fifty years ago) they'd drive the whole family from the wilderness of the Bronx to the mysterious terra incognita of Brooklyn. For shorter trips two-cylinder Renault taxicabs cruised the neighborhood.

The kids on my block played a game common in the early twenties. We'd sit on the curb and take turns identifying approaching cars as they came past an intersection some two hundred feet away. A kid would yell "Cole!" If he was right he'd win a point. If it turned out to be a Daniels, he'd lose a point. One show-off kid would yell "Elmore!" every time to prove he knew more about obscure makes. But no Elmore ever went by. I was even worse. I'd screech "Hispano-Suiza!" once in a while, although it was firmly believed that I was just making up that outlandish name. Anyhow, no Hispanos ever cruised past us. (Or "Royals-Royces," either.)

I knew there were such cars. I'd seen them on my Saturday afternoon excursions into midtown Manhattan. (In those days a twelve-year-old could float around in New York quite safely.)

Rolls-Royces (Brewster-bodied Springfield versions) sat splendidly in a showroom on West 57th Street in what was then the General Motors building. Farther east on that elegant street were places where I could see Bébé Peugeots, Lancia Lambdas (next to Carnegie Hall), and Lalique glass radiator ornaments (in Nil Melior's emporium, which sold fancy accessories to people who owned Isotta Fraschinis and such). On Fifth Avenue near 59th Street, elephantine Renault 45's with gigantic *coupé de ville* bodywork were worth a quick, bored examination. For I just couldn't wait to hurry westward on 59th to the Hispano-Suiza showroom. Not to look at Hispanos, for they, too, were invariably burdened with dull limousine bodies, but to look again and again at the little boat-tailed Amilcar which shared floor space with the Hispanos.

By the time I was old enough to buy a car, the winds of the Depression had blown the foreign-car showrooms into limbo. It would be almost twenty years before they appeared again. So what did I buy? A new Model A Ford Deluxe Roadster for $551, complete with driving lessons and a quail ornament for the radiator cap.

At about the time I bought that boring Ford a friend of mine began acquiring the kinds of cars that would change my life: first, a Type 40 Bugatti, then a 3-litre Vanden Plas-bodied Bentley Tourer. Now I rode with my moneyed friend. The Ford lay in the garage much of the time. In a matter of months I gave the Model A to my brother and embarked on an automotive spree that has never ended. Since 1932 I've been owned at various times by four Alfa Romeos, five Rolls-Royces, a couple of Bentleys, a brace of Bugattis, a Boattail Packard, a Riley, an Invicta, a Rover, two Renaults, a Welch, and several Detroit-built machines whose names escape me.

There was in New York in those days only one repair shop to which my friend thought he could trust his Bugatti or Bentley—the now legendary Zumbach's. And for the next twenty years Zumbach's would have a fatal attraction for me—and my money.

Zumbach's was much more than what it called itself, "The Zumbach Motor Repair Co." It was a club, a museum, an historical society of the motor car, a temple of automobilism. Its high priests were Charles Zumbach and Jacques Schaerley, who ran the establishment, and Werner Maeder, the chief mechanic and Merlin of carburetion.

Preceding pages: 1933 supercharged
"Mille Miglia" Alfa Romeo symbolizes virile
sports cars of the thirties. Its
engine is 2.6 litre, with twin overhead
camshafts. This is the famous
ex-Templar car that ran—and lost—in "Fastest
Sports Car" race at Brooklands in 1939.

Zumbach and Schaerley hailed from the earliest days of automobilism. Once I brought in a photograph of Gabriel's Mors making its start in the disastrous Paris–Madrid Race of 1903. Mr. Zumbach studied it for a moment, then he pointed to a youthful mechanic standing near the car. "That's me," he said. But his mechanical expertise went back before that. He carried an unusual pocket watch. I asked him once whose make it might be. "Mine," he said. "I made it as my graduation project at the technical school in Switzerland where I learned my trade." He'd whittled and filed and turned every bit of it from lumps of steel and brass.

Both Zumbach and Schaerley had been closely involved with the servicing of Mors cars before World War I, but by the time I got to know them Zumbach was king of the machine works upstairs while Schaerley struggled with the peculiar people who brought in their peculiar cars for servicing downstairs. Zumbach's department did any fancy machine work necessary on cars whose parts supplier might be in Milan or Molsheim and months away by freighter. (There was no air express from Europe thirty-five years ago.) But it also was kept busy fabricating complex devices for other purposes. At one time Zumbach seemed to be building an endless number of soap-making machines for Coty, the perfumers. Later, just before World War II, there was much to-do and secrecy while the parts for a giant all-independently-sprung eight-wheeled armored car were machined by Mr. Zumbach upstairs and assembled in Jacques Schaerley's department downstairs. Werner Maeder would then terrify the cabbies on West 54th Street when he took the noisy brute out on test.

Zumbach's went to endless trouble to minister to almost any automobilistic ailment. At 3 o'clock one awful morning my brother telephoned me. "I have your Alfa out on Long Island," he said.

"Bring it right back," I screamed, outraged.

"I can't," he said blithely. "The fender is bent and keeps the right front wheel from turning."

"Pull the fender away from the wheel, you dope, and come right home," I begged.

"The front axle looks funny, too," he admitted.

"What else is wrong?" I asked, knowing in the pit of my stomach that other horrors would be admitted bit by bit.

"There's a little body damage, too, I think."

A little body damage! When I arrived at the garage on Long Island where the corpse of my 1750 Alfa Romeo lay, the cutpurse who owned the establishment said, "I'll give ya twenty-fi' bucks for th' wreck." I brushed by him to look at my poor car. It did not look like twenty-five dollars' worth. A telephone pole had done its worst. True, the right front fender *was* touching a front wheel. But that front wheel was about a foot higher off the floor than its mate. The steering column was a bit farther aft than normal, the steering wheel bent almost double. You could say the body was damaged. The right-hand chassis member was almost touching the left-hand chassis member, making a nice K-shaped chassis frame.

Jacques Schaerley had the ruins towed to the shop. There the chassis frame was stripped bare. Body, engine, gearbox—everything was removed.

Zumbach's shop was not a pretty place. It was, I'm sorry to say, dim, greasy, and small. But it boasted amenities which few shiny, modern car-serving emporia would dream of having—a big, coal-fired forge, for example.

Zumbach's Vulcan was a genius named Mr. Hernandez, who dressed winter and summer in soot-blackened longjohn underwear above, and charred trousers below. Mr. Hernandez cleared a space on the floor near his forge and made there an accurate chalk drawing of the Alfa chassis frame. He then set the mangled frame over the drawing, removed the bent members, heated them in his forge and rushed them glowing red to the drawing where he madly hammered them back into shape. Riveted and painted that frame was as new again in a day or so. The frame job cost about $18!

The front axle was straightened cold. A cracked engine mount and the light alloy steering box (part of which was integral to the crankcase casting) were welded up. The body was sent out to a shop for straightening and repainting. A wire wheel was rebuilt. Dozens of other things had to be done. Within ten days or so I had a like-new 1750 Alfa Romeo again. The entire cost was under $400. Zumbach's charged only $1.50 an hour in those days.

But if you were crazy enough, you could spend a

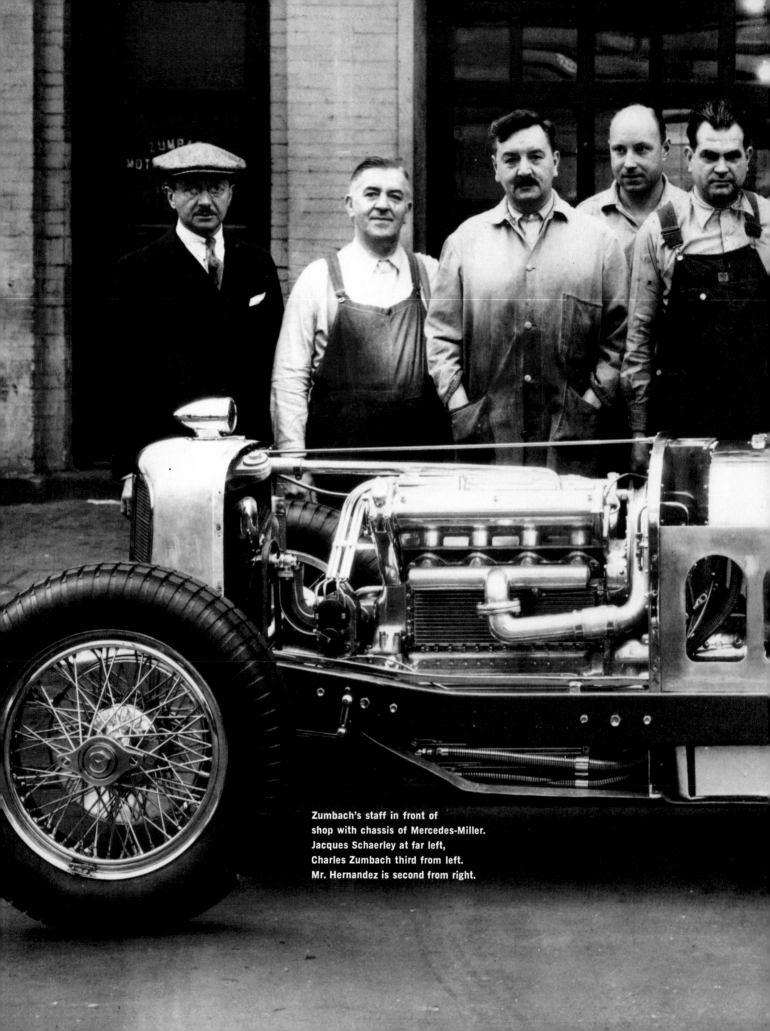

Zumbach's staff in front of
shop with chassis of Mercedes-Miller.
Jacques Schaerley at far left,
Charles Zumbach third from left.
Mr. Hernandez is second from right.

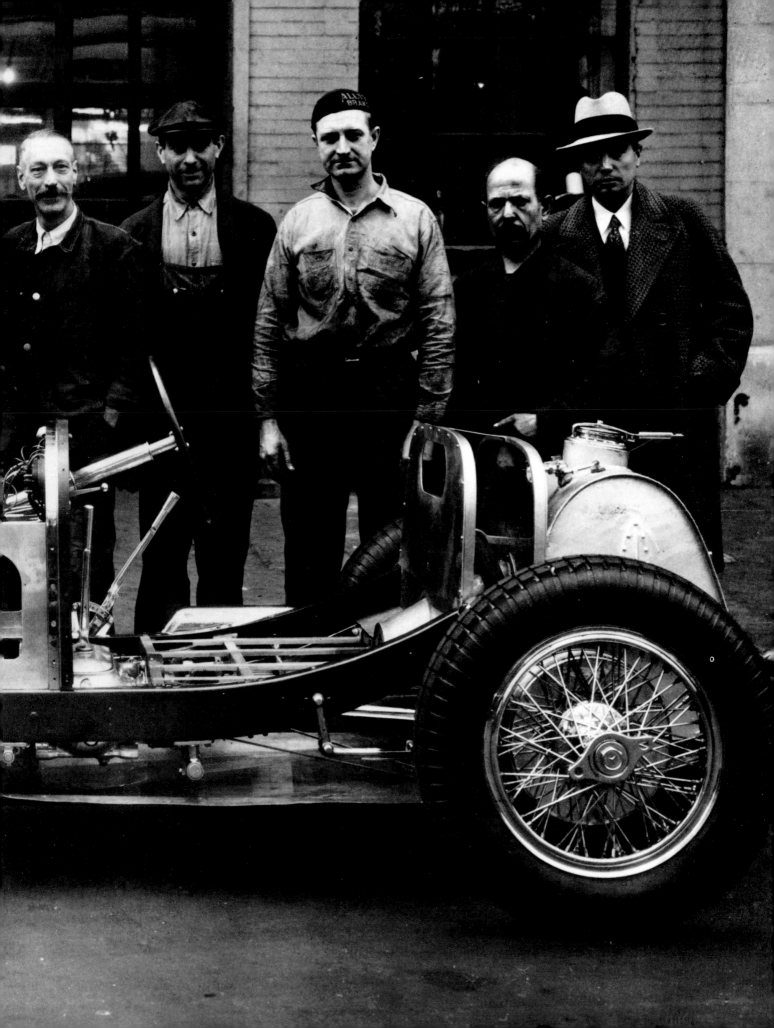

Maclure Halley had Mercedes-Miller
built at Zumbach's. American Miller engine
was installed in an old Mercedes
chassis. Body was built in New York. Photograph
above was taken at Roosevelt Raceway,
where 1936 Vanderbilt Cup Race was held. Car
was entered, but did not race.

mint of money in Zumbach's, too. A friend of mine bought a lovely Type 43 (blown, single-ohc, 2.3-litre) Bugatti Roadster. Then he decided that what he really wanted was a Type 35 Grand Prix Bugatti—but *better* than Ettore Bugatti's design. And he'd redesign that Type 43 himself. In what must have been a moment of insanity, Jacques Schaerley took the job on.

The car had to be shortened, a new two-seater body built (rather more rounded than a real Type 35, my friend insisted), a new instrument panel made up, etc., etc. Furthermore, he came up with new ideas, new drawings, changes almost every day.

The mechanic who was handed the job was a Frenchman named Lamq (Zumbach's had Englishmen working on Rolls-Royces, Italians on Isotta Fraschinis, Germans on Mercedes'). This middle-aged Gaul, complete with luxuriant handlebar moustache and collarless old-fashioned shirt with a brass collar button holding its neckband together, was a superb mechanic. For years he patiently slaved over that spurious Type 35 Bugatti. Came the great day when my friend was willing to consider the job complete.

The black Bugatti stood gleaming at the curb. Zumbach's mechanics, Zumbach himself, Schaerley, and the inevitable group of Zumbach hangers-around were assembled. Ceremoniously my friend brought out a gold watch which he presented to Lamq with a rather windy little speech of thanks and praise ending with, "And now I invite Mr. Lamq to take the very first ride in this Bugatti upon which he has worked so long and so well."

Answered Monsieur Lamq: "I wouldn' ride in th' damn thing."

Lamq was right. That peculiar "Bugatti" never handled right and broke down continually. My friend never paid Zumbach's bill. The car finally had to be sold at auction. I believe movie actor Keenan Wynn bought it. For years afterward it was known as the "Black Bastard."

The monstrous Bugatti was not the only aberrant machine Zumbach's became involved with. A star customer, Maclure Halley, who normally had them fuss with elegant Alfa Romeos, Bugattis, and a Boattail Packard which I later bought, decided once to have built what he thought would turn out to be a very superior racing machine. To this end he got hold of one of the Mercedes racing cars which had done so dismally at Indianapolis in 1923. He had the Mercedes engine pulled out and had Zumbach's install a twin-cam American Miller racing engine. But merely making such a switch was not enough for Mr. Halley. He loved chromium and engine-turned parts, especially on instrument panels. Axles, brakes, steering components, all went into chrome-plating baths. An instrument panel of astonishing shininess and complexity was installed. The slickest, smoothest body you ever saw—painted bright red, of course—was constructed.

After a long, long time the Mercedes-Miller was finally pushed out onto West 54th Street. Halley, caparisoned in white racing overalls and a cloth racing helmet, got behind the wheel and set forth. A turn or two around the block—he never got out of second gear—was enough for him. He never drove the brute again except to pose in it for a *Saturday Evening Post* cover. It was entered for the 1936 Vanderbilt Cup Race at Roosevelt Raceway but, luckily for its driver, never left the starting line. Later, under a new owner, it was involved in a disastrous accident.

Zumbach's was also the haunt of a group of gilded youths who formed the nucleus of the original A.R.C.A. (Automobile Racing Club of America). These young men were in the mid-thirties the very first to go racing in sports cars in the United States, first on the Briarcliff Manor estate owned by the father of three of them, Miles, Sam, and Barron Collier, and later at Alexandria Bay in northern New York State. They owned some wonderful machines—Amilcars, Bugattis, and a long-tailed Brooklands Riley, among others—and were continually involved in rebuilding and improving their mouth-watering mounts. One long-drawn-out bit of reconstruction involved shoehorning a Ford engine under the hood of an Amilcar, a project I looked upon as sheer vandalism. In spite of my reservations, that Ford Amilcar did very well when it was raced at Alexandria Bay.

The people who hovered outside Zumbach's to feast their eyes on unusual automobiles going and coming or parked at the curb (one guy made a hobby of photographing the cars) were shaken one day to see a thumping big mahogany racing

Author's 1934 low-chassis "100 MPH"
Invicta was frequent patient
at Zumbach's. It had 4½-litre, six-cylinder
engine. 100 mph was never quite
realized. Car had a disconcerting tendency
to wag its tail on wet roads, especially
when forty-gallon fuel tank was almost empty.

motorboat being backed in on a trailer.

This boat, so high and wide that it just barely squeezed into the doorway, was the property of Zalmon G. Simmons, the mattress king. (Guy Lombardo later owned it.) It had an engine ailment—dropped valves—the cause of which was most mysterious. The engine consisted of four Indianapolis-type twin-cam Miller engines hooked together to form a thirty-two-cylinder monstrosity. New camshafts had been made to stretch across the sixteen cylinders of each bank. Maeder and his helpers fussed with the engines, adjusting valve timing to a hairsbreadth. Then the boat was towed out to open water.

Barging his way through New York traffic in the

armored car had perhaps been fun for Werner Maeder, but this bit of testing must have been a mite nerve-wracking for a man from the Swiss Alps, whose experience with salt water was limited. Poor unnautical Maeder went flying off at 80 knots plus. The valves went kerflooey again and Maeder had the boat dragged back to Zumbach's. On each test Maeder lost more skin off his back from up-and-down friction against the seat as the speedboat pounded along. Had this gone on much longer Maeder would have had his back worn through to his ribs. But some genius in the shop discovered that the long, thin camshafts were twisting torsionally; that while one end of a camshaft was, say, closing a valve, the far end might be opening one just

1938 8C 2900-B Alfa Romeo which Maclure Halley had great difficulty prying out of Italian builders. Body was Superleggera by Touring of Milan. Halley insisted on racing engine, with valves seated on aluminum of head. Since these tended to erode, Zumbach's substituted steel valve seats.

as a piston was rising to collide with it. Thicker camshafts made in Charles Zumbach's upstairs shop were the answer.

It's not hard to understand why I and other car-crazed types loved to hang about Zumbach's. (The present chief of styling of General Motors has told me that in his youth he, too, was a Zumbach watcher.) What, for example, could be more lovely than watching a mechanic expose the intimate parts of a Bugatti or an Hispano-Suiza? Had Jacques Schaerley stood for it, his small shop would have been so crammed with spectators that no work could have been done.

Although as a regular customer I could wander into the shop, I hesitated to take too much advantage of this free-dom. I had another, more expensive, ploy—automotive hypo-chondria. I'd imagine that my Invicta, or Alfa, or whatever, was in slightly poor health. Then I could come and watch it being operated upon.

There were, of course, times when my current car needed major surgery. Then the damage to my slender purse took some of the joy out of my visits.

Saturday morning was the great time at Zumbach's. That was when the owners of exotic foreign cars descended on 54th Street, ostensibly to have Maeder "do a little something to the carburetors," but really to look at and talk about the cars parked near the shop. It was on such a morning in May, 1940,

that I first saw the S-type Invicta with which I was instantly smitten and was able to buy some three years later.

And I believe it was on such a Saturday in winter that Paul Draper, the dancer, and Paul Gallico, the writer, set forth in an open Mercedes S for Mexico City, each of them wearing fur-lined trousers from Abercrombie & Fitch. They made it to Mexico City, too, quite a feat in those days. They had a spot of trouble in Texas on the way back and left the car for repair in the garage of an honest southwestern type who sold it after a couple of weeks. He claimed he hadn't been paid for "storage."

I miss those Saturdays. But mostly I miss turning the corner from Sixth Avenue (where the New York Hilton now sits) and seeing in the distance the nose of a car with sharply cambered front wheels whose stance proclaimed it something special and sporting. Then I'd break into a run up the block.

A very narrow segment of the automobile world was visible and known to Americans in the thirties. Only the products of Detroit were familiar to them. I do not think that five cars in a million were of foreign make. Americans had almost entirely forgotten their own sports cars of twenty years earlier; the Stutzes, Mercers, and Simplexes were part of a lost mythology. They had no idea that superb sports cars—Bugattis, Alfa Romeos, Bentleys, Aston Martins—existed on the far side

**Author's Phantom I American-built
Rolls-Royces. Above, 1927 Brewster Ascot-bodied
double-cowl phaeton. Opposite: Brewster
Riviera *coupé de ville* stands behind 1937
British AC. American Rolls-Royces differed from
British-built types in having
left-hand steering and three-speed gearboxes.**

of the Atlantic. The average American's idea of a sports car was something "sporty," like an Auburn Speedster. True, in big cities, some people were vaguely aware of Rolls-Royces and Isotta Fraschinis and such—they had seen them in the movies.

At least part of this insular ignorance was due to a lack of reading material about automobiles. Magazines like *The Horseless Age* and *The Automobile* had died long before the nineteen-thirties. The only American publication still alive was Hearst's *Motor*, devoted largely to the boring problems of the garage trade.

My excitement over cars led me to wonderful and, to me, new places to read about them: the English magazines *The Autocar*, *The Motor*, and *Motor Sport*. I devoured them and a whole new world of automobilism opened to me. I read not only the current issues, but the great, dusty, bound volumes of ancient issues in the New York Public Library.

Racing had not particularly intrigued me. I had, naturally, watched the primitive dirt-track and midget-car racing that went on in the New York area. I even journeyed out to Indianapolis. But my interest was not really whetted until I discovered that a different kind of racing went on abroad —races between great makes: Alfa Romeo, Mercedes-Benz, Bugatti, Maserati. And as I read, I became familiar with the magic names of the racing men of the nineteen-thirties: Nuvo-

lari, Varzi, Caracciola, Chiron, Wimille.

The 1936 Vanderbilt Cup Race at Roosevelt Raceway, a peculiarly curvilinear artificial road circuit near New York City, brought over the European cracks with their Alfas, Bugattis, and ERA's. Most Americans were blindly certain that the foreigners could not possibly defeat the tough guys from Indianapolis and the dirt tracks. I worked for a newspaper in those days and almost the entire sports department eagerly gave me odds against the possibility of anyone with the outlandish name of Nuvolari outrunning the Americans.

I collected quite nicely when Nuvolari won in his Alfa, Wimille came in second in a Bugatti, and Brivio took third in an Alfa. Even the 1500-cc English ERA's beat the Indy boys.

I got no odds, however, in 1937 when the race was repeated and the Germans won in their beswastikaed Mercedes' and Auto Unions. One American did well that year. Rex Mays had managed to buy an Alfa Romeo from the 1936 race and took third place in it. Bernd Rosemeyer was first in an Auto Union, Dick Seaman second in a Mercedes. (The Mercedes-Benz team had brought their cars to Zumbach's for servicing. Imagine the excitement!)

1929 boattail Packard had been owned by Maclure Halley before author acquired it in 1942. Note rev counter on radiator cap. Clip-on V-shaped radiator grille and Marchal headlamps were other nonstandard modifications. Car was sold in 1943 for $350.

The racing successes of the foreigners did not cause Americans to rush out to buy themselves sports Alfas, or even MG's. You couldn't buy a new Alfa Romeo in the US, anyhow. Maclure Halley ordered a 2900-B Alfa two-seater, sent the money to Milan, and finally had to travel to Italy to camp on Alfa's doorstep to get delivery. It took eleven months. A very few MG's (PB's and TA's) were sold by the enthusiastic Collier brothers. But they cost too much in the late thirties: $1,200, almost as much as a bottom-of-the-line Cadillac.

The war changed the automobile world. The pat explanation for the postwar American enthusiasm for sports cars says that American soldiers drove MG's in England, and therefore couldn't wait until they could buy such delectable little sports cars over here. I've tried to track down this myth for years. None of the sports-car-hooked ex-soldiers I've asked about this—and I've talked to hundreds, when I was in the army and afterward—got a chance to go flitting around England's lanes while waiting to attack Hitler's *Festung Europa*. They were mostly too poor, too miserable, and too busy. The British wouldn't sell the gasoline, anyway.

I think the turn to foreign cars in 1946 was caused by two things: the British need for dollars, and the greed of dealers in American cars.

The shooting and bombing had hardly stopped when the Collier brothers started to bring in MG-TC's. Other dealers immediately began importing Austin A40's and Standard Eights (8 horsepower, not 8 cylinders!). The MG's arrived bumperless —before the war the British didn't use bumpers much—and Zumbach's was kept busy fabricating flat strips of chromed steel to help the cars withstand the shock of American-style parking. At first the MG's cost only $1,700 plus about $20 for bumpers.

They were far from being first-class sports cars; they couldn't have been at the price. But to Americans used to the obese and unwieldy vehicular objects from Detroit, they were a revelation. Here were cars that actually went where you pointed them. The tiny Austin A40's and Standard Eights sold, not because they had any sporting pretensions, but because they were an alternative to the traumatic experience of trying to buy one of the scarce Detroit cars from a vulpine American dealer. And they had a certain cachet.

As sports cars burgeoned, other makes—the XK120 Jaguar, for example—joined the pack. Clubs, magazines, and books about cars blossomed; racing became important again.

This post-World War II enthusiasm for sports cars seems somehow to have transferred itself to automobilism in general. People today are far more interested and knowledgeable about cars—even in Detroit—than they were earlier. Another facet of the renaissance is the continually rising excitement over antique and classic cars. But more about that in a later chapter.

This enhanced automotive consciousness of the past three decades is worldwide. Certainly the British and the Europeans were entirely aware of the existence of superlative automobiles; they were the people who built most of them. Grand-prix and sports-car racing was *the* big continental sport. Then why the upsurge in automobilism? The answer is simple: money. The many millions of people who were once held down by ancient class divisions now make enough money to buy cars.

An example of this upward automobility: Recently, while trundling across the Atlantic on the *Queen Elizabeth II*, I got to talking about cars with a young Irish waiter from Southampton. He was about to buy a car and wanted advice. "What kind of car were you thinking of?" I asked. "A nice, used Rolls-Royce," he answered. "I want to take my old mother driving in something comfortable."

I suppose I miss the exclusivity of owning peculiar and mysterious automobiles. I miss (although I claimed it was annoying at the time) having cab drivers pull up alongside my Invicta or Alfa to ask, "Hey, Mac, what kinda car izzat?" I miss being able to buy an Invicta for $400. (The very car was advertised recently for $15,000.) I miss being thought a pundit as I sounded off about cars no one had ever heard of.

But were those days better days? I submit they were not. We were then on a starvation diet. Today the automobilist's plate is full to overflowing. He has an unimaginable choice of sports machines, antique cars, grand tourers, family cars. New kinds of motive power—Wankel engines, turbines— and new applications of those ancient propulsors—steam and electricity—are being tried.

Dare I say the motorist's world looks bright?

The above is a representation of a Steam-Carriage, the inventio
which is so far completed that it will be re
The weight of the Carriage and propelling Machinery is two tons

W. H. James, Civil Engineer.

2.

of Mr W. H. James of Birmingham and Thavie's Inn, London, and

to start in the course of the ensuing month.

the estimated power is from 15 to 20 horses. With this power it

CHARIOTS WITH

*"The chariots shall rage in the streets,
they shall jostle one against another in the broad ways;
they shall seem like torches, they shall
run like the lightnings."*

Nahum 2:4

Back there in 600 B.C., old man Nahum must have been seeing ahead to the New Jersey Turnpike, or M1 near London, and dollars to shekels there must have been some types even then who tried to build chariots which would "run like lightnings" but without horses. But until muscle power—human or equine —was displaced by mechanical power, the idea of a vehicle which would propel itself was chimerical.

Even Leonardo da Vinci (1452-1519) addressed himself to the problem, designing several hopeless, manually powered vehicles—one of them a tank-like war carriage which looked like a wooden turtle. Inside, four soldiers were expected to labor at a pair of crankshafts geared to pins on the wooden wheels. Those poor Italian privates would have been exhausted before covering a few yards. Nor did Leonardo provide a means of steering his military machine.

Some people, kings and such, to awe their subjects, had built for themselves gaudy devices upon which they were magically self-propelled. But these machines either had horses on treadmills or pitiable servants sweating away at levers hidden inside the bedizened coachwork. Albrecht Dürer has left us a woodcut of such a "self-propelled" carriage built for the Emperor Maximilian I in 1510. Another similar toy was constructed by Johann Hautsch in Nuremberg in 1649. The poor fellows inside not only used their legs to propel it, but also had some of their muscle power diverted toward working various mechanical figures which moved and sounded trumpets. A carved dragon up front rolled its eyes and spat a stream of water at any inhabitants that dared to impede its two-mile-an-hour progress. The Crown Prince of Sweden bought it from Herr Hautsch and, not to be outdone, the King of Denmark ordered a copy.

Some inventors plumped for wind-wagons of the sort Simon Stevin built for Prince Maurice of Nassau in about 1600, a two-masted, four-wheeled, land-going sailing vessel. In 1714, a Frenchman, Monsieur Du Quet, tried another method of harnessing the moving air. He set up a windmill on his car. The rotary motion of the vanes was transmitted to two pairs of mechanical legs which walked the machine along. In a gale, I imagine, they ran like hell with it. A Swiss clergyman, the Reverend J. H. Genevois, went M. Du Quet one better. *His* windmill, being Swiss, wound up a giant clockspring which turned the wheels.

Steam power attracted inventors long before the steam engine was developed. In 1672 a couple of missionaries in Peking, a Father Grimaldi and a Father Verbiest, are supposed to have built for Emperor K'ang-hsi a car using a jet of steam from a big kettle to turn a horizontal turbine wheel geared to a pair of driving wheels. At about the same time Sir Isaac Newton was diddling with the idea of a big retort which was to expel a jet of steam and propel a car forward by reaction. By swiveling the jet, the machine would also be steered.

But it was not until steam was used to move a piston inside a cylinder that it became a really useful motive force. Newcomen in England built his first atmospheric steam machine for pumping out flooded mines in 1712. James Watt made his great improvements on it soon afterward.

The steam age, the Industrial Revolution, was just ahead. But engines like Newcomen's and Watt's—leaking steam and water, crude, big as houses, working with ponderous slowness—were hardly portable enough to power road-going vehicles.

About 1765, a Swiss engineer, Nicholas Joseph Cugnot, subsidized by the French monarchy, tried to surmount the problems of building an engine to power a machine for hauling artillery pieces. It wasn't easy. Techniques of casting and accurately machining chunks of iron like Cugnot's 13-inch-diameter cylinders and pistons were as yet undeveloped. If Cugnot's machine had been tiny, he would not have had such problems. Watches, for example, had by this time become amazingly precise. Marine chronometers already were accurate enough for navigation. Microscopes, telescopes, and other small mechanisms had reached a high degree of sophistication.

Still, Cugnot succeeded in designing the world's first machine able to propel itself. Constructed in 1769 by a Monsieur

Preceding pages: Grandiose representation of William James' steam carriage of 1829. It was claimed that it would "travel at the rate of from 8 to 12 miles an hour." This coach was never completed. Note that it has wheel steering.

UT HORSES

Brezin, it attained a speed of about three miles per hour with four passengers aboard. Its inadequate boiler, however, was capable of making only enough steam for a fifteen-minute run. Then the machine stopped to catch its breath again. Cugnot seems also to have had steering problems. The wild stories about a fire-breathing monster roaring through the streets of Paris, inhabitants fleeing before it until it smashed into a wall, are untrue, as is the tale that Cugnot was thereupon cast into a dungeon. Cugnot's creature did, however, knock over a stone wall. Although this may indicate that his car was difficult to maneuver, it also proves that it had a useful amount of muscle.

The King's Minister of War, for some reason, ordered a second version of Cugnot's steamer built at the Royal Arsenal in about 1771. It is now at the *Conservatoire des Arts et Métiers* in Paris, where I went to bow low before it. Sitting in a dim and ancient hall, it overwhelms one with its sheer size. The Cugnot is easily as big as the tractor of a modern tractor-trailer truck, although it has only three wheels. Mounted upon the single front wheel are twin 13-inch cylinders (of 50-litre capacity) and a huge copper boiler. To steer meant not only turning the tremendously thick and heavy wooden driving wheel, but also the great weight of the engine and boiler. The engine drives the front wheel, not through cranks, but by means of a ratchet and pawl. The chassis members are great rough wooden beams as big as the main beams holding up the eighteenth-century house in which I write this. Mounted on these beams is a bench for the driver in front of which is a steering column surmounted by two handles (almost exactly like that on Henry Ford's "999" racer of 1902). Slung beneath the seat is a big wicker basket for fuel—probably coke. Iron ladders help the driver and passengers climb aboard. The rear wheels are as tall as a man. As it stands now, it's doubtful whether this version ever ran. Parts are missing from its mechanism, not through attrition, but because they seem never to have been installed.

As I stood contemplating the Cugnot, about fifty small boys rushed at it, swarmed all over it, pulled levers, tried to steer. The lady schoolteacher who had brought them to the museum squeaked helplessly. Not to worry. Cugnot had not, perhaps, built a very fast or easily handled machine, but he had surely built a rugged one, which had withstood such concerted assaults for something like two centuries.

As the eighteenth century ended, steam was the magic new power source, like atomic power today. It fired the imaginations of engineers in almost every western country: Bozek in Prague, Evans in Philadelphia, Pagani in Bologna, Dietz in Paris, Dallery in Amiens were among the many experimenting with steam-driven, road-going devices.

Yet none of these inventors had anything like the success of the British engineers who rushed by the score into building steam vehicles. It was to be expected. The steam engine was a British invention. England was ahead of the world in industrial and mechanical know-how. And perhaps as important as anything else, England, unlike the countries of the Continent, had not suffered in the same degree from the traumas of revolution and the military idiocies of Napoleon.

The great Richard Trevithick, a Cornishman and the builder of the world's first locomotive, was the first of many Englishmen to prove that a steam-powered carriage full of passengers could successfully make a road journey. In 1801, Trevithick built a bare chassis to demonstrate the boiler and engine, which operated at the then remarkably high pressure of sixty pounds per square inch. By 1803, with eight people aboard a coach-like body perched high above the chassis, Trevithick was able to sail along at about twelve miles per hour. Furthermore, he could shift gears when he came to a hill.

Although Trevithick had demonstrated the first really roadable self-propelled machine, with a gearshift to boot, no one was interested in underwriting its development and Trevithick gave up. One cannot entirely disagree with the people who could see no future in a machine which might fly along at the ungodly speed of 12 mph. For in England there were few good roads on which it might travel.

After the Napoleonic wars, however, there was a burst of prosperity in Britain. The spinners of Manchester, the potters and iron founders of the North, the machine builders and the gentry, all wanted mobility. The mud holes and gullies that had served as roads in the eighteenth century, and had limited travel to horseback or slow, lumbering coaches, were no longer good enough for the new men of the new nineteenth century. They needed speed, the speed of fast four-horse

As it appeared at Hounslow

1 & 2: Cross section and model of
Goldsworthy Gurney's steam carriage of 1827–28.
It carried twenty-one passengers at 15 mph.
3. Model of Fathers Grimaldi and Verbiest's steam
turbine car, supposedly built in Peking in 1672.
4. Sir Isaac Newton's idea—a jet steam car.
5. Gurney's "steam drag" pulled a horse carriage.

A Sketch of

Mʳ GURNEY'S NEW STEAM CARRIAGE.

e 12ᵗʰ of August, with a Barouche attached, containing the Duke of Wellington and other Persons of Distinction.

Pubᵈ by T. Dickinson 114, New Bond Sᵗ.

Printed by C. Hullmandel.

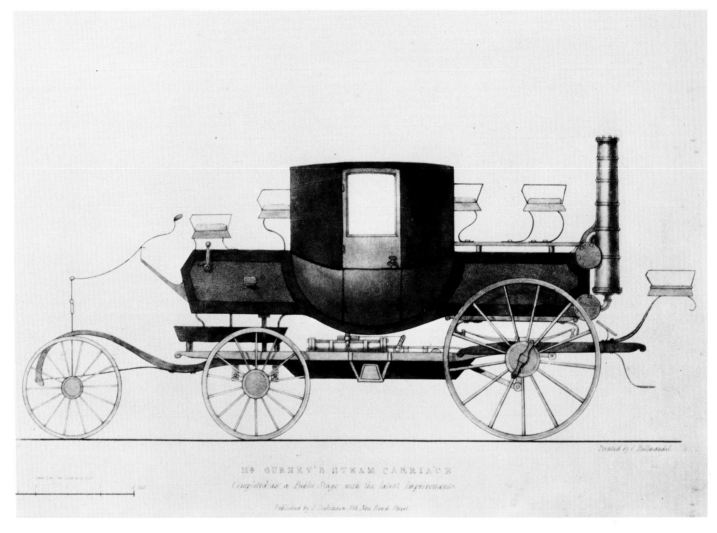

MR GURNEY'S STEAM CARRIAGE
Completed as a Public Stage with the latest Improvements

Published by J. Dickinson, 114 New Bond Street

coaches. Now came that romantic coaching era so well cele-
brated and depicted in prints. These high-speed coaches rushed
across England with hurried stops at inns for fresh horses; good
roads were essential to their schedules. Within twenty years
such roads had been built, using new methods devised and
pioneered by those road-building prodigies, Telford and Macadam (we still use the latter's name to describe a rather different
kind of road surface than the one he used).

The times seemed right for coaches faster than
four-horse post chaises; the era of steam coaches had arrived.
The eighteen-twenties and thirties saw as exciting a collection
of vehicles as ever turned a wheel.

Imagine that you're standing beside an English road
in, say, 1831. A trumpet blast announces that the Cheltenham
to Gloucester Steam Carriage approaches. From around a bend,
enveloped in steam and smoke, comes an apparition, a monster
on man-high wheels.

The machine is huge, high, thrice the length of a
long-distance coach, and is wildly painted in yellow and red
and black. Gilt coats of arms and lettering emblazon its sides.
A dozen people, top-hatted, bonnetted, some carrying para-
sols, sit precariously on benches mounted high above the body.
Two or three peer from the windows of an enclosed section.
In front a steersman struggles with a tiller. The steam coach

**Goldsworthy Gurney's steam carriages
were among the most successful.
Sir Charles Dance ran a line of Gurney-built
coaches between Cheltenham and
Gloucester from February to June, 1831,
making 396 trips during the
period. Mother-in-law seat was for fireman.**

careens past, its iron-shod wheels crunch on the flints of the road. The passengers call and wave, but are unheard over the clanking and puffing of the steam engine. Aft, a blackened stoker throws coke into a glowing firebox and a shower of sparks flys out of the chimneys. But you can no longer see the giant steam coach. Your eyes are full of cinders.

Although not a very common sight, a number of such machines constructed by optimistic engineers rumbled spectacularly over Britain's highroads for almost twenty years. The most successful ones were those built by Walter Hancock and Goldsworthy Gurney.

Hancock built nine steam carriages with lovely names: Autopsy, Infant, Automation, Era, etc. These machines, which used steam at a much higher pressure—200 psi—than was usual in their day, showed remarkable reliability. In 1834, for example, the Era and the Autopsy carried 4,000 passengers between the City and Paddington in London. Hancock's steamers were also the most sophisticated machines of their time. They had wheel steering; their vertical two-cylinder engines were in separate interior compartments where they were protected from road filth; they drove through clutches and had chain drive. More important, Hancock seems to have been the only operator to make a profit.

Goldsworthy Gurney, in 1827, built a steam coach for twenty-one passengers. This first machine had legs in addition to wheels. Gurney, fearful that the wheels, upon starting, might merely spin while the carriage just stood there, thought he ought to provide some means for giving his machine a swift kick forward. To that end he installed steam-driven legs and feet. Gurney's carriages were made for sale at £1,000 plus a royalty of sixpence a mile. Sir Charles Dance ran a line of Gurney machines between Cheltenham and Gloucester from February to June, 1831, during which period he made 396 trips.

Many other builders had fair success with their steam coaches. Scott Russell ran a line between Glasgow and Paisley. Burstall & Hill, Macerone & Squire, James & Anderson are but a few of the steam-carriage builders whose names are still remembered.

Had these inventive pioneers been able to continue, it's likely that steam would have replaced the horse in Britain by the mid-nineteenth century—at least for town-to-town coaches. And small steam machines for individual use would certainly have followed.

Incredibly, the British committed infanticide. They killed off the steam carriages. Stagecoach operators, their suppliers of oats, hay, and fodder, the yokels who grew the fodder, the drivers, grooms, horse dealers, all screamed bloody murder. Sometimes gangs of rural thugs attacked the steam coaches. Gurney and his fireman once were beaten senseless by such an oafish mob. The private turnpike owners raised their tolls for steamers to unconscionable heights. Finally, the new railroads drained away such money as might have been invested in steam road transport. By 1840 the steam coaches were gone. Even Walter Hancock gave up and set himself to designing railway locomotives.

For the next forty years or so experimenters in England, in America, and on the Continent built every possible variation of the steam road locomotive. Some, like those built by Thomas Rickett in England in 1858 and Richard Dudgeon in New York in 1853, resembled small railway engines. Others were light and delicate, like Lucius Copeland's spidery steam tricycles and high-wheeled bicycles of the eighteen-eighties. In France de Dion & Bouton in 1885 and Amédée Bollée, père, in 1878, built a number of Gallicly logical steam vehicles. And in Italy, in 1854, Virginio Bordino built a fantastic steam landau which still exists at the *Museo Dell'Automobile Carlo Biscaretti di Ruffia* in Turin.

By stretching the meaning of the word, we can call these strange devices automobiles: They did actually move by themselves. Improved, they evolved into that dead end, the steam car of the early twentieth century. (Although steam may yet return to help halt the asphyxiation of the human race.)

The car as we use it today is the offspring of two other nineteenth-century mechanisms, the bicycle (or tricycle) and the internal-combustion engine, with contributions from other discoveries, inventions, and techniques of that fruitful century, including electricity, rubber, accurate machine tools and measuring devices, petroleum, and good-quality steels.

If anyone had wanted them, automobiles might very

1

2   3

1. Scott Russell ran steam coaches
like this between Glasgow and Paisley, Scotland.
2. Walter Hancock built nine
steam carriages and engaged in a successful
passenger service in 1834, carrying
some 4,000 passengers in four months.
3. Macerone & Squire steam coach.

STEAM CARRIAGE FOR COMMON ROADS.

Patented, July 18th 1833.

by **JOHN SQUIRE** and **FRANCIS MACERONE** of

Paddington Wharf.

an 1700 Miles & still runs every day, to Edgware, Harrow or on other roads, remarkable for their hills,

d any repair. Its average speed is fourteen Miles the hour but it has run many Miles, on a level, at three minu

for coke is (at the London taxed price) from three pence to four pence per Mile. The horse coaches pay about

le for four horses more or less, according to the speed required, which never exceeds ten Miles the hour, but of

nge is much less than eight. See the Editorial reports of Morning Chronicle of Sept. 3rd, Oct. 7th, 14th, 15th, and 16th,

Observer, Times &c of same dates.

STEAM-CARRIAGE TO RUN ON COMMON ROADS, DESIGNED BY MR. RICKETT, OF THE CASTLE FOUNDRY, BUCKINGHAM.

well have appeared long before they actually did. But ordinary nineteenth-century people never gave a thought to racketing around country roads on their own. If city people wanted to go anyplace outside their towns, they had the railroad, hadn't they? Only the rich in their shiny carriages went out into the country for fun.

The bicycle changed all that. Starting in the eighteen-seventies, when muscular young men rode the dangerous high-wheelers and women and elderly gentlemen pedaled peculiar one- and two-passenger tricycles, and increasing in the eighteen-eighties, when the "safety" bicycle appeared, the urge toward individual transport made people want machines—horseless car-

riages—which would give them the freedom they had on their bicycles. But without tired muscles. The bicycle prepared people's minds for the automobile.

The idea of causing a piston to rush down the inside of a cylinder by creating an explosion (or rapid expansion) within the cylinder is as old as the wooden cannon which fired a stone cannonball. It wasn't until something less violent than gunpowder—combustible gas—came along that rapid *controlled* expansion within a cylinder became feasible. In 1804 Isaac de Rivaz, a Swiss, used hydrogen to move the piston in a primitive engine mounted on a wheeled frame. Although he seems to have succeeded in causing this vehicle to move itself, and even

Thomas Rickett built this road-going locomotive for the Marquis of Stafford in 1858. Driving was a two-man job. A fireman shoveled in coal while the Marquis steered. Opposite is the Phoenix-Daimler engine of 1899. Note the hot tube at "E" and the automatic inlet valve.

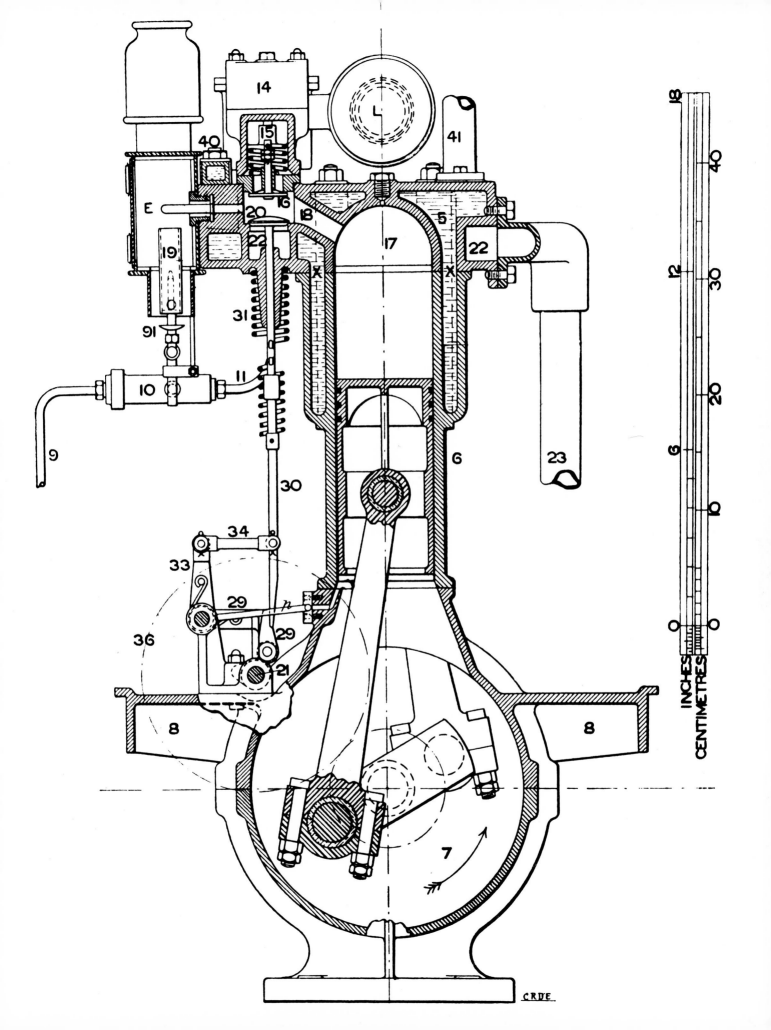

1. "La Mancelle," built in 1878 by
Amédée Bollée, still required a man to stoke
the fire. Steam engine was out front.
2. 1885 de Dion-Bouton steam
carriage was steered from amidships.
3. A British Daimler built
on Panhard lines about 1897.

3

managed to patent it in 1807, he did not further develop his invention.

The first practical internal-combustion engine was built by Etienne Lenoir. It used illuminating gas ignited by an electric spark from a Ruhmkorff coil. Although huge and greedy for fuel (100 cubic feet of cooking gas per horsepower!), it was bought by small factories where a steam engine with its boiler and fireman would be even more expensive to run.

Liquid fuel—benzene—was becoming available and Lenoir vaporized it with a primitive surface carburetor. He then hoisted one of his gargantuan engines aboard a wagon and coupled it to the wheels. This "car" actually ran in 1852 but so slowly—at about a mile an hour between Paris and the suburbs of Joinville—that he might as well have forgotten his

carburetor and dragged a long rubber gas pipe behind him. Lenoir seems thereafter to have given up on cars.

Soon after, Siegfried Marcus, in Vienna, seems to have taken a big step toward building an internal-combustion-engined automobile. In 1865 he mounted on a handcart a single-cylindered atmospheric (i.e., without a compression stroke) engine which he had invented, not to create a horseless carriage, but to test his engine. The handcart had neither transmission nor clutch, and to start the engine it was necessary to lift the driving wheels off the ground and spin them; when the wheels hit the ground again the cart took off.

Marcus, an eccentric genius, became bored with an idea as soon as he proved it could work. He didn't think there was much sense in horseless carriages, anyway, especially since they would cost too much to run. After all, benzene cost three marks for a litre bottle! He quit fooling with his motorized handcart and, of course, he didn't patent it.

There is considerable controversy about when Marcus built his second car, his *strassenwagen*. (One German pundit, a Herr Goldbeck, tried to prove that Marcus did not build it until 1888.) But it was some time between 1874 and 1878.

Marcus's *strassenwagen*, which is now a prized exhibit at the Vienna Technical Museum, is still operable at about 5 mph. Its chassis is of wood, its wheels iron-shod. Its brakes are blocks of wood pressing against the iron tires—all distressingly archaic. But Marcus's engine was not archaic. Examined today, it seems remarkably sophisticated. Its single cylinder has a capacity of 1,570 cc and develops about ¾ hp at 500 rpm. Marcus, whose specialty was electricity, designed for it a unique make-and-break ignition system powered by a magneto. The valves are actuated by a cam-like slot in a flat metal plate. The intake valve is a sliding type like a steam engine's. The exhaust leaves through a poppet valve. To assist vaporization of the fuel, the carburetor has within it a rotating brush dipped in benzol that rubs against a metal spring. The Marcus car has a clutch, a differential, and a steering wheel that swings the whole front axle.

Typically, Marcus did nothing about developing his car. Some ten years later two Germans, Daimler and Benz, would build the machines from which hundreds of millions of automobiles would descend.

Gottlieb Daimler knew as much about internal-combustion engines as anyone on earth. By the time he installed one in a motor vehicle, at the advanced age of fifty-one, he had worked with them for over thirteen years. Daimler got his experience at the Deutz engine works owned by Otto and Langen. Deutz built big, low-speed, stationary, industrial gas engines, which were far more modern than the type Lenoir had shown could be used in place of steam engines to power factories.

Daimler was not satisfied with the great lumps of slow-moving iron that Otto and Langen were selling. He pointed out the need for a light, comparatively high-speed, liquid-fueled engine that could power tramcars, boats, fire engines and—shh!—tricycles? carriages?

Otto and Langen were adamant. They'd have nothing to do with such radicalism. In 1882 Daimler quit, taking along his associate, Wilhelm Maybach. A year or so later Daimler patented a compact, "high-speed" (750 rpm) engine with hot-tube ignition and a crude surface carburetor to vaporize the benzene.

Lenoir had used an electric spark to ignite the gas-air mixture in his cylinder. We do it the same way today, but more elegantly. Otto's engine used a gas flame which was exposed to the mixture at the right instant by means of a sliding valve. Daimler's hot tube was a pencil-thick tube of platinum screwed into the cylinder like a modern sparkplug. The tube was heated red-hot by a benzene-fed Bunsen burner. The compressed mixture was forced into the hot tube by the rising piston and bang!—the engine ran. Daimler called his tube a "priming cap."

To try his remarkable engines, Daimler first installed one (¾-hp, air-cooled), in 1885, in a crude wooden motor bicycle, then in carriages (these later had two-cylinder, 3½-hp, V engines). Although these first cars of Daimler's were hardly more than mobile test beds, they were the precursors of that long line of superior motor cars which we know now by the name of Mercedes-Benz.

But those wonderful little engines played a greater role. Exported and licensed abroad (especially to France, where the great Emile Levassor built his first cars around them), they were the seeds from which most of the automobile industry grew.

Karl Benz, unlike Gottlieb Daimler, was not primarily interested in engines; he wanted to make an entirely self-propelled vehicle. Benz, too, had been a long-time expert in building stationary gas engines. But he wasn't as lucky as Daimler. Instead of having a big job with an established firm, he tried running a succession of small gas-engine companies without ever having quite enough capital. He had continual trouble with partners and greedy money men. Eventually, he put together still another company, Benz & Cie in Mannheim, to build two-stroke, electrically ignited stationary engines. But he found even the smallest of these too clumsy for the car he was itching to build, and he therefore designed a four-stroke, 8/10-

hp, electrically ignited engine to suit his purpose. Benz's first car of 1885 was a three-wheeler, not too unlike the pedal tricycles which were popular in the eighteen-eighties. Like those, it had wire wheels and a frame of bicycle tubing. It had enough size and weight, however, to support the water-cooled engine and a quite substantial buggy seat for two. The engine was mounted aft and transmitted its power by way of a belt clutch (there was but one speed) and then by a chain to the rear wheels.

From the very beginning, Benz's tri-car ran quite nicely up to 9 mph. Expectedly, however, Benz had his little troubles with it and spent all his time fiddling with this or that component. His partners were furious with Benz's neglect of the gas-engine business and threatened to pull out. Only Frau Benz encouraged him; while Herr Benz at night drew and redrew plans for later models, she'd recharge the car's storage batteries by pumping away at the treadle of her sewing machine which was hooked up to a generator.

Benz, in the next few years, built several new, more powerful, much improved models. Benz's partners still could see no future in his car, despite the fact that several had been sold and that a Frenchman, Emile Roger, had bought a license to assemble Benz cars in Paris. Luckily, two new partners, Fritz von Fischer and Julius Ganss, had more confidence. They put some money into the business and before long Benz's cars, like Daimler's engines, began to be sold throughout Europe and even in America.

None of the others had been able to accomplish what Daimler and Benz had. Not Cugnot, nor Hancock, nor Trevithick, nor Marcus, nor any of the rest. All had been brilliant men with large ideas. All had pushed back the frontiers of self-locomotion, but only Daimler and Benz at last moved the world into the age of the automobile. It remained for later men—Levassor, Lanchester, Ford, Royce, Bugatti, Birkigt, and many others—to make the motor car into the necessary and sometimes beautiful thing it became.

In the almost ninety years that have passed since Daimler and Benz first steered their feeble and faltering motorized carriages down the cobbled streets of German towns, the car has become the most commonly used mechanism on earth—with the possible exception of the clock and the small electric motor. It has changed the living experience of man; in large parts of the world only food and shelter are more important. But this "necessity," the car, also threatens us. We know by now the automobile jams our cities, poisons our air, destroys the countryside, devours our resources of metals and oil, and adds to the death rate.

Yet there are signs that this trend, which has made the automobile as much our enemy as our friend, may be coming to an end. Slowly and painfully the profit-blind corporations which spew out the world's cars (what Detroit calls "the product") will be forced to realize that cars must be safer, less polluting, smaller, and of higher quality (which does not mean they should have more gewgaws, but that they should be made more carefully and of better materials).

Expectedly, Government officials moving toward these goals do not seem to understand that safety depends on handling, on better steering and suspension and braking as much as on armoring a car's inmates with belts and airbags. Nor has the Government pressed strongly enough for the development of power sources such as gas turbines and electricity. To hang pumps and plumbing on the inherently polluting internal-combustion piston engine is to pursue a forlorn hope.

Further, nothing has been done to limit officially the size of motor cars. A smaller car uses less of the world's resources of oil and metal and preempts less space on the publicly owned highways and streets.

The small advances toward rational automobiles (which does *not* mean that they should all be of a dull sameness) are, in great part, due to the public interest engendered by Ralph Nader in his book *Unsafe at Any Speed*. Certainly, there were automotive writers who for many years deplored the vast, unmanageable, bedizened automobiles which the "sales-engineers" and ad men of Detroit foisted upon us. But only Nader, by naming names and citing accident statistics, was really effective. Today Detroit, with scars on its balance sheets from foreign competition, is at last building smaller cars. And even though these still perpetuate some of the vices of their bigger relatives (which continue to outsell them), the trend is in the right direction.

3.

THE NOBILITY

Since the earliest days of the automobile there have been some few cars which have ranked above all others. What is it, or was it, about some machines that makes us snobbishly elevate them to the peerage? Simply this: that their designers and builders conceived motor cars of great excellence and elegance and then proceeded to meticulously construct them of the very best materials and with little regard for ultimate cost.

Of the hundreds of millions of cars built during the last seventy-odd years, only a minuscule proportion was in this grand category. Surely these cars gave their rich owners pleasure. But they had another important role. They inspired the builders of lesser, cheaper cars to construct automobiles which would approach them (as far as the strictures of economics would allow) in look, in comfort, and in mechanical excellence. Even today the ad men at Ford claim the silence of Rolls-Royce for their mass-consumed vehicles. The imaginative coachwork ideas of Pininfarina, Bertone, and other *carrossiers* are pirated by the presses of Detroit into millions of Americanized versions.

Bespoke bodywork was almost entirely handwork. Hispano-Suiza or Rolls-Royce or the other great makers built no bodies. Their work ended after the finished chassis was tested and retested by fussy gentlemen who sat on crude test bodies temporarily fastened to the frame. Often these "bodies" were no more than rough wooden benches.

Earlier the customer had conferred with the coachbuilder or with the dealer from whom he ordered his car. Sometimes he ordered from designs in the coachbuilder's book but with modification to suit his fancy. But often the customer had quixotic ideas. He might want a tall roof so that he need not stoop when entering while wearing his top hat. Or a queen might require a folding rear quarter from which she would be visible as she waved to her subjects. A pope might need a throne to sit on. Indian potentates ordered special open hunting cars, complete with racks for their English double rifles, extra lights, ammunition repositories, and benches for gunbearers. Ivory, gold, silver hardware, bars built of rare woods, upholstery in petit-point, inbuilt toilets and washing facilities—the great body builders were used to any kind of demand. Some of them, like Barker, a British firm founded in 1710, had long built such

caprices into horse carriages.

Horse-drawn coachwork was of wood paneling set into a wooden framework. The earliest car bodies were of exactly the same kind of construction. As early as 1902, however, the Parisian *carrossiers*, Mm. Rothschild et Fils, started the trend toward paneling the wooden body framework in aluminum in order to construct the sexily curvilinear "*roi des Belges*" body for the Mercedes Sixty, which King Leopold of Belgium bought for the use of his very good friend Mlle. Cléo de Mérode. And for the next fifty years such aluminum paneling on a wood frame was common to almost all bespoke bodywork, both open and closed. A few builders later used a metal instead of a wood framework.

From a full-size drawing of the body made on a huge blackboard, master woodworkers constructed a skeleton of the body. Tautly fitted over this framework (it was a pity sometimes to see such elegant joinery covered) were hand-beaten panels of aluminum deftly curved to fit the skeleton exactly. Fenders were made separately, beaten and rolled out over wooden frames which were removed after the fenders had been shaped.

Before lacquer came in, in the nineteen-twenties, good bodywork was painted in the same manner as the ancient coaches. As many as forty coats of paint, hand-rubbed between coats, were carefully brushed on. Finally, in a dust-proof room hung with wet sheets to aid dustlessness, and only if the temperature was above 65 degrees, a coat of coach varnish was flowed on. The result was magnificently mirror-like. Then came the striper, a specialist with a brush called a striping dagger, who "lined-out" the body, wheels, and axles in stripes to contrast with the body color.

The great English body builders, Hooper, Freestone and Webb, James Young, Thrupp and Maberly, and the others, are gone now. Only H. J. Mulliner, Park Ward Ltd. still continues. Owned by Rolls-Royce, it builds bodies for the Phantom VI and the Corniche models. Ordinary RR bodies are stamped out and then lovingly finished.

Nor are the French any better off. Saoutchik, Binder, Letournier et Marchand, Chapron—all gone.

The USA once had custom body builders second

Preceding pages: 1911 40/50-hp Silver Ghost.
Elegant vertically striped coachwork
is by Barker. Opposite: In 1905, to allay
criticism that 20-hp Rolls-Royce
was too high-geared to stop and restart on a
hill, Claude Goodman Johnson, company chairman,
sailed up a steep grade with this mob aboard.

to none. Brewster, Locke, Dietrich, Murphy, Rollston, Holbrook. No more.

The Italians continue to build bodywork for their Maseratis, Ferraris, Lamborghinis, and Lancias. Bertone, Pininfarina, Ghia, and the rest build coachwork of supreme elegance and lightness.

Only Rolls-Royce and Mercedes-Benz build real luxury cars today. There are, of course, the stretched Lincolns and Cadillacs, fitted out with bars and television sets for oil millionaires, presidents, and TV celebrities. But under their svelte and not too well-finished skins lurks Detroit machinery.

It is not only the perfection of construction that puts a car into the topmost class. Its performance must excel all others in the framework of its time. I stress time. Although a 1902 Panhard et Levassor was certainly in the first rank in its day, we cannot fairly compare it with, say, an Hispano-Suiza of 1937.

Performance today means speed and acceleration, but it should have a larger meaning. There should be smoothness in the control of engine speed, gear-shifting, steering, and braking. All these systems should operate like sensitive extensions of the driver's nervous system. This is true performance. Certainly we want speed and acceleration, but not at the expense of roughness and unpleasant noises caused by mechanical crudity.

Here then, with their orders, decorations, and pedigrees, are some of the nobility among motor cars.

ROLLS-ROYCE

I have lived intimately with four Rolls-Royces. The first one to share my board, in 1937, was American, a 1927 Springfield (Massachusetts)-built Phantom I with a double-cowl Ascot tourer body by Brewster. The last, in 1960, was a real British Royce, a 1935 Phantom II Continental with a drophead body by Henry Binder of Paris. Between these two came another Phantom II, with British Barker coachwork, and a Phantom I Springfield model of 1927 with a *sedanca de ville* body—the Riviera—by Brewster.

I loved them all, but unequally. Thinking back, I realize that it was the P-II Continental drophead that I was most enamored of.

I had bought that one in a peculiar way (almost every car I've ever owned was acquired in odd fashion). I saw it advertised one Sunday morning in 1958 in *The New York Times*, its price a mere $1,000. The address was Avenue Foch in Paris. Normally, I would have ignored the advertisement, for inevitably the avid members of the Rolls-Royce Owners Club would have beaten me to it. But this was a special Sunday: The eager Roycers were far away at a Rolls-Royce meet in Montreal. I telephoned the owner in Paris, begged him to hold the car until the morning when a friend, the late illustrator Leslie Saalburg (then in Paris), would arrive with the money. I then got Leslie on the phone, told him I was wiring him money to buy me a Rolls-Royce, but not to buy it if the car was a dog.

Monday afternoon I had a call from Saalburg. "You've got a nice car," he said, "but what am I supposed to do with it? The concierge is raising hell about my keeping it in the courtyard." (Leslie lived in an apartment in a sixteenth-century house complete with a cobbled courtyard.) "Every time I start it up the neighbors raise a fuss because it roars so." (I worried: a roaring Rolls?)

"Call American Express and have them deliver it to New York," I said. Leslie delivered the car to the express company in a Paris railway yard. After a trip on a flat car, then a

wait in Le Havre, then an ocean voyage aboard a freighter, the Rolls finally arrived in New York.

After the usual hassling on the pier (with long-shoremen, customs men, Department of Agriculture men), I set out for home. Leslie had been right: That Rolls *did* roar embarrassingly. And no wonder. The after-end of the muffler was gone, burned away after twenty-three years of muffling. Somehow I made the hundred-odd-mile trip home to eastern Connecticut without trouble with the police, and proudly switched off and climbed out as my wife and kids swarmed into the driveway.

"Hey, Pop," said my youngest, "what makes that funny bubbling sound and why is white smoke coming out around the gas cap?" I flipped open the filler cap. The fuel was nicely on the boil. The flames from that open-ended muffler had done a fine job of heating the fuel tank.

A temporary welding job on the muffler ended my fears of the Rolls becoming a flaming rocket. A new "silencer" from London (cost: a thumping £70, including customs duty) made the Rolls a quiet gentleman again.

That 1935 Phantom II Continental (187 TA) was the last model of the big 40/50-hp Rolls-Royce (taxable horsepower) cars. Its six-cylinder 7,668-cc (about 460 cu. in.) engine must have developed over 160 hp (Rolls-Royce Ltd. never talks about horsepower). The Continental differed from the standard model in having a slightly higher rear-end ratio (3.41 to 1), a

Preceding pages: 1905 10-hp, two-cylinder Rolls-Royce.

Top left: Two-cylinder engine of 1905 Rolls-Royce.

Top right: C. S. Rolls in his 1907

Silver Ghost, specially built to hold his balloon.

Far right: Eric Platford, chief tester

for Rolls-Royce, driving Silver Rogue in 1908

Scottish Reliability Trials.

higher compression ratio for the engine, and flatter springs. Further, the Continental was always built on the "short" 144-inch-wheelbase chassis. (The long chassis was 150 inches.)

My Continental was somewhat Frenchified. In addition to its French coachwork, its instruments read metrically, its lights were great staring Marchals, and its instruction book was a condensed version in French. Most Gallic of all, however, was a complex auxiliary shock-absorber system in addition to the regular RR hydraulic dampers. Twin nickel-plated cranks on the steering column, one each for front and rear, tensioned a cat's cradle of steel cables which tightened four friction shock absorbers. Fully wound, these shockers could stiffen things into the rock-like immobility which people once considered necessary for high-speed roadholding.

Continentals usually had such auxiliary shock absorbers, but most of them were British André-Telecontrols which were operated hydraulically via pipes and rubber bags in the shock absorbers.

But the Continental was a long-legged machine for open spaces and long, fast runs. Its very name suggested that here was a motor car not for the twisting lanes of England, but for the long, straight, poplar-lined *routes nationales*, a car to run from Boulogne to Nice between dawn and dusk, tirelessly, quietly, and in regal splendor.

The Connecticut Highway Department does not supply poplar-lined *routes nationales*, and rural Connecticut is no

place for regal splendor. Still, my P-II adapted itself very nicely. Despite its age (it was twenty-three years old when I got it), and its size, and its almost three-ton weight, it was agile and quick. One hundred and sixty km showed often enough on its speedometer, although zero to 60 mph took about 20 seconds. Its four-speed gearbox (synchro on the top two speeds) was sheer delight, the right-hand lever moving with oily, silent smoothness. And if I felt lazy, I just did not bother shifting down at all, even at 5 mph. From which speed, in top gear, the big engine picked up with uncomplaining smoothness.

The P-II had its little foibles. Its servo brakes, energized from the gearbox through a clutch (a much-vaunted Rolls-Royce device built under license from Hispano-Suiza), did not have quite the stopping power they ought to have had, since the clutch discs, "being designed to function with no lubricant" (the Rolls-Royce handbook said), somehow managed to get themselves oily.

If the brake servo was *too* oily, the kingpins upon which the front wheels pivoted were not oily enough. This dryness and consequent wear and rusting (dare I use those words about a Rolls-Royce?) were due to too little oil coming down the pipes from the RR's central oiling system, which theoretically, upon the operation of a plunger from the driving compartment, fed metered amounts of lubricant even to the farthest reaches of the chassis.

These seem like small matters, easily remedied, but

Left: Cockpit of 1923
American-built Silver Ghost.
Right-hand drive was
unusual in Springfield RR's.
Top: Frontal aspect
of same Brewster-bodied
Pall Mall phaeton.
Above: A similar Springfield
Rolls-Royce built in 1922.
Earliest RR's built
in Springfield, Massachusetts,
were close replicas of
cars built in Rolls' Derby
factory. Later models
gradually departed
from British designs.

Rolls-Royce's stuffy agents in New York (they've since been replaced) either couldn't or wouldn't bother with a twenty-five-year-old car. They said there were too many new Rolls-Royces to worry about.

I fixed them good. I sold the Royce for $3,000 (about £1,200), or perhaps $2,000 less than the car finally cost me after repainting, rechroming, reupholstering, etc. If I had the car today, I'd ship it back to RR's service station at Hythe Road in London, where they're reputedly not too busy to fuss with *sixty*-year-old Royces.

The other type of Rolls which owned me was the Springfield version of the Phantom I. (The Phantom I was at first called the New Phantom; it didn't get a number until the Phantom II arrived on the scene in 1929.) These machines were somewhat Americanized models built in the Massachusetts factory for the ten years from 1921 to 1931.

If I had never driven the British-built Rolls, I would have thought these Springfield Phantoms truly wonderful machines. But, although they were meticulously built, they somehow just missed having the superb feel of their English cousins. The Springfield P-I differed from the British model in several important respects. It had a three-speed instead of a four-speed gearbox. Since it had left-hand steering, its long, thin gear lever sprouted from a ball in the center of the front floor. (This alone was less pleasurable than moving the beautifully designed, stiff gear lever in a visible gate which the British P-I had.) Further, the American Rolls, although it had twin ignition, used two coils instead of a coil and a magneto. Electrics—starter, generator, etc.—were by Westinghouse. Instruments, too, were American, as were the wire wheels. In fact, practically no part of the car was imported, except for the engine crankshaft. The American cars were, in my opinion, superior in one respect: Most of them had Brewster-built coachwork, which in design and construction is second to none. Brewster bodies forty-years-old are tight and rattle-free, while much of the old wood-framed, English coachwork dries out and wobbles with every breeze in the more arid American climate.

The Ascot double-cowl tourer was, with top furled, a delight for summer journeys, but our special joy—my brother's and mine—was long excursions in winter when, with top

erected, side curtains buttoned on, and chains on the rear wheels, we'd make long passages over empty, snow-covered roads. With the snow crunching under the Rolls' big wheels (700 x 21) and a cloud of snow in our wake, we'd charge along at fifty or so with confidence in the surefootedness of that big battle cruiser of a car. I don't remember even a hint of a skid.

When necessary, a Springfield P-I could move quite quickly. In 1954 I drove the 1927 Riviera to Springfield, Massachusetts, for a meet of the Rolls-Royce Owners' Club. My wife at the same time was visiting nearby Northampton for a class reunion. There she fell seriously ill and it became necessary to transport her in an ambulance to Long Island. I drove the Rolls to Northampton, had her bundled into the ambulance, which then screeched off, siren howling and red lights flashing, into the Sunday traffic. The ambulance bulled its way along at a steady 70 plus—sometimes much faster on straight, open stretches. I followed close behind. A few times on the parkway I had to mount the curb and take to the grass in order to pass a slowpoke (this on twenty-five-year-old whitewall tires). Still that huge old P-I stayed right with the ambulance. Average speed for the 150-odd miles to the hospital was 50 mph, top speed reached, 80 mph.

The Riviera P-I was oddly acquired, too. I had heard that a V-12 Cadillac tourer was for sale on a Long Island estate. The Cadillac was there, all right. But at $750 it seemed, back in 1952, high priced. I stuck my nose into another garage on the place—and there, sitting in the middle of a vast and spotless wood floor that looked as if it belonged in a ballroom, was a very large something—a car? One could not be sure, because it was entirely wrapped in brown paper glued together with gummed tape. I turned to the family chauffeur who had shown me the Cadillac. "What's that?"

"The master's Rolls-Royce, sir," he answered.

"May I look at it?"

"I can't unwrap it, sir."

"Just a peek?"

"You may tear a small hole in the paper, sir. I can tape it up again."

I tore a small opening in what looked like the radiator end of the package. A huge, shining Marchal headlight stared

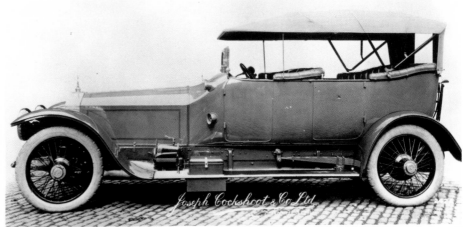

1. 1905 two-cylinder Rolls-Royce, C. S. Rolls at wheel.
2. Rolls-Royce armored cars performed
in both World Wars. Silver Ghost chassis were used.
3. Silver Ghost with coachwork by Joseph Cockshoot.
4. 1927 Phantom I with boattail body,
purportedly built for an Indian maharajah. Lockers on
running boards supposedly held ammunition.

The Premier "Straight Eight"

Above: British advertisement for Isotta Fraschini. Right: 1938 4¼-litre Bentley. This Rolls-Royce-built model was based on the 25/30-hp Rolls-Royce, but had a twin-carburetor engine and a lower chassis. Known as "the Silent Sports Car," it was capable of over 90 mph. This example, once the author's, had Thrupp and Maberly drophead coachwork.

back at me. To its right was a gleaming Rolls radiator shell. Stretching into the brown dimness was an awful lot of Rolls-Royce.

"Is it for sale?"

"Perhaps, sir."

After complex and devious negotiations with the chauffeur and his employer, Rolls-Royce number S184PM with Riviera *coupé de ville* coachwork by Brewster became mine for $400. It required nothing but a new muffler and an oil change. I didn't like its odd, blue color, so I had Gus Reuter repaint it in primrose and gray.

The Phantoms I and II were the last series of Rolls-Royces that Henry Royce was involved with. After his death in 1933, other brains and hands carried on to build the Phantom III, the Wraith, the Silver Dawn, and the other great machines down to the fine Silver Shadow of today.

Henry Royce was already past forty when he constructed his first car. He had by then built up a business in electric cranes and dynamos. Royce's electrical devices, built with the same precision and superlative finish that his cars would have, sold very nicely in those spacious Victorian days when British manufacturers had the world to themselves. But toward the end of the century, the United States and Germany, began to give the British stiff industrial competition. Further, England after the Boer War found itself in a recession. Things didn't look too rosy at Royce Ltd. in Manchester.

Royce had some experience with a rather fearsome little device called a de Dion Quadricycle and also a more sophisticated machine, the 10-hp, two-cylinder Decauville. Neither of these vehicles was any great shakes. Why, Royce must have reasoned, shouldn't Royce Ltd. build a *properly* engineered machine and get into this new business of motor cars? Royce, after some arm twisting, brought his directors around to a similar view, and by April 1, 1904, the first two-cylinder car of Royce quality (which meant the very best) was ready to roll onto the Queen's highways.

But it wasn't until after Hon. Charles S. Rolls and Mr. Henry Royce had lunch together at the Great Central Hotel in Manchester that the car got that onomatopoeic name, so oilily suggestive of smoothly turning and gliding surfaces.

It would be hard to find two more dissimilar characters lunching together, Royce the rugged, self-made mechanic-cum-engineer, Rolls the elegant young cosmopolite and son of Lord Llangattock. Rolls wanted a new car to sell in his London showroom (C. S. Rolls & Co. already were the agents for the Panhard et Levassor and the Minerva, among other makes). Royce needed an outlet for his car. But Rolls thought that the new Rolls-Royce car ought to have more than two cylinders. Three- or even four-cylindered machines would sell better.

In 1904 the *dernier cri* was the six-cylinder car. Although a fair number of car builders were already building sixes (starting with Spyker, the Dutch firm), it was the English Napier that had the most noise made about it. Selwyn F. Edge, its windy promoter, trumpeted that his car was "the Best Car in the World" and, in fact, was defeating all comers, including such giants as Mercedes and Mors, in competitions he dreamed up to prove it.

It was high time for Rolls-Royce to show how a six *ought* to be built. Unfortunately, the first Rolls-Royce sixes—the 30-hp's of 1905—were less than perfect. Among their vices was a nasty crankshaft vibration at certain speeds. Some crankshafts broke, too. Only thirty-seven were built before Royce and his draftsmen designed an entirely new six, the great 40/50-hp Silver Ghost.

At rare intervals an artifact appears which by a happy combination of circumstances turns out to be exactly right in look, in utility, and above all, perhaps, in its ability to fire the imaginations of people, not only at the time of its appearance, but for years afterward. The early Leica camera was such an object. The Mercer Raceabout car was another. The DC-3 airplane comes to mind, as does the Spitfire. There are but a few other names on this short list, and unquestionably the Silver Ghost Rolls-Royce belongs among them.

In 1907, when the Ghost first appeared, most cars were noisy. They vibrated. They smoked. The Ghost was silent, not because Henry Royce had discovered some revolutionary secret means of combining rapidly moving metal parts—Royce seldom was an innovator—but because each of those parts was carefully designed for its purpose and then painstakingly made of the very best cast iron, steel, aluminum, or bronze. Slow,

meticulous assembly helped, too. A Ghost engine was quiet also, because Royce did not demand that it run rapidly in order to deliver the power that its cubic capacity (7,036 cc before 1909, 7,428 cc thereafter) might lead one to expect from it. Its small carburetor and small valves kept the revs (and the horsepower) down, as did its big and perhaps overzealous muffler.

Royce, as a youth, had been an apprentice in the locomotive shops of the Great Northern Railway and, not surprisingly, railway engineering practice showed in his work. High-speed locomotives had hollow crankshafts through which their oil was forced under pressure from a pump. The Ghost, too, used such a system when most cars' engines still had a total-loss oiling system. These received oil from an external pump, an "oiler," which bathed their parts in lubricant that then dripped into the crankcase. This naturally became overfilled after a time, since the oil could not return to the pump. You had to get under a car to let some out (into the road, usually) while adding fresh oil to the oiler.

Some cars had drip-fed regulators on their instrument panels which purportedly metered the correct amount of oil going to various parts of the machinery. Drivers, fearful of run bearings, usually fed too much oil. This fouled plugs, carboned cylinders, clogged mufflers. A white cloud of greasy smoke usually followed most cars down the road. No such effluvium accompanied a Silver Ghost.

The Silver Ghost was almost perfectly suited for the Edwardian world into which it was born. Its 70-mph top speed was more than quick enough for the leisured rich of those leisurely days. And if the tremendous amount of labor necessary to keep it greased and serviced seems shocking to us, we must remember that the income-taxless upper classes were up to their ears in underpaid servants—chauffeurs and footmen and grooms.

In 1926 the Silver Ghost became the New Phantom —the P-I—with overhead valves instead of the side valves of the Ghost. In 1929 the P-I became the P-II with an open drive shaft instead of the heavy torque tube of the first Phantom and with normal half-elliptic rear springs instead of the outboard cantilevers aft.

Charles Rolls never saw any Rolls-Royce model beyond the Ghost. An early aeronaut, he was killed in the crash of a Wright biplane in 1910. Royce, in poor health for years, suffered a serious collapse in 1911. After that, until his death in 1933, he had little to do with the actual running of the factory, although he continued to do much designing at his country homes at Canadel in the south of France and at West Wittering in Sussex, where he had small staffs of draftsmen.

The loss of Rolls and the invalidism of Royce might well have wrecked the company if it had not been for Claude Goodman Johnson, who had been a partner of Charles Rolls since 1903. Johnson, more than anyone, had made the Rolls-Royce famous. He had pushed Rolls-Royce into contests and competitions. He had coined the name Silver Ghost after painting a 1907 40/50 (the thirteenth one built) silver, and silver-plating its bright parts as a publicity ploy. In fact, he really ran the show at Rolls-Royce, and it was he who, when Royce was stricken, forced him to leave the factory before he died of overwork.

Above: 1955 Rolls-Royce Silver Wraith with coachwork by H. J. Mulliner.
Above right: 1935 Continental Phantom II with drophead body by Henry Binder. This is the machine whose importation from Paris is described in the text. It could reach almost 100 mph.

It has been said that Johnson's insistence that Royce leave the works may have saved the company from Royce's fanatic perfectionism, which caused continual changes in design and raised hell with the costs of production.

The present-day Rolls-Royce stems neither from the great 40/50 sixes—the Ghost, the P-I, the P-II—nor from the big P-III, that complex and wonderful V-12 of 1936–1939, but from a smaller automobile, the 20-hp Baby Rolls of 1922, which was brought out as an "economy" car at £1,500! This lovely, if sedately slow, little machine developed into the more powerful and quicker 20/25-hp of 1929, the 3½-litre Rolls-Bentley of 1933, the 25/30-hp of 1936, the 4¼-litre Rolls-Bentley of 1936 and, finally, the Wraith of 1938. All had engines with a 4½-inch stroke. Bore diameter and power went up over the years.

Postwar Royces—the Silver Wraith of 1947, the Silver Dawn of 1949, the Silver Cloud I, and the various Bentleys until 1959—still had six-cylinder engines with the same 4½-inch stroke of the Baby Rolls of 1922. By 1959 that was about all that was left of the little ancestor. Starting in 1959 Rolls-Royce went to V-8's (there had been a straight-eight engine in the snobbish, only-for-royalty Phantom IV of 1950 of which only sixteen examples were made).

The current V-8 Silver Shadow has an engine of indeterminate horsepower, an automatic transmission, a self-leveling chassis, and disc brakes; it's as modern as modern can be. Is it still "the Best Car in the World"? Yes, it is, if you mean is it the best five- or seven-passenger device for going from here to there. Maseratis and Lamborghinis and such are really different animals.

The elegance not merely of the Shadow's coachwork, but of small details like the hand-finished, chrome-plated buttons for locking the doors, the switches on the lovely wood-veneered instrument panel, even the Yale lock for the glove-compartment door, are second to none on any car on earth.

Still, the things I loved about the old Royces—the beautifully polished machinery under the floorboards, the felt-lined mahogany floorboards themselves with their bronze hold-down screws running in bronze bushings, the wonderfully contrived gear lever in its gate, that mass of precise gadgetry at the hub of the steering wheel, over-all an infinity of pleasurable mechanical details—are gone, as are the artisans who were willing to labor over such beautiful (if not necessarily functional) complications for a couple of shillings an hour.

Probably this is why so many Rolls-Royce enthusiasts love the old Royces—the Ghosts, Twenties, Phantoms; they venerate the sheer elegance of their mechanisms. An elderly Rolls-Royce engine does not look particularly beautiful to the uninitiated. To them it is a mass of black-enameled machinery with an aluminum or brass bit here and there. There is not the ooh-ing and ah-ing that the polished and fettled aluminum sculpture under a Bugatti's bonnet is sure to evoke. But the dedicated Roycer is smugly happy with the knowledge that mechanical beauty hides under the paint; that, for example, every control rod, from the carburetor or the magneto or whatever, fits every other control rod exactly, without shake or play.

Flat-out speed means little to a Roycer. If it did he

would be looking at Ferraris or their like instead. *He's* proud of how *slowly* a Rolls-Royce P-II will glide along on a whiff of throttle with no bucking or fuss. He likes the feeling of small-ness even the biggest models have when threading their way through traffic. Above all he loves the indefinable feel of quality transmitted to his hands on the wheel, to his feet on the pedals.

Until a few years ago this kind of Rolls-Royce lover was not necessarily rich. Some I knew were quite poor men who'd buy an elderly Rolls for very little money and then spend years of labor making it into a gem. Today almost any Rolls costs too much for such impecunious types.

Fewer than 8,000 Ghosts, both British and American, were built in the nineteen years of their production. People who could afford one bought a Rolls because it was more reliable and quieter and, oddly, because it was more economical to main-tain than other first-class cars of its day. Later, as it became established as *the* car of the knowledgeable rich, the cachet of the name became important to those people who must always have the correct possessions.

Today the Silver Shadow's base price of $28,400 is really less in our debased money than the $8,000 price of a 1907 Ghost. Some people say they are buying Rolls-Royces for the same reasons Ghost owners did sixty-five years ago: econ-omy, reliability, and the pleasure of owning a well-made article. Perhaps a Rolls *does* begin to be economical if you keep it for twenty years.

Preceding pages: 1907 six-cylinder, 60-hp Napier. The British Napier was the first successful six-cylinder car and was, for a time, the great rival of the Rolls-Royce. Above: A similar Napier touring Newfoundland.

ISOTTA FRASCHINI

If I were allowed but one word to describe the Isotta Fraschinis which could be seen in surprising numbers on New York's Park Avenue and Hollywood's Sunset Boulevard in the fateful year of 1929, that word would have to be "arrogant." How else might one describe a giant of a car whose brightly polished hood stretched more than seven feet from radiator cap to wind-shield, whose wheelbase exceeded twelve feet, whose straight-eight engine had a cubic capacity of 7,350 cc and yet trans-ported but one person other than the driver. Such a roadster with a Castagna body was ordered by Rudolph Valentino for $25,000 (£5,000). And at least one limousine with ivory and silver fittings is said to have been sold for $40,000.

The 8A Isotta Fraschini was by no means a large lump of flashy trash. It was no Auburn. It was built quite as well as its fellow aristocrats, the Rolls-Royce and the Hispano-Suiza. And like them it had noble forebears (but few descend-ants).

Cesare Isotta and Oreste Fraschini had exhibited their first car in 1901 in Milan. It was a 5-hp, single-cylindered gas buggy. By 1906 they were important constructors exhibiting in Paris. By 1908 they were winning the Sicilian Targa Florio and taking second place at Long Island's Vanderbilt Cup.

The variety of models built by IF before the Kaiser War is mind-boggling. It doesn't seem possible that the jewel-like overhead-cam-engined 1,200-cc voiturettes of 1908–1911 came from the same factory as the elephantine 12-litre IM model of 1910 or the 11-litre brute of 1914, the KM.

Still, all of the Isottas of those days had one important thing in common: four-wheel brakes. Isotta Fraschini was the first in the world with them—in 1909.

After World War I the multiplicity of types gave way to one model, the world's first production straight-eight, the Tipo 8 of 1920. This was superseded by the 8A in 1925. Shorter-chassis "sports" versions, the Spinto and the Superspinto, became available in the late twenties.

The 8B Isotta Fraschini came out during evil times —1932—and few were sold. Its chief advantages were a stiffer frame of deeper section and a Wilson preselector gearbox instead of the three-speed box of earlier models.

Isotta turned to other fields in the mid-nineteen-thirties—aircraft and torpedo-boat engines, military hardware.

In 1947 a Tipo 8C was shown at the Paris Salon. Called the Monterosa, it had a 2½-litre V-8 engine in its tail, independent suspension, and well-constructed but bulbously ugly bodywork. It failed to bring Isotta Fraschini back from the dead.

NAPIER

Until the Silver Ghost Rolls-Royce came along to push it off its throne, the lordly six-cylinder, 60-hp Napier was *the* British car of the Edwardian rich.

Although Montague Napier was the man whose name was engraved (yes, engraved) on the radiator, it was another man who made the name famous: Selwyn Francis Edge. I'm sure that the British hoped that Edge someday would be unmasked as an American, for he was the kind of blatant, publicity-seeking promoter that the English think of as very American.

D. Napier and Son Limited had been engaged in building coin-minting machines, printing presses, scales, and other precise devices since 1808. In 1899 S. F. Edge approached Montague Napier and asked him to build a new 7-hp, two-cylinder engine for his 1896 Panhard.

Napier had already been intrigued by motor cars and was building one of his own when he was sidetracked by the persuasive Mr. Edge. The new Napier-Panhard took the road in November, 1899, and thenceforth, until 1912, Napier and Edge were inextricably combined.

In 1900 the first wholly Napier-built two-cylinder chain-drive car appeared and was immediately entered in the legendary Thousand-Mile Trial, where it won a medal.

Napiers first became really famous for winning the Gordon Bennett Trophy in 1902, but an exploit, begun in 1901, also was making the name Napier well-known in the United States. This was Charles Glidden's world tour of 1901–1908, in which he used up four Napiers and drove some 45,000 miles through forty-odd countries. In roadless places Mr. Glidden fitted his Napiers with flanged wheels and took to railroad tracks. (The indefatigable Glidden was, of course, the man who started America's famous Glidden Tours, revived in recent years by the antique-car people.) Glidden's success also resulted in an American-built (in Boston) Napier, a few examples of which still exist.

It is the great, long-nosed Napier Six that we best remember today. Edge first trumpeted the six-cylinder car as far back as the autumn of 1903. He was even brash enough to make the claim that the six-cylinder engine was his own invention; this despite the fact that six-cylinder engines had been built by Spyker and Sunbeam among others. Fernand Forest in France had shown a six as far back as 1889. Admittedly, however, Edge was the first man to successfully market a six.

The 60-hp 1907 Napier was a typical example. The L-head engine consisted of three blocks each of two cylinders with a 5-inch bore and a 4-inch stroke. Ignition was by coil, and provision was made for a magneto if a customer wanted one. Although rated 60 hp, some 100 hp was said to have been developed. It was the prodigious length of this engine that gave the Napier its ungainly look, for the radiator was mounted far forward, overhanging the front axle. The tall "water-tower" radiator filler was another Napier peculiarity.

The chassis of the Napier was typical for its day— a simple ladder-type frame with two leaf springs forward and three in "platform" configuration (one spring athwartships) aft. Unusual for a car of its power in 1907 was shaft drive. A six cost £1,465 in 1907.

A friend, Ronald Barker, the noted English motoring writer, owns a similar car. I visited him recently, and, although he invited me out for a drive, I declined. My excuse was the weather—too cold. In reality I was just too frightened of his exuberant driving style. You wouldn't believe it possible to throw a big machine around the way Barker does. His big Napier handles like a modern sports car. At least it does for Barker.

Edge, ever eager for kudos, continually campaigned his cars. Brooklands Track was barely completed in 1907 when Edge took a 60-hp six out on the fresh cement. (The trouble with bumps on the track's surface for the next thirty-five years has been attributed to Edge's run on the uncured concrete.) He ran the Napier, following a line of kerosene lamps, for twenty-four hours, covered 1,582 miles, and became the first man in history to average a mile a minute around the clock.

Edge was particularly proud of the Napier's top-gear performance and had cousin Cecil Edge drive one from Brighton to Edinburgh in top gear. In another stunt, designed to prove that Napiers were controllable despite blowouts, a car was driven at high speed over broken soda-water syphons. Naturally Napier took a crack at the London–Monte Carlo record—everyone did in those days. One A. E. Paul broke the record in 33 hours and 34 minutes.

Edge departed from Napier in 1912. Then the Kaiser War turned Napier to aeroplane engines and no new car appeared until 1919. This, the overhead-cam-engined 40/50-hp, failed to take hold and Napier concentrated on aero engines, which—as part of the English Electric aeronautical combine— it still does.

What did Edge think of the Rolls-Royce? In 1911 he said it was "certainly quite a nice car."

DAIMLER

When I hear the name "Daimler" I don't, in my mind's eye, see the svelte, low, ultramodern, ohc-engined luxury machines that British Leyland Motors now builds and which, except for their prows, are much like Jaguars. I see vast, tall, maroon-and-black equipages occupied by kings in top hats and queens wearing even funnier hats. These huge automotive devices seem always, in my imagination, to be silently proceeding down the Mall from Buckingham Palace and to emit a hint of oil smoke from their exhaust pipes.

British royalty did proceed in such Daimlers for years and years (they also use other marques today), because of some hassle with Rolls-Royce which is now largely forgotten. And obviously, attuned to the cachet of such royal patronage, lesser denizens of the *Almanach de Gotha* could do no less than ride behind their chauffeurs and footmen in machines similar to those their monarchs chose.

Daimler today has no connection with Daimler-Benz of Germany, the people who build the Mercedes-Benz. British Daimler got its name from an 1893 licensing arrangement between Daimler-Motorengesellschaft and the British Daimler Motor Syndicate Ltd., which had been set up to build Daimler engines.

The first British-built (in Coventry) Daimlers appeared in 1897. Earlier Daimlers shown at the first automobile show at the Imperial Institute in London had been German-built in Cannstatt. It had been in one of these that the Prince of Wales (later Edward VII) had his first ride in a motor car, thus starting the long involvement of the House of Hanover (later Windsor) with Daimler cars.

Between 1897 and 1903 Daimlers of some twelve different configurations and sizes of engine came popping out of the Coventry factory. Some had two cylinders, some four. Although some had the tiny capacity of 1.1 litres, engines as big as 4½ litres powered a few models.

The early Daimler quickly made a name for itself, winning no fewer than sixteen awards in that first important English event, the Thousand-Mile Trial of 1900. After this success the Prince of Wales bought himself a 6-hp model with coachwork by Hooper. This was still an open model, but Hooper would later build those towering motorized greenhouses from which queens would wave.

Until fairly recent times most Daimlers looked pretty stodgy. But there was often very innovative engineering under their conservative skins. In 1908 Daimler was one of the first to adopt the quiet sleeve-valve engine invented by Charles Knight. Mercedes, Panhard, Minerva, Voisin, Willys, and Stearns for a time also used the Knight design, but Daimler continued long after the others gave it up. That little plume of oil smoke was the Daimler-Knight trademark. The most remarkable use of the Knight sleeve-valve engine was in the famous and fabulous Daimler Double-Six. This 7,136-cc V-12

Opposite: 1899 12-hp Daimler.
This was the first
four-cylinder Coventry-Daimler.
Owned by Hon. John
Scott-Montagu, it took third
place in the Tourist Class
of the 1899 Paris–Ostend race.

1

first appeared in 1926 and in various smaller sizes was built until 1937. Coupled with another Daimler first, the Fluid Flywheel, still used in modern automatic transmissions, it was one of the smoothest, quietest power plants of all time, even by modern standards.

Most Double-Sixes, including those King George V added to his stable, were uncompromisingly square. But a few were taken in hand by Reid Railton of Thomson and Taylor (the racing-car specialists who used to supply me with Alfa Romeo parts at dime-store prices) and made into the longest-hooded sporting cars ever seen anywhere. With only 150-odd hp their speed was unexceptional, but it was possible to go from 2 to 82 mph without touching the gear lever. Later models used the famous Wilson preselector gearbox.

There have been many, many models of Daimler since the days of the Double-Six. One of them was, perhaps, the ugliest looking sports car ever built but also one of the very nicest to drive that I've ever known. This, the 2½-litre V-8 SP250, would reach 120 mph with acceleration to match. It was built between 1959 and 1964. Yet today's V-12 Vanden Plas Daimler will leave the SP250 standing. And it's the best-looking luxury car in the world.

HISPANO-SUIZA

I have long (in earlier books) sung the praises of Hispano-Suiza cars—the lovely four-cylinder T-15 Alfonso which appeared in 1912, and the Hispano that I consider one of the very

1. King Edward VII with
Hon. John Scott-Montagu
in 1901 22-hp Daimler.
2. 1932 Daimler double-six
sports saloon with
coachwork by Martin Walter.
3. Four-cylinder Daimler
stuffed with toffs
in a Coventry street c. 1902.
4. Current svelte V-12
Vanden Plas Daimler.

2

3

4

great motor cars of all time, the H6 37.2-hp (and 45-hp) over-head-camshaft six.

Recently, however, I had a ride in another Hispano-Suiza, the property of Mr. William Harrah, who, among many other interests, operates the giant Harrah Automobile Collection in Reno. This Hispano is the Type 68, a fabulous 9½-litre, V-12-engined supercar of a magnificence the world will never see again. I quickly realized that I had not in past writings given this supreme example of the marque Hispano-Suiza its due.

The V-12 Hispano-Suiza first appeared in 1931, two years after its designer Mark Birkigt had decided to build it to replace his superb H6 37.2-hp six, which he was convinced was becoming a bit long in the tooth. Birkigt's V-8 ohc aero

engines had been the most successful of all those powering the warplanes of the Allies in World War I, and his overhead-camshaft six in the H6-series cars had been based on these military engines. Before the war ended he had a V-12 on the stocks, and he used this new aero engine as the basis for his new car engine—but with one important difference. The engine in the cars would have push-rod-operated valves instead of an over-head camshaft. This he did in the interest of quiet running, for that earlier H6 engine had been, it must be admitted, a bit on the noisy side.

The twin blocks and heads of the V-12 were of aluminum alloy beautifully enameled black under pressure—an Hispano tradition. Cylinder liners of nitrided steel were screwed

1. Badge and radiator cap of 1912 "Alfonso" Hispano-Suiza. Note engraved top of cap.
2. 1912 four-cylinder Hispano-Suiza was developed from successful racing voiturette.
3. 1937 V-12 Hispano-Suiza with owner William Harrah at the steering wheel. Engine displacement is 11 litres.
4. Hispano stork was modeled after that on Spad fighter flown by French flying ace Guynemer in World War I.

1

2

3

4

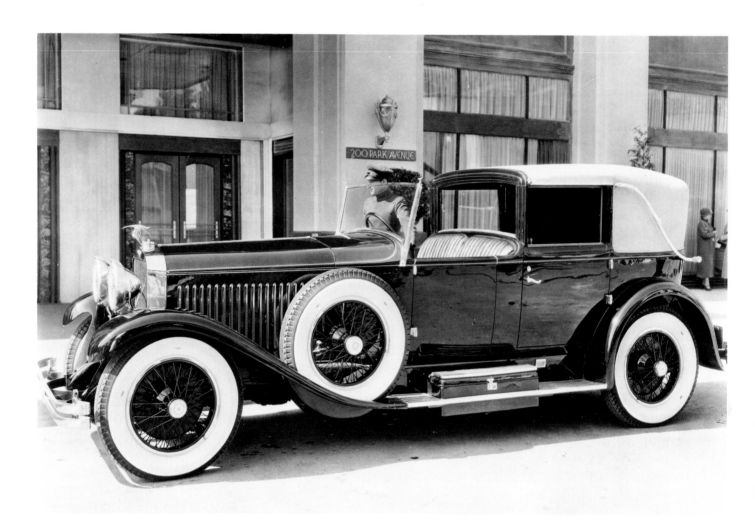

1

2

3

1. 1928 six-cylinder Type H6
Hispano-Suiza limousine.
2. 1907 four-cylinder Barcelona-built
Hispano-Suiza touring car.
3. André Dubonnet, the apéritif king,
often raced Hispanos. This
wood-bodied example is a six-cylinder model.

into the blocks. Ignition by twin Scintilla magnetos supplied the sparks to two sparkplugs per cylinder. Twenty-four sparkplugs! (Some early examples used coil ignition.) At a mere 3,000 rpm and a low compression ratio of 6 to 1, 220 hp was produced.

A later version of this engine, the 68 *bis*, had a cubic capacity of no less than 11,310 cc and produced 250 hp. And these were real hairy horses quite unlike the horsepower of Detroit fairy tales.

The chassis of the V-12 Hispano was of simple ladder-type but of great depth and rigidity. It had conventional leaf springs all around, torque-tube drive, and a three-speed gearbox whose top gear was a high 2.72 to 1. Shifting was almost redundant anyhow, considering the great torque of the huge engine.

The V-12 Hispano-Suiza's brakes, like those on the earlier ohc six, were of Birkigt's patented design—the gearbox-driven mechanical servo type, also used by Rolls-Royce under license. Operating ribbed drums of great diameter, they were remarkably efficient for mechanical brakes, considering the fact that the car, with luxury coachwork on a 146-in. wheelbase (even longer ones were offered), might weigh close to three tons.

The V-12 Hispano had a remarkable performance for its day—zero to 60 mph in 11 seconds, a top speed of about 110 mph.

The Harrah Hispano-Suiza in which I rode had a very pretty body by Letournier et Marchand and was registered as a 1937 model. I sat next to the driver as he negotiated heavy home-going Reno traffic. There was no drama in his driving—no fancy shifting, no revving of the engine in the gears, but we slipped through that traffic with eel-like ease. Nothing passed us. Serenely, in silence, with barely discernible movements of the steering wheel, that almost forty-year-old Hispano-Suiza moved through the Detroit cattle like the superior animal it was.

V-12 Hispano-Suizas were not cheap. In the mid-thirties a chassis cost £2,800, a complete car with a quite good bespoke body cost circa £4,000. I recall reading of an Indian potentate who demanded the height of luxury and paid £8,000 for his Hispano.

The V-12 was built until 1938. In the mid-thirties Hispano-Suiza took over the Ballot factories and from this union came some lesser cars of no great interest. After the war, at the 1946 Geneva Auto Show, Hispano showed a front-wheel-drive V-8, but nothing came of it.

Warning: When talking to an Hispanophile never refer to an Hispano-Suiza as a "Hisso." He will become angry.

PACKARD

Real estate speculators who've made their pile, oil men, suppliers of military hardware, and other such examples of modern success seem in some cases to feel a cultural lack unless they collect artifacts of the past. Early cars are among the objects of their acquisitive instincts. But not too early. For reasons which elude me, they covet mostly classic American cars of the nineteen-thirties (also, more understandably, Rolls-Royces of that period). Their favorites are Packards and Duesenbergs.

You can't fault them for being hot after Packards, for the Packard was for a very long time—from about 1907 until World War II—among the very best of American cars. For a time it had two great rivals, Peerless and Pierce-Arrow, and the three American greats were called the "Three P's." In later years only the Lincoln was the Packard's peer; Cadillac was never quite up there except perhaps for the short period during which the V-16 Cadillac was produced.

The Packard goes way back to 1899, when the first car, called an Ohio, was produced. By 1907 (it had been called a Packard since 1900), the four-cylinder Packard Thirty was—as it remains—a supremely desirable car. It was beautifully put together, easy to start, a pleasure to shift—although shifting was hardly necessary—and fast for its day, easily reaching 60 mph. A Thirty (its horsepower was nearer 60) would suit me fine as my only car today—except for two serious shortcomings common to all of the fine cars of its time. Its two-wheel brakes make it dangerous in today's murderous traffic, and it requires cranking by hand. The Thirty was built until 1912 when it was superseded by the Forty-eight, a six-cylinder model which had gone into production in 1911. The last of the Thirties were expensive enough, at $4,200 for a touring model, but the Forty-eight cost even more: $5,000 (£1,000) for a tourer, $6,450 for an "Imperial Limousine."

By 1925 the Packard company was something very unusual. It was a giant builder of luxury cars. The terms "giant" and "luxury" had never before been coupled. Usually, if you were a "giant" you built many cheap cars, and if you built "luxury" cars you only built a few. But America was booming; Packard had made untold millions out of World War I and was spending $57,000,000 on improving and expanding its factory.

Much of this prosperity was due to the phenomenal success of the Twin-Six V-12 Packard which had been announced in 1915 and immediately sold like mad. In 1916 alone some 10,000 were sold. Much of this success was due not only to the simple fact that the Twin-Six was a very good car. It was also a phenomenal value at $2,600 for a touring car—half of what the previous Model 48 Six had cost.

The collectors of today, however, are mostly interested in Packard's straight-eights, which arrived in 1923 when the Twin-Six departed.

I owned a typical eight for a while—a Model 734 boattail roadster, which cost $5,210 in 1929. It was one of the famous Seventh Series line of cars and was built at the time when Packard was riding the crest of the wave that was very soon to break so disastrously on the rocks of the Depression. Packard was then selling half of all the prestige cars in the world. The royal houses of Japan, Belgium, Egypt, Yugoslavia, and a half-dozen other of the now happily defunct monarchies used Packards for state occasions.

While I was in the Army in 1942 I bought my boat-tail Speedster Eight for about $400 in practically new condition—which gives you an idea of how prices go down when things get rough. I kept it for about a year. Although it looked sporting as all get out, it was, compared to the 1750 and 3-litre Alfa Romeos I had owned previously, an unresponsive barge. It was quick enough—about 90 mph from its 145-hp engine—but it was too phlegmatic compared to the lovely, nervous Alfas. I sold it to buy a 4½-litre Low-Chassis Invicta.

Packard started to build V-12's again in 1931 and built them until 1939. These were as magnificent looking cars as have ever been built in the United States—especially those bodied by coach builders like Brunn, Dietrich, Rollston, and the rest of the now long-gone American *carrossiers*. They cost enough, too. A

Brunn all-weather cabriolet cost $8,355 (£1,670) in 1939.

But Packard's decay had already been long underway by then. To stave off disaster during the Big Slump, cars like the cheap $795 Model 120 of 1935 were rushed into production.

War work saved Packard for a time. Then the postwar car shortage kept things going. In 1952 Packard was merged with another sick company, Studebaker. The end came in 1962.

DUESENBERG

That other darling of the money-is-no-object American collectors is the Duesenberg, which they revere as the most prestigious, most beautifully constructed, most glamorous car ever built in the United States. Also, the most expensive then and now.

Although you could buy a very nice Duesenberg for about $15,000 in 1928, a fellow I know recently turned down $90,000 bid at an auction for his double-cowl touring car. As was pointed out, this Duesenberg was like new, and to build a replica of it, bolt for bolt, casting for casting, couldn't be done for twice $90,000 today. If you could find somebody to do it. Which you can't.

The straight-eight Duesenberg engine displaced some 7 litres. It had twin overhead camshafts and four valves per cylinder. Connecting rods and pistons were of light alloy. Its crankshaft was a lovely piece of chrome-nickel-steel jewelry which rotated on five unusually wide (2¾-inch-diameter) main bearings. A 7-litre engine is a pretty big one. Five main bearings are not many for a huge straight-eight; nine bearings would be more usual in a high-quality engine. The secret was meticulous balancing. Every con rod, every piston, was weighed to make sure that it was *exactly* the same weight. Every revolving part was carefully balanced (especially that wonderfully machined-all-over crankshaft). To damp out any hint of crankshaft vibration, cartridges ninety-four percent full of mercury were fastened to the shaft between the two forward cylinders. The sloshing of the mercury damped out vibration. A broken crankshaft on a Duesenberg is unheard of.

The Duesenberg chassis frame was only slightly more rugged than that on a Pullman car (remember those?) and was 8½ inches deep. The semifloating axles were of 2³⁄₁₆-inch diameter, but hollow to save weight. The gearbox had only three speeds, but downshifting a Duesy merely to gain acceleration was

Preceding pages: 1903 12-hp
one-cylinder Model F Packard.
1. 1899 single-cylinder Model A Packard.
2. Driving compartment
of 1907 Model 30 Packard.
3. 1914 105-hp six-cylinder Packard.
Note the unusual aluminum wheel discs.

1

2

3

2

1. 1912 Packard still had
acetylene gas headlights. By
then Cadillac already had
electric lighting and starting.
2. Model 734 eight-cylinder
Packard boattail speedster was
capable of 95 mph. It cost
$5,200, but a similar car was
sold for $51,000 in 1972.
3. 1933 eight-cylinder Packard
with Dietrich victoria body.
4. 1931 Duesenberg Model J.
Twin-ohc, straight-eight engine
produced 265 hp. Top speed
was 116 mph. Convertible roadster
coachwork was by Murphy.

3

4

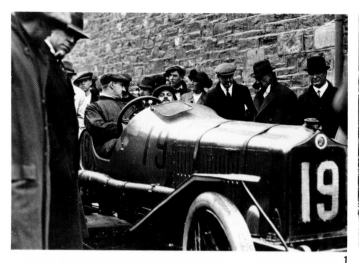

1

2

3

1. 3.3-litre racing Minerva
at the 1914 Isle of
Man Tourist Trophy Race.
2. 1907 40-hp, six-cylinder Minerva.
3. 1930 Minerva AL with
unusual double-cowl phaeton
coachwork by Murphy of Pasadena.

not looked upon as necessary.

The factory claimed that a J Duesenberg's engine developed 265 hp and would reach 116 mph (90 mph in second gear). The SJ Duesenberg which came out in 1932 boasted a centrifugal supercharger which was claimed to boost the horsepower to 320 and to increase top speed to 129 mph and second speed to 104 mph. Zero to 100 mph in 17 seconds was claimed.

I don't know how true all these claims of power and speed may be. I've never dared to drive a Duesenberg very fast. However, at the risk of incurring the wrath of owner-investors of Duesenbergs, I must say that I think a Duesenberg is nicer to look at than it is to drive at speed.

The Duesenberg brothers, long involved with racing cars, built their first passenger car, the Model A, in 1921. Developed from racing practice, it had a straight-eight ohc engine, which developed 90 hp, and hydraulic brakes. But the Model A didn't sell well, and stock-market manipulator and builder of the Cord and Auburn, E. L. Cord, took over the ailing company. It was under Cord's regime that the grandiose Duesenberg was born in 1928. Production ceased in 1937.

MINERVA

It was a not too uncommon sight in the late nineteen-twenties to see a man drive his own Duesenberg or Rolls-Royce or even his Hispano-Suiza. But to see an owner behind the wheel of a behemoth of an AL model Minerva—perish the thought. A Minerva owner rode behind his chauffeur when he didn't ride behind a chauffeur *and* footman, both in high-collared livery in a color to match the paintwork. That photograph of a sporty tourer which accompanies these words is of a most unusual Minerva. Minervas were not always so fancy.

The Minerva stemmed, as so many cars did, from bicycles and motorcycles built in Antwerp by a M. Sylvain de Jong. De Jong not only built his own motorcycles but got rich building engines for half the cycle builders of Europe and Britain.

The first actual Minerva cars appeared in 1904, but these voiturettes, starting at 1.6 litres for the one-cylinder models, were hardly precursors of the luxuries to come. Between 1904 and 1909, when de Jong embraced the sleeve-valve Knight engine, there was a multiplicity of Minerva models, even Minerva racing cars which performed on Europe's road circuits with notable success.

It was the Knight sleeve-valve engine which made the Minerva a stately goddess like its namesake. For the big advantage of sleeve-valve engines was their ability to propel a car in a stately hush. True, they laid down a small smoke screen, but that was of more concern to the people in cars following than to the inmates ensconced in the quiet luxury of a Minerva limousine.

At first, Minervas had four-cylinder sleeve-valve engines—big ones of 6.3 litres as well as a gaggle of smaller sizes. Sixes in various capacities followed them. But it was the grandiose AL type that we remember as the Queen of all Minervas. She swept into sight in 1929.

Her engine was a gigantic straight-eight with sleeve valves, a bore of 90 mm and a stroke of 130 mm (6,625 cc), nine main bearings, and both magneto and coil ignition. Of superb finish, it was a joy to behold. About 150 hp was developed.

The rest of the AL Minerva's specification was, although of impressive quality, quite conservative—a ladder-type frame with four leaf springs, a four-speed gearbox, and four-wheel mechanical brakes. There was however an unusual Adex stabilizer incorporated in the chassis—an arrangement of rods and levers which connected the rear axle to the frame and was claimed to improve roadholding.

The AL Minerva was one of the biggest cars of its time. The chassis was 17 feet, 6 inches long. With a typical limousine body it weighed about three tons. Still, people who have driven it swear to have seen better than 90 mph on the clock.

An AL Minerva was not cheap. At the Minerva agency in New York a bare chassis cost about $10,000 in 1929. Have one clothed by any of the better coach builders who did Minervas, like Hibbard and Darrin or Vanden Plas, and you'd spend another $10,000 or so. A Duesenberg complete at $15,000 was cheaper.

As it had done to other conveyances for the rich, the Depression killed off the AL Minerva. The company came up with smaller, still excellent Minervas, like the AP, which cost only £895 in England. But the times were against it. In 1935 the great *Société Nouvelle Minerve* went under.

HORNS, LIGHTS &

Pity the poor modern automobilist. There's hardly any lovely utilitarian gimcrackery he needs to buy for his new motor car. He can't even buy much stuff he *doesn't* need. Things like sporty wood-rimmed steering wheels, quartz-iodine driving lights, and the shiny chrome junk small-town kids buy to fancy up their cars are about all he can find to attract him.

In the early days speedometers, horns, lights, and other appurtenances were not molded-in parts of a new car, as they are today. They were separate pieces. If a manufacturer included lights, or even a top, in the price of a car, he loudly proclaimed such unusual benisons in his advertising.

Take lights, for instance. The very first cars to venture abroad after dark used candle lamps, the kind horse carriages and hearses had used for years, imitations of which are now seen flanking the front doors of suburban houses. The long stem hanging beneath the body of such a lamp held the candle. But candles did not cast their gleam far enough even for 10-mph speeds, and kerosene lights were little better. Acetylene gas was the answer. Bicycles had already been fitted with tiny, nickel-plated acetylene lights, and small cars like early Curved-Dash Oldsmobiles often used them. These were "self-generators." The base of the lamp held gravel-size pieces of calcium carbide and a separate reservoir for water. The water dripped through a valve into the carbide, and acetylene gas resulted. The gas was led to a burner similar to those used in the then-popular gas-lighting fixtures, and like them it was lit with a match. The people of this gas-lit world thought it perfectly natural.

Very soon manufacturers in London and Paris and Chicopee Falls and in dozens of other places leaped into the business of making wondrous big brass lamps with a hundred ingenious methods of accomplishing the simple task of dripping water on carbide. Some had cylinders that slid out sideways for refilling, some had drawers, some doors. To amplify the gas flame, some used mirrors as reflectors, others mounted beautifully ground and polished lenses ahead of the flame. But self-generating lamps posed a problem. The used carbide formed a cement-like mass of lime if allowed to dry before being removed. A chisel was then a man's best recourse. The next step was to separate the gas generators from the lamps. These were mounted on the running boards and the gas was led to the lights through tubes. The generators were simple for simple cars but wildly gorgeous and complex for the embellishment of big machines like Mercedes' and Panhards and Simplexes. Still they, too, suffered from the hard residue of spent carbide.

The Prest-O-Lite Company solved that problem. It went into the business of selling cylinders of compressed acetylene gas. Empty a cylinder and the man at the service station exchanged it for a full one. You bought only the contents, the company owned the cylinders. I still have such a cylinder, half full, on my 1908 car. It was last exchanged in 1920. When it's empty I can get a full one from Prest-O-Lite, which still offers them for the use of welders and safecrackers.

On rare occasions I drive behind a pair of huge brass gas lights made by BRC in Paris when my car was new. The beam they project through their lenses (mine use no mirrors) are no competition for sealed-beam electrics. I dare not drive more than 20 mph behind them. Yet there were people back there sixty-odd years ago who complained of being blinded by the deadly glare of similar acetylene lamps.

At least one English maker rushed to their aid. He manufactured semaphore-like blinkers to be mounted inside his "Autoclipse" lamps. By operating a control, the driver meeting another car or wagon could swing the blinker between the gas flame and the reflector.

Lighting a gas headlamp in wind or rain was delicate. Matches blew out, the gas flames, unprotected for a moment by the open glass fronts of the headlights, also blew out. A genius of the day, bemused by the wonders of electricity, invented a device which would light the lamps by remote control. The driver first opened valves to cause gas to flow to the burner. Then he pressed a switch which caused an electric spark near the burner. If he was a bit slow and allowed the headlights to fill with gas before pressing the switch, a spectacular, headlight-bursting explosion was not unlikely.

Despite their foibles, autoists loved the beautiful brass headlamps. Hanging the biggest, shiniest ones they could afford on the bows of their motor cars was somehow like hanging expensive jewelry on a beautiful woman. And the making and selling of headlights seems to have been very lucrative for one French lamp manufacturer, Louis Blériot. He made enough

**Preceding pages: 1910 Oldsmobile
stares brassily at
photographer, who is reflected
upside down in parabolic mirrors of
acetylene headlights. Gas
burner in left lamp is correctly
oriented. Other one is slightly askew.**

LICENSE PLATES

Manufacture and advertising of brass headlamps and sidelamps was a big business until 1912 when the gas headlight became electrified and nickel-plated. Left: Front and rear doors were openable.

Solar Lamps

OIL SIDE-LIGHTS

GAS HEAD-LIGHTS

"SHOW THE WAY"

CATALOG OF LATEST MODELS SENT ON REQUEST

BADGER BRASS MFG. CO.
KENOSHA, WIS.

EASTERN BRANCH

11 WARREN ST. NEW YORK

MANZ

Brass headlights were made
in shapes to please every whim.
1. The headlamps on this
1907 Napier were "Neverouts" of
American manufacture.
2. Sidelamps burned kerosene.
3. The headlights of this
1903 Winton are of the
self-generating type. Calcium
carbide and water were
put into separate compartments.
Water dripping on carbide
generated acetylene gas.
4. Lamps on this 1912 Packard
were fed from replaceable
Prest-O-Lite gas cylinders.

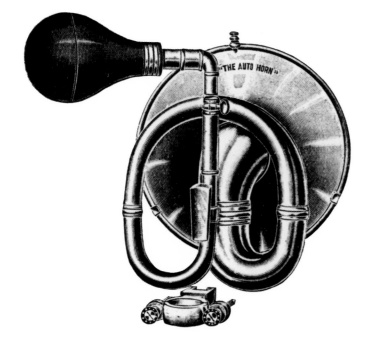

money from headlights to finance his aeronautical pursuits, including that first flight across the English Channel in his monoplane in 1909.

The early cars needed no noisemakers to warn people of their approach. As cars quieted down (especially electrics and steamers), foot-operated bells came into use.

But such gentlemanly tintinnabulation was not arresting enough for the rambunctious Mr. Toads. Horns, sirens, whistles soon joined their voices in a scalp-raising cacophony. The bray of the bulb-operated horn was not too nerve-wracking. But here utility was not enough for automobilists proud of the brave show of brass on their cars. The more showy and convoluted the trumpet of such a horn, the more it was desired. Another much-wanted, albeit expensive, horn was the "Boa-Constrictor," whose long, shiny, tapering body of brass coils lay full length along a front mudguard, and whose business end was a brass, open-mouthed snake's head complete with tongue and fangs.

Hand-operated sirens still were legal in the early years of the century, but more popular were various horns and whistles operated by the exhaust. One was the "Gabriel," a sort of organ pipe, which was attached just aft of the muffler. Exhaust gases could be diverted into the Gabriel by way of a wire controlled by the driver. More musical drivers attached four Gabriels of varying notes and could, by operating a sort of switchboard of controls, create musical havoc on the highway. Less ambitious types merely fitted various makes of piercing whistles to their exhaust system. My favorite horn is the French "Testaphone" of about 1910 which, depending on your choice of "selector barrels," could by a series of squeezes on its rubber bulb play anything from *Die Wacht am Rheim* to "In the Shade of the Old Apple Tree." But the era of curling brass and rubber bulbs came to an end in 1911, when the "Klaxon" arrived, and that peremptory outrage of the twentieth century, the electric auto horn, became part of our lives.

A fast-pedaling constable aboard a bicycle could catch a turn-of-the-century automobile. But, before long, a miscreant exceeding the speed limit on Main Street could outdistance any cop, no matter how hard he pumped the pedals. Frustrated, the police insisted that every car carry a number, so that a lawbreaking autoist might be identified even if he outran a pursuing policeman.

These earliest license plates weren't plates at all. They were made of leather and had numbers (the kind you can

1

2

Cars were once bedizened with brass:
1. Controls of 1912 Simplex.
2 & 3. Running-board gas generators
of a 1909 Pope-Hartford and of
a 1908 Stearns. Brass boxes
contained compartments for water
and calcium carbide, whose
combination produced gas to light
car on its way at night.
4. 1907 Napier's name and address
were hand-engraved
into the car's brass radiator.
5. Brassy décor in
cockpit of 1905 Rolls-Royce.
6. Stirrup on 1911 Mercer.
7. Hubcaps needed polishing, too.

3

4

5

6

7

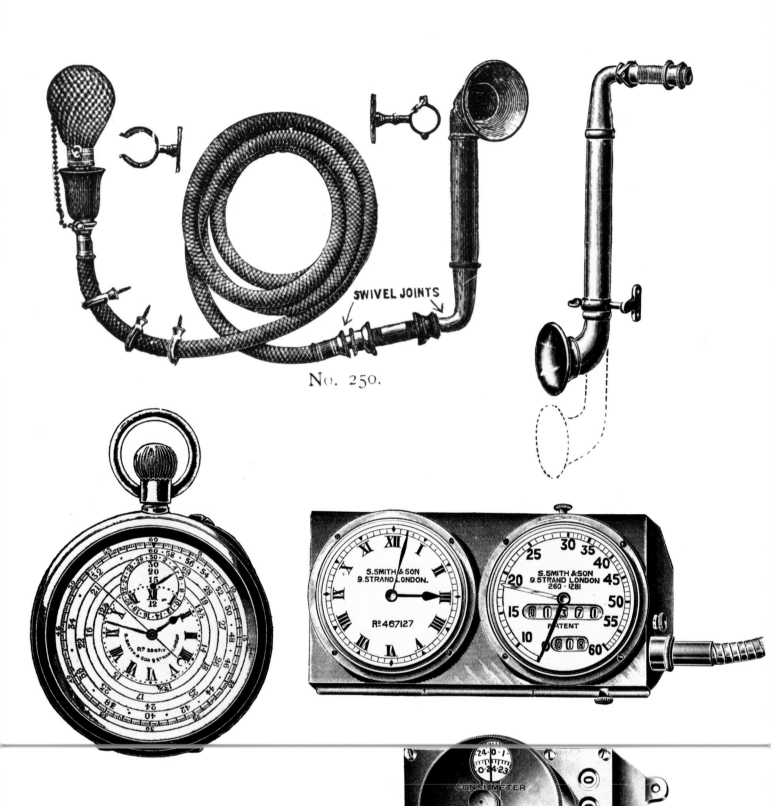

No. 250.

SWIVEL JOINTS

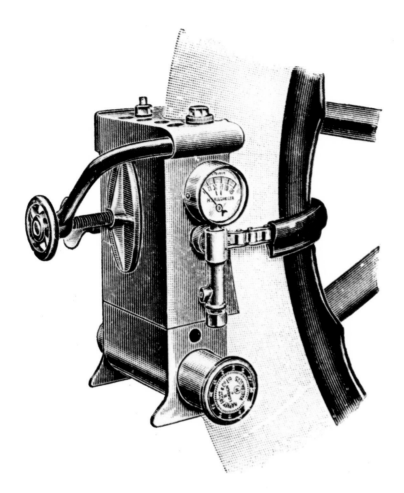

still buy in hardware stores as house numbers) affixed to them. And you made your own; officialdom did not supply them.

The first proper license plates were made of metal, but not like our thin and flimsy present-day affairs stamped out by the million in prisons. They were about an eighth-of-an-inch thick, and the numbers on their colored backgrounds were of baked enamel, thick and beautiful, but fragile when bumped. There are countries—England, for example—where cars' license plates are not supplied by a government bureau. To have some made you go to a specialist.

Tires drove the pioneer autoist to distraction. He was continually removing them (demountable rims and wheels came later), repairing them, pumping them up. Accessory manufacturers supplied not only tire-demounting tools that looked like Spanish Inquisitors' torture instruments, but offered intriguingly complex devices for tire repair and inflation. One lovely gadget, made in England, was the "Harvey Frost Vulcanizer." This could be clamped to the car's running board for repairing either tires or tubes. Putty-like raw rubber was applied to the tire's wound. The tire and its poultice were then gripped by the Harvey Frost vulcanizer and cooked until healed. A contemporary book glowingly called the running board vulcanizer "a small steam boiler of convenient shape."

Engine-driven air compressors were one way to pump a high-pressure tire up to eighty pounds or so, but one type I covet was a small, four-cylinder air compressor which could be attached to a car's running board (next to the vulcanizer?) and cranked by hand.

If all else failed, it was possible to buy a "tire gaiter," a sort of corset-cum-bandage, to be strapped tightly over a tire's lesion.

Of all the gimcracks available to our automobilist ancestors (and there were hundreds—from sparkplugs with built-in petcocks for supplying fuel directly to the cylinders on cold days, to odometers which measured a car's progress not through any connection with the wheels but by counting bumps in the road), the one I most desire is a "nail-catcher," a device which hung from a rear mudguard and caressed the tire in order to remove any objects which had not yet entirely embedded themselves in the tread.

THE GENTRY

There is a class of motor cars which, if not quite bluebloods like Rolls-Royce and Hispano-Suiza, are yet highly desirable machines. True, some are from factories noted as mass-producers, but there were times in their pasts when such organizations as Renault, Chrysler, and Fiat built truly fine automobiles.

Why then do we allow these superior cars only the rank of gentlemen instead of promoting them to the peerage? First, of course, they were generally less expensive. Quality is built into them but not with the fanatical perfectionism of the great-car builders who spent money with abandon, and the performance of these cars reflects this. Still, their position above the hoi polloi of automobilism is secure. They were assembled with much more care than is possible on the high-speed assembly line. Aimed at a large and prosperous middle class, their designers had a certain freedom and more money to spend. Engines in cars like the 1922 Wills Sainte Claire and the 1912 Austro-Daimler not only had overhead camshafts, they were something a man could enjoy looking at.

This good kind of car—neither pretentious luxury machine nor super sports car, nor yet a stamped-out Detroit appliance—is happily still with us, albeit in small numbers. The current BMW's, the better Fiats (higher-priced models that are not brought into the USA), most Mercedes-Benzes, and top-of-the-line Citroëns are—considering that first-class craftsmanship has practically disappeared—about as close as we can get to the high-quality construction of cars in this class built before World War II. Despite the lack of meticulous finish on their mechanisms and the disappearance of hand-built coachwork and wire wheels (which I dearly loved), the present-day automotive gentry are in important ways better than their forebears. They are faster, they have greatly increased visibility, they hold the road better, and they are, generally, more comfortable to ride in.

Here, then, are cars of a most superior kind, the gentry of automobilism. Some of them are so good that, I must admit, there may be arguments for setting them above that station.

PANHARD ET LEVASSOR

Certainly Gottlieb Daimler and Karl Benz are the true fathers of the automobile. But there is another name to add to theirs: Emile Levassor. For he was the Frenchman who, using Daimler's engine, built around it the practical car from which descended the many generations of motor cars. With its up-front engine driving a gearbox through a clutch, Levassor's car of 1891 was the archetype still followed by our cars of today.

Emile Levassor and René Panhard owned a successful metalworking factory in Paris which manufactured power saws. The firm, Panhard et Levassor, entered the age of the internal-combustion engine through the efforts of an old friend of Levassor's, a lawyer named Edouard Sarazin, who was also a friend of Gottlieb Daimler and who had, as Daimler's agent in France, patented Daimler's new high-speed engine there. Sarazin, not without difficulty, succeeded in persuading his dour and pessimistic friend Levassor to build a few of Herr Daimler's engines for test and demonstration purposes. But Sarazin never saw the fruits of his efforts. In December, 1887, he died, with Levassor at his bedside holding his hand.

Sarazin, with Daimler's friendly approval, had registered the patents for the engine in his own name and now his widow inherited them. Madame Sarazin, a handsome and charming woman with a well-developed sense of business, soon convinced Daimler that she ought to succeed her husband as his agent and patentee in France. While convincing Herr Daimler, she made several trips to his Cannstatt establishment. Levassor went with her on one of these excursions and there examined Daimler's motor-quadricycle (and a boat and a streetcar), which was powered by a new Daimler two-cylinder, narrow-V engine. Levassor was lukewarm toward the quadricycle but loved the engine. Crusty Levassor had also fallen in love with Madame Sarazin and in May, 1890, she became Madame Levassor, bringing a wonderful little engine as her dowry.

Levassor would not only build the Daimler engine but would build what he thought the proper car to do it justice. Within a few months, the first Panhard et Levassor left the gates of the factory on the Avenue d'Ivry with Emile Levassor at its tiller. He was headed for Point-du-Jour, six kilometers away, and he meant to make the round trip without an involuntary stop. This was not to be. Time after time he set out, and time after time he broke down. It was early in 1891 before he succeeded in a round trip without a *panne*. And for that memorable occasion Tricolor flags flew from the factory in fine

Preceding pages: 1949 Type 175 Delahaye *coupé de ville.* The fat Saoutchik body on this car took a year to build. Interior appointments are plated in 14-k. gold. Carpets are of lamb's wool. The sun roof comes off. The whole ensemble is ridiculous.

celebration.

Levassor's first machines were not like his front-engined car which later made the *"système Levassor"* famous. They had their engines amidships and transmissions forward. They suffered from vibration and steering problems, and did not, oddly, incorporate Daimler's newer V twin engine but his earlier single-cylinder design instead.

In 1892, however, when Panhard et Levassor issued its first catalogue of "carriages powered by petroleum motors on the Daimler System," it pictured the front-engined machine, six of which had been sold the year before.

Panhard et Levassor was not the only firm using Daimler's engine. Armand Peugeot, who was in the hardware business, making everything from pepper mills to bicycles, became fired with the idea of building automobiles. Hearing about this, Daimler and Levassor visited Peugeot, an old friend of Levassor's, and offered to sell him some engines. Peugeot bought a single engine and, in 1891, built a car incorporating it. Although successful, and the precursor or the fine present-day Peugeot, its rear-engined design, albeit ingeniously built of bicycle tubing which also carried the cooling water, was a dead end. Later models, like almost everyone else's, were laid out like Levassor's.

What exactly were Levassor's early cars like? First, they had chassis frames designed for automobiles; Levassor abandoned the horse-carriage concept. And everything about his cars was solidly and perhaps too heavily built. After all, Levassor is remembered for the phrase *"Faites lourd, vous ferez solide."* ("Make it heavy and you'll make it strong.") Up front (of course) was Daimler's V twin engine of 75-mm bore and 120-mm stroke. This developed some 3½ hp at 750 rpm. Between the engine and the transmission gears, which were fully exposed to the mud and grit of the road, was a clutch. This was at first a sort of brush made of stiff steel wires that engaged a disc at the front of the transmission. Levassor soon abandoned this type for a leather cone clutch. Neither the gears nor the leather clutch were invented by Levassor; both had long been used on lathes. Another oft-quoted phrase of Levassor's is, *"C'est brutal, mais ça marche."* ("It's brutal, but it works.") Levassor was talking about his gearbox of the eight-een-nineties, but for the next forty years manual transmissions were not much less brutal. Still, Levassor proved that even a hard-to-shift, noisy jumble of toothed wheels was better than a cat's cradle of belting which slipped and slid erratically, especially when stretched with use or wet with rain.

The rear wheels were chain-driven (one chain at first, later two). A foot pedal applied brakes attached to the sprockets on the rear wheels. A crank at the driver's right could be turned to apply a horse-wagon type of block to the rear tires, but this had no ratchet and was useless for parking. Steering was controlled by a tiller and the front wheels had a lock of no more than 30 degrees. A greater steering angle on the short chassis of less than 60 inches would have been downright dangerous, even at the low speed of which a Panhard car of the nineties was capable—about 12 mph. Levassor considered himself more experienced than other drivers and allowed that it was safe for him to have a faster car—one which would do 13 mph!

In 1895, Levassor, working with Daimler and his associate Wilhelm Maybach, designed a new vertical two-cylinder engine, the Phénix, which now also had a proper float-feed carburetor instead of the somewhat erratic surface carburetor of the V engine. The new car to which the Phénix engine was fitted also had a casing over the transmission gears.

It was such a Phénix-engined Panhard et Levassor car that Emile Levassor, accompanied by a mechanic, drove in the Paris–Bordeaux–Paris Race of 1895. Incredibly for 1895, this involved the great distance of 732 miles.

The race started from Versailles just after noon on June 11, 1895. Drivers had to check in at controls but did not have to stop racing at night. A change of drivers was permissible, and Levassor had placed a man at Ruffec who would take over from him, drive to the control at Bordeaux and thence back to Ruffec, where, refreshed by sleep, Levassor would take the car back for the dash to Paris. It didn't work that way. Levassor on Panhard No. 5 soon passed a gaggle of steamers which had shot away from the start in clouds of steam but then started breaking down. At Vouvray, Levassor led the pack. At dusk, just before 9 o'clock, Levassor lit his candle sidelights and kept going by their dimly flickering light. At 3:30 in the morning

LE PETIT POUCET MONTAIT UNE PEUGEOT

AUTOMOBILES
PEUGEOT

Left: 1902 Panhard et Levassor.
Panhard still retained radiator of
bent, finned tubing, when
other makes, like Mercedes, were
using honeycomb radiators.
Entrance to tonneau is via rear door.
Panhards of this vintage
were available with either
two- or four-cylinder engines.
Posters of early manufacturers are
now collector's items.

FIG. 99.—PANHARD & LEVASSOR DAIMLER MOTOR CARRIAGE, 6-HP. RACING TYPE.

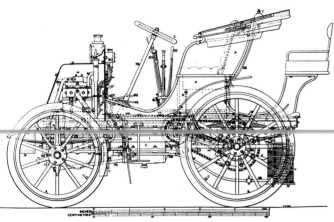

1

3

4

5

1. 1891 Panhard still had tiller steering.
2. 1908 Panhard et Levassor limousine.
3. Sleeve-valve 1914 Panhard et Levassor
with remarkably advanced Labourdette body.
4. Plan of 1896 "racing" Panhard.
5. Early (c. 1901) racing Panhard with
lamps and fenders added for touring.

he reached Ruffec, so far ahead of time that his relief driver was still snugly in bed. Levassor, not wanting to waste time waking him up, kept going. He was able to snuff out the candles at Angoulême at 5:30 in the morning. At 10:30, twenty-two hours out of Versailles, Levassor rolled into a wildly excited Bordeaux. The pavements, the sidewalk cafés, the windows of houses were packed with cheering thousands.

Levassor stayed in the car at the control as he drank a glass of champagne. Ten minutes later he was back on the road toward Paris. This time the relief driver at Ruffec was dressed, ready and eager to take the tiller. Levassor waved him off, pressed on. At 12:57.30 P.M. on June 13, forty-eight hours and forty-eight minutes after he started from Paris, Levassor braked and shut off the supply of fuel to the hot-tube burners of his engine. He had arrived at the finish line at the Porte Maillot of Paris. His average speed for the 732 miles was 15 mph.

In the *North American Review* for September, 1899, the Marquis de Chasseloup-Laubat, an eminent early automobilist, wrote: "He supervised the machine himself constantly, except when ascending an occasional incline, when the rate of speed was comparatively slow, and then he had entrusted the lever to his mechanic. M. Levassor remained on his machine about 53 hours, and nearly 49 of these on the run. Yet he did not appear to be over-fatigued; he wrote his signature at the finish with a firm hand; we lunched together at Gillet's at the Porte Maillot; he was quite calm; he took with relish a cup of bouillon, a couple of poached eggs, and two glasses of champagne; but he said that racing at night was dangerous, adding that having won he had the right to say such a race was not be run another time at night."

One advantage of putting the engine up front was the ease with which it was possible to add cylinders. The first four-cylinder Panhard appeared in the 1896 Paris–Marseilles–Paris Race, which it won. But the two other Panhard cars in the race still had 8-hp, two-cylinder engines. And two-cylinder cars were offered for sale until after the turn of the century. By then, too, it was possible to order electric ignition, although P & L preferred the old hot-tube type. Early Panhards had no radiators; water from a tank did the cooling. In 1897, Levassor fitted a radiator of finned tubing to the rear of his new, two-

cylinder, 6-hp car. It wasn't until 1898 that P & L thought to move the gilled-tube radiator up front. Tiller steering had given way to wheel steering by then, too.

In September, 1896, driving a two-cylinder Panhard in the 1,062½-mile Paris–Marseilles–Paris Race, Emile Levassor hit a dog and his car was overturned. In spite of the injury he suffered in this contretemps he kept on working at his usual pace. But he never really recovered; he collapsed while working in his drawing office one night and died, at age fifty-three, on April 14, 1897. On that day Gottlieb Daimler's wife Lina gave birth to a daughter. The Daimlers named her Emilie. Today Levassor and his Panhard stand sculpted in a stone memorial at the Porte Maillot.

Until 1906 the Panhard et Levassor dominated the racing scene. From that first run of Levassor's in 1895 until Panhard gave up racing, Panhards took no less than twenty-one first places in the thirty-one races the firm entered, plus many more second and third places. These included the great Paris–Vienna Race of 1902, when Farman drove a big 70-hp Panhard to victory, and the first American Vanderbilt Cup Race of 1904, when Heath won with a 90-hp monster of 15.4 litres.

It was these wins plus the Panhard's reputation for superb construction and unparalleled reliability that made the Panhard *the* car for the ultrarich. During the early years of this country no other car would do (except perhaps a Mercedes) if you were an American millionaire, an English milord, or a French music-hall star. In 1904, a 24-hp Panhard-Levassor was sold in New York by Smith and Mabley (who also built the American Simplex) for $8,250, equal to over $40,000 in our debased money. In London, it was Charles S. Rolls, later of Rolls-Royce, who was the Panhard agent.

After Levassor's death, *Commandant* Arthur Krebs took over at P & L. It was Krebs who was to be responsible for the monstrously engined racing machines. Before that, however, he developed the four-cylinder Centaur engine, which by 1903 was available with electric ignition. The famous Krebs carburetor gave it a flexibility remarkable in a day when most other engines ran at an almost fixed speed and changes in road speed were not accomplished by varying the throttle opening but by shifting gears—a most demanding way to drive. If the early four-cylinder Centaur engines were small (40 x 134 mm), Krebs' 1906 Centaur racing engine was almost incredibly huge: 18,279 cc, 130 hp.

Under Krebs the old wood-framed chassis was dropped in favor of pressed steel. On some models chain drive gave way to shaft drive. And in 1905 the gilled-tube radiators were supplanted by the almost universal honeycomb type.

In 1908, when René Panhard died and his son Hippolyte became manager, Panhard et Levassor was still, with Mercedes, Rolls-Royce, and De Dietrich, one of the world's top luxury cars. But its greatest days were almost over.

Like every other important car builder, Panhard was producing six-cylindered cars (it started in 1905). And, like Daimler, Mercedes, Minerva, Stearns, and others, Panhard turned toward the sleeve-valve engine of the American Charles Y. Knight. After 1912, Panhard went all-out for sleeve valves, which consist of thin sleeves which line the cylinders and are pierced with ports for intake and exhaust. These sleeves move up and down to expose the openings either to the inlet manifold or to the exhaust system. (It's really rather more complicated than that.)

In any case, sleeve valves were much quieter than poppet valves (the kind we still use today), but they had disadvantages. Much more oil was needed for lubrication, so sleeve-valved cars smoked. Cooling was more difficult and, since there were more and heavier reciprocating parts to move, rpm and acceleration suffered.

Like every other car builder, Panhard et Levassor busied itself with the usual military hardware during World War I. Afterward Panhard returned to building sleeve-valve models in a multiplicity of sizes—fours, sixes, and eights, all of them beautifully built, nice to drive, but rather boring.

There were, however, some few flashes of the old Panhard brilliance in the years between the wars. In 1930 the famous Panhard rod, now widely used, became standard on P & L cars. This is the transverse rod which prevents too much sideways movement of the rear axle in relation to the chassis frame. And Panhard, surprisingly, after so many years of somnolence, decided to go in for record breaking to show off its car's stamina. In 1926, a special high and skinny single-seater

dubbed "the Razor Blade" broke the record for an hour's run at 118 mph. After this mark was broken several times again in 1934, George Eyston, later famous as holder of the Land Speed Record, put the hour mark up to 130 mph in a new Panhard with a 300-hp engine under its hood.

In 1938, Panhard came out with a supercar, the ugly Dynamique with a low-built, windcutting monocoque body, trick three-piece *panoramique* windshield, and torsion-bar suspension. Two engine sizes were offered, 16 hp and 27 hp. Both were sixes. (These ratings are by the peculiar French measurement which has no relation to actual horsepower.) Both, of course, had sleeve valves.

It was too late. By the beginning of World War II, Panhard was a very sick company. During the war, it built no cars, but Paul Panhard (René Panhard's nephew, who had joined the company in 1906 and become president in 1916) took the opportunity to think things over and decided to start fresh.

In 1946, a brilliant little two-cylinder, air-cooled, light economy car, designed by Jean-Albert Gregoire, was brought out. This Dyna-Panhard, modified and remodified, was produced for more than twenty years. In 1955, Citroën took virtual control of Panhard et Levassor. But Panhard's greatest days were really over when the Uhlans cantered into Picardy in 1914.

AUSTRO-DAIMLER

Your modern Porsche buff may be happy to learn that Dr. Porsche not only gave his name to that delectable little bomb he's driving but also designed what some people consider to be the world's first sports car: the 27/80 Austro-Daimler of 1910. No one called it a sports car back there before World War I; the term wasn't used until much later. And I submit that the English Vauxhall and the American Mercer Raceabout, which were contemporaries of the 27/80 Austro-Daimler, were quite as sporting.

Porsche's Prince Henry Austro-Daimler, built by the Austrian offshoot of the German Daimler Company, first created a sensation in the German Prince Henry tours sponsored by Prince Henry of Prussia, brother of Germany's Kaiser William II. These "tours," run from 1908 to 1911, were fairly wild events—combinations of rallies, speed trials, and out-and-

1. ALPENTYPE Austro-Daimler on the Turracherhöhe in the 1914 Austrian Alpine Trials.
2. 1924 ADM Austro-Daimler had overhead-cam engine.
3. Instrument panel of the 1932 ADR.
4. 1932 "Alpine Eight" ADR Austro-Daimler had backbone chassis, 4.6-litre overhead-cam engine. Heavy, teutonically-styled coachwork hurt performance.

1

2

3

4

out road racing. The Teutonically complicated rules included a handicap formula (which the losers always loudly maintained had been rigged against them) and a stipulation that the cars were to be touring machines with four-passenger coachwork, complete with mudguards and lights.

In 1910, Ferdinand Porsche, then thirty-four years old, had for four years been chief designer at Austro-Daimler's Wiener-Neustadt factory. There he had worked on the Maja car—Austro-Daimler's answer to the Mercedes and named after Mercedes Jellinek's younger sister (just as the Mercedes had been named after the older sister)—and on various electric cars and trucks. More important, Porsche had been involved with building engines for the Parseval, a nonrigid airship.

When Austro-Daimler decided to enter the Prince Henry tour, Ferdinand Porsche designed a remarkable car for it, the engine of which owed much to the high-efficiency airship engine. It had four individually cast cylinders (its only archaic feature) of 5,714 cc. A vertical shaft drove an overhead camshaft which operated large-diameter valves that were inclined at 45 degrees and held in quickly detachable cages. Instead of the usual heavy cast-iron pistons, Porsche used lightweight steel pistons. The vertical shaft also drove twin Bosch magnetos set at an angle rearward to allow for a narrow engine hood. Surprisingly, Porsche did not use a pressurized engine lubrication system, which other makers (like Rolls-Royce) had already used for years; instead he used the old-fashioned total-loss system from a belt-driven lubricator.

The engine of this Austro-Daimler has been of particular interest to me, for it is almost a carbon copy of that in the 1908 American-built Welch which I drive. Like the Austro-Daimler, it too has an overhead camshaft, inclined valves in cages, rearward-canted, vertical-shaft-driven magneto, even the same kind of total-loss oiling system. My Welch, I'm sorry to say, only develops some 50 hp at 1,800 rpm. Porsche's engine, only slightly larger, is about twice as powerful. The Welch engine was first produced in 1904. Might Ferdinand Porsche have seen one?

Aside from its engine, the 27/80 Austro-Daimler was fairly conventional for its day. It had a 120-inch wheelbase, four semielliptic springs, and two-wheel brakes. Chain drive was used at first, shaft drive after 1912.

Peculiarly ugly "tulip" bodies were common to several of the Prince Henry entrants. The tour organizers, in order to discourage freakishly narrow, wind-cheating coachwork, gave all entrants drawings which specified a minimum body width. But the drawings showed only the dimension at the top of the doors and failed to say anything about the lower parts of the body. The sharper entrants, taking note of this lapse, and seeking the advantage of a small frontal area, then narrowed the lower parts of the bodywork to such a ridiculous extent that the poor inmates must have played an uncomfortable game of kneesies for the length of the tour, the organizers having insisted that all four seats be occupied. Furthermore, Porsche had the front axle, the chains, and other parts of his cars faired in with streamlined shields. Even the brass gas lights had bullet-shaped covers over their lenses.

The 86-hp Austro-Daimlers proved to be very fast for 1910 touring cars. Almost 90 mph was reached on long, straight stretches. And they were, in addition, reliable enough to run away with Prinz Heinrich's brouhaha.

Porsche, accompanied by his wife and a couple of mechanics, himself drove one of the eleven Austro-Daimlers entered, and, with two others driven by factory drivers, finished first, second, and third. Many of the other AD's came in among the top twenty. Considering that they were competing against the great marques of their day—including Benz and Mercedes—driven by top drivers, and that the 27/80 was not a special one-off job (except for the bodywork) but a production model of which hundreds were later built, the AD's spectacular triumph had great impact on the automobile world of 1910.

The 27/80 was in production until Prince Henry's brother Willy (der Kaiser) got a war named after him in 1914, and there were other successes to add luster to its name until that year. Nor was the 27/80 the only successful Austro-Daimler. In 1911 a team of less exotic Alpines with 2.3-litre, 30-hp, four-cylinder, L-head engines ran off with top honors in the tough Alpine Trial over the appallingly high passes of the Austrian and Italian Alps.

During the war years Austro-Daimler, now amalgamated with Skoda, busied itself with trucks, artillery tractors, and Porsche-designed aeroplane engines.

Afterward Porsche designed the rather dull 4.4-litre, six-cylinder ADV which evolved by 1923 into the excellent AD 617, a first-quality six with a light alloy block into which iron cylinder sleeves were screwed *à la* Hispano-Suiza.

Like Hispano-Suiza this engine, too, had an overhead camshaft. This was the first of a series of sporting and luxury cars, including the 2.6-litre overhead cam ADM, which continued the name until 1935, by which time Austro-Daimler was part of Steyr, the big Austrian arms and motor company.

Porsche's enthusiasm for racing and sports cars resulted, in 1922, in the Sascha, a delightful little four-cylinder, 1,100-cc (later 1,500-cc) overhead-camshaft-engined sports machine capable of quite high speeds for 1922: 89 mph over a flying kilometer in Holland. A Sascha won its class in the 1922 Targa Florio and did very well indeed in the Irish Tourist Trophy. Porsche also built out-and-out racing Austro-Daimlers and campaigned them all over Europe.

The directors of Austro-Daimler saw little sense in the expenses and dangers of racing. In 1922 at Monza, in the Italian GP, a factory driver was killed in a 2-litre Austro-Daimler and the directors raised hell with Porsche. It didn't help when Porsche pointed out that in one year Austro-Daimlers had started in fifty-one events in fifteen countries, had won forty-three times, and been second eight times (that record *did* strain credibility). Anyhow, Porsche finally got sore, quit, and went over to Germany to develop the superb S-series Mercedes-Benz.

The greatest Austro-Daimlers since the 1910 27/80 were built after Dr. Porsche joined Mercedes. These were the ADR's built both as sixes and as straight-eights. The smaller six was known as the "Bergmeister" in honor of Hans Stuck, the great race driver and hill-climb king. Stuck won forty-three races in four years and in 1930 set a record (in a special ADM) of 42.8 seconds at Shelsley-Walsh, the important English hill-climb venue. This record stood until three years later when Whitney Straight, on a Grand Prix Maserati, climbed in 41.2 seconds. The ADR Alpine Eight had a 4.6-litre overhead camshaft engine and dual ignition—sixteen sparkplugs! The block was of light alloy with cylinder liners and the crankshaft turned

on nine main bearings. Most unusual was the backbone chassis frame and the trick rear suspension.

There haven't been any new Austro-Daimlers for some thirty-five years. But there is at least one 1913 model Prince Henry you can look at in the Frederick C. Crawford Automotive and Aviation Museum in Cleveland, Ohio.

WILLS SAINTE CLAIRE

For some reason I cannot divine, people who have no great interest in cars, who don't know a Pierce-Arrow from a Pontiac, but who think they must make small talk about the subject with me, almost invariably say, "Remember the Wills Sainte Claire?"

Why always the Wills Sainte Claire?

The Wills Sainte Claire was, in a way, a violent reaction against Henry Ford and his Model T by a genius who had worked with Ford since the days when Ford was a hungry mechanic—and not too good a one, either.

Childe Harold Wills (he never used the "Childe," a name wished on him by a mother hooked on Byron) was brought up using machine tools. His father was a master mechanic for a railroad. But Wills, while still in grade school in Detroit, wanted to be a cartoonist. Luckily, he was persuaded that cartooning could be a very chancy profession, and when he left school he got himself apprenticed as a toolmaker for the Detroit Lubricator Company at $7.50 a week. Four years later, he was making only $10 a week. He quit and got himself a new job at $18 per. He must have known his stuff, for three weeks later he became foreman of the shop, and three months later superintendent at $50 a week—big money for a twenty-one-year-old in 1899. But ambitious young Wills wanted to be more than a successful toolroom boss. He signed up for night school and worked hard at courses in drafting, engineering, and metallurgy.

There was a mechanic in Detroit struggling to build automobiles who had certain serious gaps in his knowledge. He needed someone who knew how to make engineering drawings, who knew more than he did about metals, and who at least knew how to read a blueprint, a skill beyond him. In desperation he ran an advertisement for such an assistant. He signed it "Henry Ford."

Wills got the job, but he was cautious. He held on

1922 Wills Sainte Claire roadster
had V-8 overhead-cam engine which
developed 65 hp. Remarkably
advanced for its day, it had some
features reminiscent of the
Hispano-Suiza. Note the resemblance
of its radiator shape to
that of the Hispano. The Gray Goose
badge, too, is not unlike
the Flying Stork ornament of the
Hispano. The Wills Sainte Claire
was built until 1927.

to his regular job and arranged to work for Ford from 5 till 7 in the morning, then from 7 in the evening until midnight. It was cold work, sitting over a drawing board in Ford's unheated loft. Every half hour or so, Wills and Ford put on boxing gloves and sparred for a while to warm up.

At this time Ford was involved with his big, crude race cars, "Arrow" and "999," hoping to get some publicity through them and thus attract money for his return to car manufacturing. The publicity worked; A. Y. Malcolmson, a Detroit coal tycoon, put up the cash for Ford to start building passenger cars again.

Wills now quit his job and went to work full time for Ford at the munificent sum of $15 a week. He didn't even have the title of chief engineer. Ford didn't believe in titles. You worked for Ford, period. For the next fifty-odd years no Ford employee had a title. Wills had no money to buy stock, so Ford made a trick deal with him. He agreed to pay Wills ten percent of whatever Ford personally made plus Wills' salary. It wasn't too many years before this ten percent became more than a million dollars a year. Ford then made another deal. A million a year was to be Wills' limit. Plus his salary, naturally. Wills quickly became a multimillionaire.

But Wills had been worth it. He, more than anyone else, had been responsible for the design of the Ford cars, from the Model A of 1903 right through the alphabet to that fabulous gold mine, the Model T of 1908. The design of the T's planetary transmission was his. And the use of vanadium steel to lighten and strengthen the T seems to have been his idea, in spite of Henry Ford's story (in his book *My Life and Work*) that he first learned of vanadium steel after picking up a bit of it from the wreckage of a French racer at Ormond Beach. Metallurgy was Wills' special field by then.

Wills stood Henry Ford's peculiarities for almost twenty years. He might well have quit after one tantrum in 1912, when Ford, after returning from Europe, was shown a much-improved, lower, better-looking Model T designed by Wills and his men in the experimental department. Ford instantly ordered it smashed to bits on the spot. Or he might have told Henry where to go after being ordered to show up in the shop at 8 A.M. sharp, as if he were an assembly-line hand instead of the man

who had done so much to make Ford a billionaire. By the time World War I broke out, relations between Ford and Wills were strained. It was only a matter of time before they broke off.

But Wills performed one more big task. Ford had signed a Government contract in 1917 to make cylinders for the 26,000 much-publicized World War I Liberty airplane engines the automobile industry was to build. If these cylinders had been made in the usual fashion of machining them out of solid lumps, or even by finishing rough cylindrical forgings and then welding on their complex heads, they might not have been ready until Hitler's war instead of the Kaiser's. Wills figured out a way to make the cylinders out of welded steel tubing which was then, by means of special machinery, shaped to form a head, complete with valve ports. Wills' method was not only faster, it cost less than a third as much. Ford then got a contract to make *all* cylinders for the Liberties and also to build 5,000 complete engines. Wills took over a half million square feet of the Highland Park plant, installed some 1,500 machine tools, and set 11,000 men to work. Nearly 4,000 engines were built by the time the war ended.

Wills, a multimillionaire and just over forty, quit Ford in March, 1919. Another Ford man, John R. Lee, left with him. They enthusiastically announced that C. H. Wills & Co. was going to build a new and revolutionary car "ten years ahead of its time."

Those were great days, back there in 1919. The big war "to make the world safe for democracy" was at last over. People felt, somehow, that the world was new again. Americans were certain that they could do anything, build anything better, faster than anyone on earth. People, except of course those who had been clapped into uniform, had pockets full of money. And everyone was sure that any new mechanisms, especially automobiles, would have unheard-of improvements springing from what had been learned in the war.

Perhaps C. Harold Wills was a victim of this euphoria. Before he started building his new automotive gem, he decided to found a model town at Marysville, Michigan, which would have modern housing for the workers, parks, playgrounds, a model sewage system, and a superfactory in which the Wills Sainte Claire car would be built. Before any production was

1. 1935 540K Mercedes-Benz
at London Auto Show.
2. 1900 Benz racing car.
Engine was in rear. Note
vertical finned-tube radiator.
3. 450 SE Mercedes-Benz has
4½-litre, overhead-cam, V-8 engine.

started, $3,500,000 was spent on this 4,000-acre dream.

Molybdenum was the brave new metal of the brave new post-Kaiser War world. It had never been produced in useful quantities until 1918. Wills, the metallurgical enthusiast, decided to use it in his new car. Molybdenum is fine stuff. Alloyed with steel and cast iron, it increases their toughness, hardenability, and strength. Wills' publicity pictures showed axles twisted like pretzels without breaking.

Wills had hoped to be in production by August, 1920. He had planned on a run of 10,000 cars in the $2,000 price class. But Wills was a perfectionist. He fussed, changed things. There were production problems. Cars didn't appear on the market until March, 1921, and they cost $500 more than had been hoped. And, although demand was good, only 500 cars were built before the end of the year.

The Wills Sainte Claire was indeed years ahead of most American cars of its time. The model A-68 of 1921 had a V-8, 60-hp (at 2,700 rpm), 265-cu. in. (4½-litre) engine with an overhead camshaft for each bank of cylinders. The two vertical shafts which drove the camshafts formed a V. The crankcase was of aluminum but, oddly, Wills still stuck to cast-iron pistons at a time when advanced designers were turning to aluminum.

The crankshaft was of molybdenum steel. Wills rightly felt that driving a cooling fan, even the beautifully cast one on his engine, took too much horsepower, and so he had a clutch automatically disengage the fan at 40 mph. Only recently have some advanced sports cars adopted this method.

Wills probably had studied the Hispano-Suiza aero engine when he worked on the Liberty. And, after 1919, the Hispano car as well. For not only was his engine reminiscent of Hispano-Suiza, but the shape of the radiator shell, the gray-goose badge, and flying-goose radiator ornament echoed Hispano motifs, too.

The rest of the chassis was not unconventional, with a ladder-type frame, a 118¾-inch wheelbase, three-speed gearbox, and semielliptic springs. It was, however, lower slung than in most cars of the period.

American cars of the early twenties were uncompromisingly stodgy in appearance. The Wills Sainte Claire looked better than most. But not much. Happily, it went better than it looked. Compared to other cars of its class, it was light—not much over 3,000 pounds—and it handled nicely up to its top speed of about 75 mph, which was fast in 1921. The car had a couple of faults. The gearing for the ohc was noisy and its en-

1

2

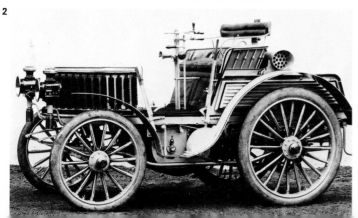

3

Top: 1929 SSK Mercedes-Benz
has British-built drophead coupé
body by Corsica Coachworks.
Supercharged, six-cylinder, 7-litre
engine pushes it at 120 mph.
Left: 1949 Type 175 Delahaye has
4½-litre, six-cylinder engine.
This car cost $20,000.
Delahaye ceased production in 1954.

gine was difficult to work on due to its nondetachable head.

The postwar boom turned into a nasty little postwar slump in 1921. Wills had poured millions into his model city and his new car. Suddenly he found that C. H. Wills & Co. owed $8 million on short-term notes. The bankers took over and a receivership ensued. John R. Lee left. But Wills was able to convince Kidder, Peabody & Co. that there was a solid demand for his car. In 1922 they lent him the money to buy his company back. Reorganized and with bankers on the board of directors, it was now to be known as Wills Sainte Claire, Inc.

Wills started building his V-8 again but also got to work on a new model—an in-line six. The new car appeared in January, 1925. It still had an ohc engine but now with a detachable head. It developed slightly more power than the V-8: 67 hp from its 273 cu. in. (4½ litres) at 3,300 rpm. Wheelbase was increased to 127 inches (the later V-8's also had a 127-inch wheelbase), and weight went up to 3,410 pounds.

In 1925 a fancier, but short-lived V-8—the C-68 Vogue Series—was introduced. These deluxe versions included a limousine at a formidable $4,285.

The six, however, became the mainstay of the company. In 1925 its toughness was proved by a cross-country run from New York to San Francisco. The drivers, Louis B. Miller and C. I. Hansen, were not professionals; nor were there supply depots and repair facilities set up along the route as was usual for such attempts. Nonetheless, a record of 102 hours and 45 minutes was set.

In 1926 Kidder, Peabody made a survey of the automobile business and came to the wonderfully forward-looking conclusion that, since there were already almost twenty million cars in use in the United States, no more would be needed. Therefore it would be silly to put any more cash into an industry which had reached a dead end. Wills got no further financing. The 1926 recession didn't help, either. In 1927 the great Gray Goose folded its wings forever.

C. Harold Wills had sunk some $14 million into his dream. He had built some 16,000 cars of which about seventy-five still exist, a surprisingly small number. Wills was still under fifty years old when his company evaporated. Broke, he kept on working. At first he did metallurgical work for various com-

1

2

panies, including Timken Roller Bearing. He even tried to get a job with Ford again. But Henry and the hard-boiled characters surrounding him gave him the cold shoulder. Then he became involved with the design of the legendary front-drive Ruxton, whose chance for survival faded with the appearance of the Cord. Wills did best at Chrysler where, in 1932, he was hired at $100 a week with no set tasks. He earned his money. Wandering around the plant, he saw ways in which to save the company money—$200,000 in the first six months. He immediately became more important. At first he had only desk space. Now he was given a big office and his old secretary from Marysville was hired to work for him. Wills' most important work there was with the famous Oilite bearings, a Chrysler development.

Childe Harold Wills died in 1940, aged sixty-two.

MERCEDES-BENZ

In the mid-thirties, when I spent so much time loafing in Zumbach's among dismantled examples of the world's most delectable motor cars, it was only that fire-breathing giant, the Mercedes-Benz S (and its younger sisters, the SS and the SSK) that could pull me away from my contemplation of Alfa Romeos and Bugattis.

I never really wanted to own one of these monstrous Mercedes' anymore than I wanted to own one of the Hudson-type locomotives that drew the Twentieth Century Limited. But each had a look of brute power that fascinated me.

The S, or 36/220, Mercedes-Benz, was designed by Ferdinand Porsche in 1927. Under its long, louvred, and strapped hood lay a big, 6.8-litre, overhead-camshaft engine and a supercharger of magnificent bulk. With this *Kompressor* disengaged, the engine developed 120 hp at 3,000 rpm. With the *Kompressor* in action, 180 hp would instantly become available.

The Mercedes-Benz method of supercharging was unusual. On most other blown cars—and they were much more common in the nineteen-twenties and thirties than today—the superchargers were continually working. A Mercedes *Kompressor* only worked if you pressed the accelerator right down. At that moment a clutch engaged the supercharger. This blower was a Roots type but, unlike similar superchargers in other cars, it did not pump a gas-air mixture from the carburetor to the engine. It *blew* air through twin carburetors to the engine. And

it howled like a thousand banshees in the process.

Owners were warned not to overdo their indulgence in this noisy delight. Twenty seconds of foot-on-the-floor stuff while accelerating—never in bottom gear and never at top speed in high gear—were all you were supposed to enjoy lest you sicken the engine.

The S Mercedes was not only a powerhouse, it was also an aesthetic delight. Its pointed radiator in gleaming German silver, its polished exhaust headers curling from the impossibly long hood, its frankly exposed front axle and steering mechanism, all added to an ensemble of classic perfection.

A Mercedes-Benz S was as mechanically excellent as its appearance promised. The finish of its engine and gearbox—of every bit, in fact—was as good as human hands could accomplish. Light alloys were used to keep down avoirdupois, but the 36/220 was no lightweight.

Still, the S was fairly nimble for its size. Steering was lighter and quicker than you might expect, except when you tried to park.

The S was a success, and with the great Rudolf Caracciola at the wheel it won race after race. Within a year, however, more potent versions appeared—the SS 38/250 and the short-chassis SSK ("K" for *Kurz*).

The SS had a slightly larger engine than that in the S—7.1 litres—and a slightly higher compression ratio; it now put out 170 hp unblown, 225 hp with the supercharger engaged. Normal top speed was about 110 mph. It was an SS upon which Caracciola won the Tourist Trophy in the rain in Belfast in 1929.

An SSK won the Italian Mille Miglia in 1930. The model's top speed—over a flying kilometer during the Oostmale speed trials near Antwerp in 1930—was 120 mph. Another lightened version, the SSKL ("L" for *leicht*), reached 147 mph, but this was with a special oversized "elephant" blower which gave the SSKL 300 hp.

The line of hard, lean Mercedes-Benz cars came to an end when Hitler came to power. The British magazine *The Motor* commented in 1944: "Modern Germany has often accused the British of effeteness. It is amusing to remember that the rise of the Nazis coincided with the replacement of that real he-man's

1. 1939 V-12 Delahaye had curvaceous coachwork by Figoni et Falaschi. Windshield could be wound down flush with the cowl.
2. V-12 Delahaye coupé had engine similar to those used in racing Delahayes.
3. A six-cylinder, push-rod engine powered this Figoni et Falaschi Type 135 Delahaye.

1

2

3

4

5

1. 1932 Marmon convertible coupé has custom
body by Le Baron, 200-hp, V-16 engine.
2. Rumble seat was inescapable in 1932.
3. Marmon's styling was by Walter Dorwin Teague.
4. 1913 Pope-Hartford had four-cylinder, 50-hp engine.
5. 1909 40-hp Pope-Hartford touring car.
6. 1913 Pope-Hartford boasted brass electric lights.

1   2

car, the 38/250, by the relatively effeminate and woolly types 500 and 540K."

The fat and vulgar 500 and 540K pleased not only the Nazi bigwigs of the thirties but still please certain tasteless collectors of classic cars. They had push-rod engines of 5 and 5.4 litres and were blown on the same principle as their forebears. A 540K could reach 105 mph from its 180 hp.

A 540K cost about $10,000 (£2,000), rather less than the $15,000 asked for an SS.

Mercedes-Benz, which not only had helped Hitler's rise, but also had powered his war machine, was almost exterminated by Allied bombers, but not quite. Almost immediately after the war, it was in business as usual making dull but well-built and overpriced family sedans, plus a few vaguely sporting models. I can, however, think of at least one outstanding car, the gullwing 300SL of the early fifties, which did well in sports-car racing. More recently, the quadruple-Wankel-engined C-111 sports-car prototype seemed to offer a promise that Mercedes-Benz might build something more exciting than excellent status symbols for retired stock brokers.

DELAHAYE

I had, for many years, a friend who was just crazy about Delahayes. This was the late and much-missed Bob Grier, who collected unusual cars at a time when that pursuit was still uncommon. He owned mostly Types 135, and I rode in them with him for many miles. And sometimes, nervously, he let me drive.

I was then, and I still am, much impressed by those Delahayes. Dressed in *carrosserie* by Chapron, Figoni et Falaschi, Saoutchik, Letournier et Marchand, the Delahayes were as

svelte-looking cars as ever graced a *Concours d'Elégance*. But Delahayes had much more to them than mere handsome looks. They were tough. They handled well, and they were surprisingly quick for their day.

Unlike some marques which delighted us by the beauty of their mechanisms, the Delahayes disappointed anyone who might raise one of their hoods. For the engine looked, as someone said, like "a Chevrolet six with three carburetors." In reality, a 1936 Type 135M Delahaye was powered with an adaptation of one of the firm's notably rugged truck engines. A six, it had a capacity of 3½ litres, three Solex downdraft carburetors, and push-rod-operated overhead valves. It developed 160 hp at 4,200 rpm. To give you an idea of the beefiness of this power plant: The 135's connecting-rod and main bearings were no less than 2½ inches in diameter. Wrist pins were about an inch thick.

Most Delahayes had Cotal electric gearboxes shifted by a finger-light lever in a miniature gate on the steering column. But for more sporting driving—since the Cotal had wide ratios—some cars were delivered with excellent four-speed, synchromesh boxes.

Chassis had independent suspensions forward and leaf springs in the rear. A 135M in good tune could better 110 mph. Zero to 60 could be accomplished in under 14 seconds.

The Type 135 was notably successful. In 1934, at the Montlhéry Autodrome, a specially bodied example broke seven world's records at an average of 110 mph. In 1939, in a match race at Brooklands for the "fastest sports car," a Type 135 with a light body won over a Talbot-Lago and a 2.6-litre

1. 1938 Type 328 BMW was powered by an 80-hp,
2-litre engine, had excellent road manners.
2. 1936 Type 319/55 had 2-litre engine
of earlier type and exceedingly ugly bodywork.
3. Bob Grier and his BMW which won a
shortened version of the Italian Mille Miglia in
1940. Grier raced his machine in the 1950's.

Alfa Romeo. Delahayes won the Monte Carlo Rally twice and Le Mans once.

In 1937, when the Germans in their Mercedes' and Auto Unions were winning everything everywhere, a 4½-litre, triple-camshaft, V-12-engined Delahaye appeared to give them battle. An award, the *Prix du Million*—a million francs—had been offered to the manufacturer who could better the time set by the Germans at the Montlhéry Autodome. Bugatti entered a blown, 4½-litre, straight-eight. A SEFAC, the result of a French-Government-sponsored attempt to build a race car, was another entry. The Delahaye, driven by René Dreyfus, was the third entry. Dreyfus broke the German record and collected the prize for Delahaye. In 1938, Dreyfus in the Delahaye twelve won the Pau GP, defeating Caracciola in a blown Mercedes.

Several Delahaye sports cars with V-12 engines were offered for sale just prior to World War II, and I was able to drive one of them (pictured herewith) when it reached the US in the nineteen-fifties. The photograph makes it look rather larger than it was—in reality it was quite a handy, easily maneuverable little beast with a sparkling performance, despite being out of tune.

After the war, Delahaye produced several models: the 4½-litre 140-hp with Dubonnet front suspension and de Dion rear, and the 175S, a sporting version on a short chassis whose engine produced 185 hp. The types 178 and 180 were other variations using the same six-cylinder, 4½-litre engine. The last Delahaye was the Type 235, which was not unlike the old 135, but with a more highly tuned engine delivering 152 hp.

Delahaye was in the car business a very long time,

from 1895 until 1954. Until the mid-thirties it made cars and trucks that were solid, bourgeois productions. Its great days began when management woke up to the fact that the stodgy image of the Delahaye would inevitably result in disaster. In the end it was the opposite of stodginess that ruined the marque. For the French Government decreed that an expensive-looking car was evidence of high income and thereupon piled on the taxes. And that's why the builders of high-quality French cars and coachwork are no more.

FIAT

Since 1899, when Giovanni Agnelli built the first F. I. A. T. (Fabbrica Italiana di Automobili Torino), until today, all Fiats (the capitals, except for the first, were dropped in 1906) have had one thing in common: They hold the road. This virtue is expected, for Turin, where Fiats have been built these seventy-odd years, is within spitting distance of the Alps, a natural testing place for prototypes.

The first Fiats were, naturally, tiller-steered gas buggies. But by 1902 and until about 1909 most Fiats were almost indistinguishable from the Mercedes: honeycomb radiators, chain drive, T-head engines and all. But from about the time of World War I—although large, powerful cars continued in production—the emphasis turned toward lighter, more economical machines.

Fiat was for years very important and successful in racing. A Fiat driven by Vincenzo Lancia took second place in the 1906 Vanderbilt Cup, and in 1907 Felice Nazzaro won the Kaiserpreis, the Targa Florio, and the French Grand Prix.

In 1910, an American company started manufacturing Fiats in Poughkeepsie, New York. These were not assembled

1

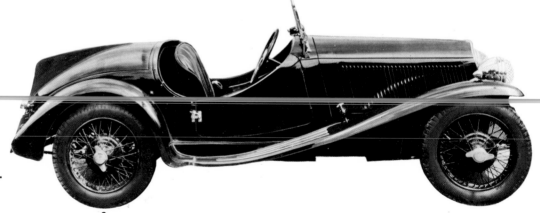

2

1. 1915 American-built Fiat had
4½-litre engine, 60-mph top speed.
Fiats were built in Poughkeepsie,
New York, from 1910 to 1918.
2. 1935 Fiat Balilla was small
sports car named after
Italian Fascist youth group.
3 & 4. 1906 20/30-hp Renault town
car has Windsor of Hounslow
coachwork, stands over eight feet.
5. Then, as now, curvy young
ladies helped advertise automobiles.

3

5

4

from Torinese parts, but were built entirely in America and were quite exact copies of their Italian relatives. Italian engineers from Turin made sure that Fiat standards were not debased. (The accompanying photograph is of a 1915 American Fiat.) In 1918, the Fiat Motor Co. factory was sold to Rochester-Duesenberg, which had war contracts to build airplane engines.

Fiat had always built sporting versions of some of its utilitarian cars, and today its low-priced sports cars, some with ohc engines, are second to none in their price classes.

Back in 1934 Fiat had great success with the Balilla, a sort of poor man's Zagato Alfa Romeo whose lines it aped. Although its 995-cc, four-cylinder engine developed only 36 hp at 4,000 rpm, it was capable of about 76 mph. It was a sure-footed little machine, weighed only 1,300 pounds, and had such amenities as Lockheed hydraulic brakes and center-lock wire wheels. It cost only $1,200. In 1952, Fiat brought out a far more sophisticated sports car with a V-8, 110-hp, two-litre engine. Its chassis-cum-body formed a double-walled structure of great strength and lightness. Independent suspension was used all around with the springs enclosed in oil-filled aluminum casings. A top speed of 125 mph was possible.

Fiat today is one of the world's great industrial giants. Among other things, it builds aircraft, ships, railroad rolling stock. And its cars, of which more are sold in Europe than any other make.

BMW

BMW—Bayerische Motoren Werke—produces cars that must be among the most surefooted, well-built passenger transports in the world. One—the BMW 3.0 CSL coupe, which is not at this writing imported into the USA—is also one of the quickest, its six-cylinder, 3,002-cc, fuel-injected engine propelling it at up to 150 mph. BMW also builds those sturdy, shaft-drive motorcycles. During World War II (as in World War I), BMW built airplane engines for the *Luftwaffe*, notably those which powered the Focke-Wulf 190's.

As fine as their present-day productions are—and they are very fine, indeed—I do wish that BMW still made an open two-seated sports machine like the Type 328 which was so successful before World War II. I first saw a BMW 328 in Zumbach's in about 1938. It had been imported by a man who wished to substitute it for a very nice Type 44 Bugatti fitted with a pretty four-passenger fabric body built in England. I thought the fellow was out of his head. "What, get rid of such a fine Bugatti for this stamped tin sports car?" Anyhow, I found him a customer for the Bugatti (the Bugatti buyer left it out in the weather and six months later it looked as if it had been stored at the bottom of a swimming pool), and I was permitted to try out the BMW. It was a revelation. The BMW might not have had the kind of hand-finished look that was then expected in a first-class sports car, but it certainly went like a first-class sports car. It weighed only 1,800 pounds, and was very fast—about 100 mph; it accelerated from zero to 60 in 11 seconds. It steered and held the road beautifully. At that time, the late thirties, it felt entirely different from the rather brutal sporting machinery we were used to. What we didn't know was that it was, in fact, a precursor of a type of car which we would not see until the fifties.

The 328 first made its debut in 1937. It had a 2-litre engine with hemispherical combustion chambers and inclined valves operated through an ingenious system of push rods from a single camshaft down inside the engine block. Three down-draft Solex carburetors were mounted between the high rocker boxes. In its pre-World War II form in the 328, this engine developed about 80 hp. Afterward the BMW engine was built in England, where it was called a Bristol engine and powered various British cars, including the Frazer Nash, the Bristol, the AC Aceca. Later verisons of the BMW engine often developed up to 125 hp.

The 328's chassis was advanced for its day, with ultra-sensitive rack-and-pinion steering, independent front suspension, and very powerful Lockheed hydraulic brakes. A BMW 328 cost about $3,000 (£600), much less than a Bugatti or Alfa, but more than twice the price of an MG. For a time before the Hitler war, it was marketed in Britain as a Frazer Nash BMW.

In 1940, an aerodynamicized BMW won a shortened version of the Italian Mille Miglia at an average of 103.53 mph. My friend, the late Bob Grier, bought this car in the fifties and raced it in amateur contests without great success, despite its reputed ability to better 130 mph. Grier used it as a street car, and when I rode in it with him I found it unbearably hot, noisy, and unpleasant.

Before their present successful series of cars, BMW built, among other machines, one which has become a classic: the beautiful Albrecht Goertz-designed 507, which had a 3.2-litre V-8 engine. BMW also built the tiny Italian-designed bubble car, the Isetta. Both these vehicles were commercial failures and almost put BMW out of business.

It's hard to realize now that the first BMW car built in 1929 was a Baby Austin built under license.

POPE-HARTFORD

The Pope-Hartford, built in Hartford, Connecticut, was the kind of solid bourgeois car a successful businessman might buy if he was not quite rich enough for a Pierce-Arrow or a Packard. But the Pope-Hartford was hardly a cheap car: In 1912 a 50-hp model cost more than $3,000 (£600).

Built from 1903 until 1914, it was the best of those machines with hyphenated names that Colonel Albert Augustus Pope constructed in his many factories. These were the Pope-Toledo, the Pope-Tribune, and the Pope-Waverly (an electric). He also built the Toledo Steamer and the Pope motorcycle and was closely involved with another car, the Columbia.

Pope was the tough, sharp Yankee who had dominated the American bicycle industry (he had been building bicycles since 1877), and he had visions of getting a stranglehold on the budding automobile industry as well. Together with an unscrupulous crew of millionaires who had been his partners in an outfit called the Electric Vehicle Company, Pope got control of the Selden Patent, which was issued by the Patent Office in 1895 and which, in their view, meant that no one else but George Baldwin Selden or his licensees could build or sell a car. They formed the Association of Licensed Automobile Manufacturers and forced almost every American car builder and importer to pay them tribute. Otherwise they sued. They made the mistake of suing Henry Ford, who licked them in 1911.

Pope's ethics were perhaps no better than the piratical business methods of his times, but the cars he built were honestly constructed of the very best materials. The Pope-Hartford was, unlike most cars of its time, built entirely in its own factory. The engine, transmission, all bearings and gears, frame, body, wheels, even the bronze carburetor, were built by Pope. A tire

factory was bought to make Pope tires. Each Pope-Hartford chassis went out on a test run before the body was mounted. And before an engine went into a chassis, it was run in the factory.

Although Pope-Hartford cars were not primarily sporting machines, they did fairly well in races and hill climbs in the hands of Bert Dingley and other well-known drivers of the time. But the Pope management was aware that, although its engines were capable of sustained high speeds, its chassis were not of racing caliber. It therefore installed modified 50-hp, four-cylinder Pope engines in Fiat chassis and called the hybrid a Portola. The engines had oversized valves, high-lift cams, lighter pistons, and higher compression.

Over the years there were Pope-Hartfords in all sizes from one-cylinder, 10-hp machines to big sizes rated at 60 hp. The car in the illustration is a 1913, 50-hp, four-cylinder Model 33. Its engine looks peculiarly tall, and its exposed valve gear with long push rods outside the cylinders gives a false look of complication. Much of the engine, except for the cylinders, is of cast aluminum. Dual coil and magneto ignition is fitted. Valves are in detachable cages. Exhaust pressure is used to force fuel from the tank to the carburetor. Power is transmitted by a leather-lined cone clutch, a four-speed gearbox, and shaft drive.

Such a meticulously built car at so high a price could not compete with the cheaper cars flooding out of big combines like General Motors. Nor did the Pope-Hartford have the snob appeal of makes like Packard and Pierce-Arrow. The end came in 1914. But one healthy survivor of Colonel Pope's empire still rolls along our roads. The Columbia Bicycle.

MARMON

The first Marmons go back to 1902, when Howard Marmon, of Nordyke & Marmon in Richmond, Indiana, which had been in the milling-machinery business since 1851, built a car with a four-cylinder, air-cooled engine. Despite their unusual features—cast-aluminum bodies, air-cooled engines, and flexible chassis which offered a primitive sort of independent suspension—the successful touring cars which Marmon built for years afterward are half forgotten. What are remembered are the 5.2-litre Model 32 Marmon speedsters, open two-seaters in the same tradition as the Mercer Raceabout and the Stutz Bearcat. These, built from

1. Early Citroëns were not quite as elegant as their ads.
2. 1922 5-cv Citroëns with three-seater "cloverleaf" bodies, were often painted lemon-yellow *(citron)*.
3. *"Traction Avant"* Citroëns were first built in 1934, were beloved as getaway cars by French gangsters. The cops used them, too.
4. Sophisticated Citroën SM has V-6 Maserati engine.

3

4

1909 until 1913, were the basis for a series of highly successful Marmon racing cars. In 1910, for example, Marmons entered 93 races and won 25 firsts, 24 seconds, and 13 thirds. And, in 1911, Ray Harroun and Cyrus Patschke won the first 500 at Indianapolis in the Marmon "Wasp."

The Model 32 was before my time. The Marmons which intrigued me were the Model 34's, especially the pretty sporting roadsters. The six-cylinder, 75-hp, ohv, 5½-litre-engined Model 34 was a sensation when it was first shown in 1916, mostly because of its extensive use of aluminum. The cylinder block, the hood, the radiator shell were all of light alloy. In 1923 front-wheel brakes were offered. Model 34's sold well, especially right after World War I, even at their high price of $5,000. On July 24, 1916, a Model 34 was sent off on a transcontinental run. Its parts marked and sealed to prevent replacement, it made the New York–San Francisco run in an incredible five days and eighteen hours—an average of 25.1 mph over nonroads. Variations of the Type 34 were built until 1927.

Somehow, Marmons seemed to lose some of their high quality as the twenties waned. But in 1931, Howard Marmon brought out a supercar—the incomparable Marmon V-16. The overhead-valve engine of this mighty machine displaced 491 cu. in. (8 litres) and produced 200 hp at 3,400 rpm. Its light weight—930 pounds—was due to the considerable use of aluminum alloys. The cylinder block, cylinder heads, crankcase, and many other parts were all of aluminum. "Wet" cylinder liners of case-hardened nickel-molybdenum steel were pressed into the block.

Mr. Edmund L. Robinson, who has enthusiastically owned four V-16 Marmons, wrote me concerning his present Waterhouse-bodied Marmon Phaeton: "My Marmon sixteen engine runs with incredible smoothness—in fact, it is like a turbine. I have placed a dime on its edge on top of the engine while idling. It remained there for as long as five minutes without falling."

The 145-inch wheelbase chassis was ladder type with leaf springs all around. A three-speed synchromesh transmission and a hypoid rear axle transmitted some 400 foot pounds of torque.

The design of the V-16 Marmon's sharp-edged body was far ahead of its time. Designed by Walter Dorwin Teague, a famous industrial designer, it was laudably free of excrescences and decoration. Expectedly, the big Marmon was very fast for a car of more than 5,000 pounds. Each buyer received a certificate stating that his car had exceeded 100 mph for at least five miles on the Indianapolis Speedway. Owners have claimed speeds of over 125 mph.

For a car of such evident magnificence, the price of $5,000 seems surprisingly low. But, at about three times the cost of a Cadillac in 1933, V-16 Marmons sold poorly. Only some 400 were built. According to Mr. Robinson, sixty-two Marmon V-16's are still in the hands of happy owners.

When Marmon stopped building cars in 1933, a V-12 was on test. This one is said to have had an independent front suspension, a tubular backbone frame, and a de Dion rear axle.

CITROËN

No matter what I've said about other cars in this book, I think the Citroën SM is *the* car without a peer. It is the ultimate motor car. Certainly, its many superb features—its V-6, 2,670-cc, 180-hp Maserati engine, hydropneumatic self-leveling suspension, big four-wheel disc brakes are impressive. Further, the bodywork which envelopes this remarkably sophisticated machinery and which was developed by careful wind-tunnel research, is, in my opinion, functionally beautiful. (But I thought that the coachwork of the older DS Citroën looked right, too, in spite of remarks by Philistines who called it "The Angry Clam.") Inside, too, the SM is not only eminently habitable but gives the driver near-perfect visibility, comfort, and a feeling of being in absolute control.

It is the lightning-quick steering of the Citroën SM that I found the most satisfying of its features. It enables a driver to take avoiding action instantly and prevent accidents before they can happen. From full lock to straight ahead takes but one turn of its oval wheel. And due to an ingenious hydraulic device, the steering is self-centering to an unusual degree. The faster you go the more this mechanism takes hold to keep the car on a straight and steady course.

Last I heard, an SM cost about $13,000 in the US.

The first Citroën appeared in 1919. It was Europe's first mass-produced automobile, the result of André Citroën's fascination with American mass-production methods. With a four-cylinder, 1,327-cc, 18-hp engine, conventional chassis, and ugly bodywork, it was not much of a car. But it was cheap—only 11,000 francs (the gyrating franc was worth only pennies in 1919)—and it set M. Citroën on the road to success.

Until 1934, when Michelin took over, André Citroën pursued a policy of turning out less-than-spectacular, albeit highly salable, cars, as well as very spectacular publicity. Among other stunts, he sent Citroën half-tracks across the Sahara Desert, into Alaska, and on a trip from Beirut to Peking. (Some cars on this "Yellow Journey" were taken to pieces and carried across the Himalayas by porters.) And in 1936 I watched as an electrician did a very French wiring job on the huge "Citroën" electric signs that stretched from the top to the bottom of the Eiffel Tower.

Before André Citroën had lost control of his company, he had directed his engineers to design a new kind of car. By 1934 they had succeeded with a machine that was years ahead of anything else around—the 7-cv "Traction Avant"—and until 1957 this front-drive car in various sizes and configurations was one of the most successful automobiles ever built. (It was especially cherished by French gangsters as a getaway car.) In 1956 the first of its svelte descendants, the front-drive ID19, came upon the scene to succeed it.

There is one other Citroën I must mention—the lovably ugly 2-cv, the most successful and practical utility car ever built. Made of flat sheets of corrugated metal, with minimal amenities, and sprung like an acrobatic kangaroo, it could have been a wonderful antistatus symbol in America. Unfortunately, it is too slow for our turnpikes.

That chevron-shaped device on Citroëns? It symbolizes the first mechanism André Citroën was associated with—the herringbone gears he manufactured at the turn of the century after buying the rights to their invention from a relative in Lodz, Poland.

RENAULT

Today Renault builds cars of admirable utility. They are modern and solid, and they sell prodigiously in France, the country which also controls the Renault Factories.

I have owned two of them. One was a "Quatre-Cheveaux," a car which, purportedly, Dr. Ferdinand Porsche helped develop. I was fond of that little 4-cv until it broke my arm when I tried to hand-crank it while its ignition system was deranged. The other Renault I owned was a 1957 Dauphine, similar to one in which I was a passenger when its driver rolled us over a few revolutions and almost into the River Loire. I lost enthusiasm for my own Dauphine after that.

Louis Renault built his first prototype car in 1898. M. Renault powered his machine with a little 1¾-hp, 273-cc, one-cylinder de Dion engine under a hood out front. But the car was ahead of its time, with shaft drive to a back axle incorporating a differential and a gearbox with direct drive in high.

Renault Frères (Louis, Marcel, and Fernand) was immediately successful and sold some sixty cars in its first six months. The brothers Renault did well on the race courses, too. Marcel won second place over-all in the great Paris–Vienna Race and also took first in his class. In 1903, his luck failed and he was killed in the Paris–Madrid fiasco. Later, François Szisz won the 1906 French Grand Prix on a 13-litre giant.

Renault's unique dashboard radiator behind a shovel-nosed hood and a sealed engine compartment remained a feature until the late nineteen-twenties. Perhaps the best remembered of the many Renault models using this configuration were the famous *taxis de la Marne* which helped move some of General Gallieni's troops to stop von Kluck's army before Paris in 1914.

Of the multiplicity of Renault models, the most impressive was that mastodon, the "45," which I remember seeing in a Fifth Avenue showroom in the twenties. These huge, shovel-nosed machines had 9.1-litre, six-cylinder engines and were capable of over 90 mph. Their wheelbases stretched an incredible 158 inches. One of them, fitted with a light, aerodynamic body, was sent out on a track in 1926 and became the first car to average over 100 mph for twenty-four hours.

After the twenties Renaults became less spectacular and more like the products of Detroit, with which they were competing.

Louis Renault, who had been imprisoned for suspected collaboration with the Germans, died in jail in 1944. Since then Renault has been under French Government control.

Renault still maintains a good head of sporting steam. A Renault Alpine won the 1973 Monte Carlo Rally.

No envelope of metal and glass shielded the early automobile tourist from the rigors of weather, the gale caused by his car pushing its way through the atmosphere, or the dust raised from the unpaved roads of his day. Instead, the primitive autoist and his female passengers sat atop their wide-open, windshieldless machines swathed in such strange armor of wool, rubber, fur, and leather as to terrify the inhabitants of the small towns in which, like people from a distant planet, they might alight. But these were adventurous, second-generation autoists.

The very *first* motorists had no such forbidding aspects. Their flea-powered horseless carriages progressed slowly, created little wind and dust. As for rain and snow, their con-

ductors had enough sense to avoid such dreadful inclemencies. We see them photographed in bowler hats, celluloid collars, and business suits as they desperately grip their steering tillers.

In the next stage, especially among drivers with pretensions to sportiness, the *de rigueur* costume consisted of a black peaked cap, like that of an engineer on a steam locomotive, a black leather jacket, and goggles, which could be worn, at low speeds, above the cap's peak.

People didn't begin to bedizen themselves with weird-looking motoring costumes until cars became big enough and fast enough for touring at respectable speeds. If some of their wilder looking getups—the floor-length bearskin coats and leather face masks—seem extreme to us today, it's because most of us don't know what a drive in a touring car of, say, 1905 was like. I often drive such a big, open, windshieldless machine. In July, on an 80-degree summer afternoon, a passenger who insists (against my admonitions) on wearing summer clothing is soon begging to be taken home to put on a coat. The reason is simple. At fifty miles an hour, the effective temperature, because of the wind-chill factor, becomes about forty degrees. On a nice brisk autumn day when walkers are strolling along in sport jackets, the occupants of my car must bundle up like Arctic explorers. Only once did I essay a drive on a snowy winter's day. We froze no matter how much clothing we put on. If we'd had some of those peculiar 1905-style coats and face masks we might have managed.

The 1902 British Badminton Library of Sports and Pastimes book, entitled *Motors and Motor Driving*, contains some definitive advice on "dress for motoring" by Baron de Zuylen, president of the *Automobile Club de France*. Some of his ideas: "Leather may be used as a lining to cloth clothes provided that it is bored with many small holes through which the moisture of the body may evaporate. A suit of cloth lined with punctured chamois leather will be found agreeable for both winter and summer. . . . If the automobilist does not use a thick rug to protect his legs, gaiters should be worn with knickerbockers. . . . As regards underclothing . . . silk is perhaps the best material for retaining the warmth of the body. . . . On the Continent a coat made of rough fur is worn with the fur on the outside. In addition to the heat-retaining qualities of the fur,

Preceding pages: Poster for Paris garage recognizes problems of dressing correctly while motoring. Above: Rugs over legs, heavy coats still failed to keep motorists from feeling cold. Right: Young lady has her own isinglass windshield to protect her face and coiffure.

1. Scarf enveloping lady's head
renders her incognito and dust-free.
2. Long motoring coat kept Madame
warm and cozy but also invited
disastrous entanglement with pedals.
3. This well-masked young lady
is waiting patiently for her young man
to return to his 1903
single-cylinder de Dion-Bouton.
4. Peaked caps and fur coats were
correct attire for this brace of
Rothschilds in 1900 Cannstatt-Daimler.

1

2

926   MOTORING AT THE CAPITOL, WASHINGTON

Automobiles—1902   © 1911

such coats have the advantage of readily shooting off rain. . . . In the summer, when the weather is very hot, provided that a thick suit of clothes be worn, a greatcoat is sometimes unnecessary, except as a protection from dust."

De Zuylen describes a device for defeating the effects of rain: "It consists of a flat, circular, leather-covered cushion about 15 inches in diameter, by, say, 2½ inches thick, having a hole 2 inches or 3 inches in diameter right through the centre . . . In wet weather you put the cushion inside your coat and thus preserve a dry seat. Should you at any time leave the cushion exposed to rain, the water will not form a pool in the centre and saturate it, but will run away at once through the hole."

De Zuylen then goes on to describe various "India-rubber" kilts, greatcoats, and whatnot. He was evidently unaware of a great American invention—a sort of poncho big enough to cover the whole car. This had four holes punched in it to allow the heads of the driver and his passengers to protrude.

The duster, that long, dust-colored coat of canvas-like material, was also an American garment. For, though dust clouds followed cars in Europe and Britain, American dust clouds were, as usual, bigger and better due to the shameful fact that few American roads were paved.

Everybody wore goggles, including even Bud, the small bulldog who rode the 1903 Winton driven by H. Nelson Jackson on its sixty-four-day trans-American run. Bud refused to start off mornings until his goggles were in place. Still, Bud, due to the shape of his face, couldn't wear the type of goggles that high-speed autoists often affected. Those were part of a leather face mask reaching to the chin.

It wasn't only in the earliest days that people dressed oddly in automobiles. In the twenties and thirties, European drivers of open Mercedes-Benzes and Bugattis thought it *trés sportif* to wear white cloth racing helmets and goggles in imitation of racing drivers. More recently, when the British MG's and Jaguars became popular in the early fifties, bank clerks and real-estate salesmen dressed themselves in what they thought sporting Englishmen wore when motoring. Checked caps and tattersall vests such as British turf accountants might don when drunk became common in suburbia. And RAF moustaches proliferated.

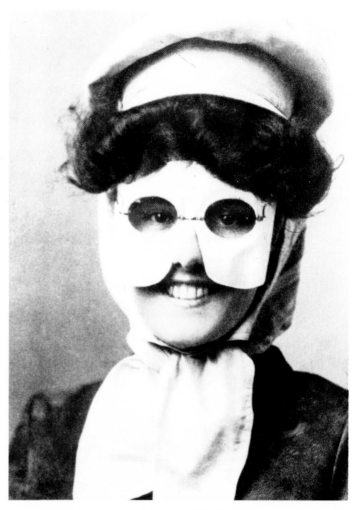

We doubt if the lady in the lithograph opposite dared drive her snappy 1912 model speedster while wearing that wind-catching hat.
Top: Face masks like this disappeared when windshields (called "glass fronts") became common.
Above: The huge hats on this bevy of beauties must have caused speed-cutting wind resistance.

ON HIGHWAYS

A sports-car driver reveling in his car's ability to negotiate the twists and turns of a country road almost certainly does not ponder the fact that the bit of curving road he so enjoys was originally engineered by a moose or an elephant—depending on whether he's driving in New England or East Africa. Hunters —Mohicans or Masai—followed animal trails. And the roads we now use in many places still follow the old paths that were first widened to accommodate carts, and then in time—only recently, in fact—were paved.

In Western Europe and Britain it was, of course, the Romans, intent on moving their legions as quickly as possible, who ignored the twisting cow paths and built fairly straight, all-weather roads on bases of masonry. Interestingly, the ruts worn into these stones by Roman cart wheels are still close to the standard 4-foot, 8-inch gauge of modern railway tracks and, until very recently, of almost all automobiles. The imperial roads of ancient China were not unlike Roman roads in purpose and in masonry construction.

The great French *routes nationales* were in many instances based on old Roman roads. Even in medieval times, when Roman roads were allowed in other countries to sink into desuetude, French roads were maintained by serfs forced to spend several days' labor each year in highway-repair work. Napoleon improved these roads for his bloody purposes and did what was beyond even Roman engineering abilities. He built across the steep western Alps roads suitable for heavy wheeled vehicles. Neither Hannibal nor Caesar had anything but trails usable by foot soldiers or pack animals. Napoleon's roads across the Simplon, Mont Cenis, and Mont Genèvre passes, built between 1800 and 1810 mostly by brutally overworked Italian laborers, allowed Bonaparte to windily announce "that there were no longer any Alps" and to feel that he had northern Italy firmly locked in his grasp.

In Britain, the 2,655 miles of Roman road started to disappear soon after the legions left in A.D. 406. Bridges collapsed, roads were buried under sand and earth and overgrown with trees and brush. Later generations who had forgotten their builders attributed the remains of the roads to heathen monsters and legendary beings. They dug out stones from the roads to build convents and monasteries.

Until the nineteenth century most British roads were morasses in wet weather, choked with dust and stones on the rare dry days. Then enormous changes were wrought on Britain's roads, due mostly to the efforts of the two great road-builders Thomas Telford and John Macadam. Telford, known mostly for his construction of the famous Holyhead road, built his roads almost in the Roman style, on stone blocks. But Macadam, whose name is still attached to some of our highways today, is the real father of the modern road. Instead of a costly masonry foundation, Macadam put a layer of small broken stones about an inch in diameter directly on the subsoil. A carpet of much smaller stones was spread over the lower stratum. The wheels of coaches and wagons crushed some of these smaller stones into a powder which, when rolled and watered, served to cement the road surface.

The Macadam roads were functional during the early nineteenth century. Coaches and post-chaises whirled over them at speeds up to 14 mph. But before the century was out something much better was needed. The motor car had arrived, and cars tore up the water-bound "macadam." The powder which had held the roads together took to the air as dust. Pot holes formed.

The answer was tar. And the now familiar tar-macadam road came into being. Other types of coating have since been used successfully, too, notably oil and asphalt. But one type of mixture—an emulsion of petroleum and ammonia used to lay the dust during some early car races—raised hell with the drivers, burning their eyes and skin and almost asphyxiating them.

America had few such problems with road surfacing. For there existed hardly any highways to surface. Although there were some two million miles of publicly owned "roads" in 1904, only seven percent were "improved." "Improved" usually meant that a horse pulling a scraper had leveled most of the hump in the middle of the road (along with the grass and weeds growing on the hump), and that most of the tree stumps had been uprooted. Sometimes a wheelbarrow-load of stones was dumped into the mud holes. The only paved roads were the streets in towns, and many of these were surfaced with bone-jarring cobblestones.

Preceding pages: The workmen seem to be ready—at last—to pave the town street over which the man is driving his big 1909 Premier. Streets in cities were surfaced long before anyone paid particular attention to country roads. Right: Pavement ended at the edge of town.

Opposite: Building a cement section of the Lincoln Highway west of South Bend, Indiana, in 1915. Below: Model 30 Packard traverses a dirt road in 1907. Bottom. A drawing by A. B. Frost, famous American illustrator, portrays a group of tourists on a typical unpaved highway. Such roads, though dusty, were not too difficult to drive on in dry weather, but rain turned them into bottomless quagmires.

It wasn't until the eighteen-nineties that people started griping about our ridiculous roads. These were mostly bicyclists caught up in the cycling craze of those days. Led by Col. Albert Pope, the manufacturer of Columbia bicycles and later an early automobile magnate, they started the "Good Roads" movement. Sadly they didn't get very far, not having much clout in state legislatures controlled by conservative rural types who detested city slickers on wheels.

Automobilists, naturally, were the ones who forced state and federal authorities to move toward building decent highways on a national scale. In fact, the very first resolution passed by the American Automobile Association after it was first organized in 1902 was startlingly ambitious. It called for building a coast-to-coast highway from New York to San Francisco, no less!

At first all the pressure to build better roads came from city people, rich people with big cars who drove mostly for pleasure. Farmers, who thought the muddy tracks over

Opposite: A 1910 Pierce-Arrow fords a stream. The stream bottom was often hardly less deep in mud than the road crossing it. Above: A distressing scene in 1911. People sometimes waited for days in order to let roads clear before setting forth. Remedy for this impatient winter traveler would be a horse.

Above: Horses or mules, like team at 1920's
fuel-and-oil depot here, were the
best means of extricating cars from ditches,
mud, or snow. Right: Turn-of-the-century
English print, showing early motorists
in Panhard-like car, memorializes the passing of
the four-horse London and Brighton coach.

Right: It wasn't until the 1920's that gas stations became as fancy as this one. Electric pumps were still in the future, and the attendant hand-pumped the gasoline up into a glass section of the pump before the fuel went down the hose to your gas tank.
Below: This 1904 Packard will have to travel a long way before finding a paint shop or drug store at which to buy gasoline.

which they drove their wagons to town were good enough, resisted costly frills like well-graded, paved roads. Their taxes were high enough. That didn't stop them from taking advantage of dudes from the cities in fancy cars, though. They managed to make a few dollars when their mules were hired to haul a car out of a deep mudhole—a mudhole often carefully watered by the farmer as a source of income. And it was not unknown for farmers to bury big saws athwart the road. A saw's teeth just below the dusty surface was death on tires and gave the mules some work even in very dry weather.

It wasn't "Good Roads" propaganda that at last filled in the muddy gullies and removed the boulders from the roads. It was Henry Ford's Model T. Ford had built that car with the farmers in mind, and they bought it by the millions. As soon as the farmers became motorists they too screamed for better roads. And since the men in the bib overalls controlled the state legislators, they soon got them.

It was supersalesman Carl Fisher, head of the Prest-O-Lite company and the promotor of the Indianapolis Speedway, who in 1912 first tried to put across the idea of a coast-to-coast highway, which he called the Ocean-to-Ocean Rock Highway. It was Fisher's idea to have the auto industry tax itself one-third of one percent of its gross and thus raise part of the money to build the highway. The rest would come from private individuals, states, and cities. He hoped to raise $100 million and get his road finished in time to connect New York with the Panama-Pacific Exposition due to open in 1915.

Henry Ford wrecked this grandiose plan. He'd have had to put up most of the auto industry's share since seventy-five percent of the cars sold in the country were his Model T's. He hated the people in the auto industry and he wouldn't give a red cent. But the industry tycoons persevered. They changed the name of the road from "Rock Highway" to "Lincoln Memorial Highway," formed the "Lincoln Highway Association," and started the biggest publicity campaign the country had ever suffered. Elaborate tours were sent out to struggle across the country to San Francisco over what was to be the "Road." But no roads at all existed in some sections. There were no road maps or road signs west of Chicago, except those put up by local boosters. These super-Babbits sent out crews to paint colored bands on telegraph poles along miserable stretches of country byways. One bunch would paint yellow bands on their poles and call their route the Yellow-Pole Road. A competitive chamber of commerce might use white paint and call their "road" the White-Pole Highway. In some places the road west was merely a right-of-way across privately owned fields, and motorists had to open and close gate after gate in the fences surrounding the fields.

Every tank town in the country wanted the highway to go down its main street. Battles continued for years as to where the highway would go. President Wilson wanted it to loop down through Washington, D.C. Senator Warren G. Harding got into the act in Ohio. The Automobile Club of Southern California fought angrily to have the western terminus at Los Angeles instead of San Francisco. Cleveland accused the Association of leaving it off the route because Detroit's auto builders wanted to freeze out Cleveland's car makers. Utah's Mormons were still sore at President Lincoln for sending troops to Utah because they had sympathized with the Confederacy and didn't care for a road named "Lincoln." The association gave Utah $100,000 to help in building the road. Utah kept the $100,000, but didn't build anything.

It wasn't until 1921 that the Federal Highway Act at last made enough money available to actually help the states complete Fisher's dream. The Lincoln Highway Association existed until 1927, when it voted to use the money still in its treasury to put up insignia forever identifying the Lincoln Highway. Three thousand markers, complete with Lincoln's portrait in bronze, were set in place from coast to coast, after which the "Lincoln Highway" almost immediately ceased to exist as such. The Federal Highway Act, which had helped to complete the road, then brought in the numbering system. Those Lincoln Highway markers are collector's items now. Dismembered, parts of the highway became sections of US 1, US 30, US 40, and so on.

Parts of that old Lincoln Highway have died and been buried like the Roman roads of ancient Britain. But the concept of long, superroads lived on to become the German autobahnen, the Italian autostradas, and the huge American federal highway system. For a long time such roads represented progress. Do they still?

THE SPORTS CAR

These are the athletic motor cars; they are built to show their muscle and agility, and to delight us while doing so. Not only can we exult in mastering and controlling such machines, we can take pleasure in merely looking at them. For sports cars, more than any other type, allow body designers free play to conceive aesthetic and wind-cheating shapes with fewer concessions to the practicalities required in more mundane machinery.

In *Sports Cars of the World*, a book I wrote in 1951, I said: "In the beginning, some sixty years ago, all cars were sports cars. . . . The mere act of climbing aboard one of the shaking, smoking, high-wheeled monsters of the nineties was certainly a most sporting proposition. Driving one of them was the same kind of desperate nineteenth-century adventure as scaling the Matterhorn or going up in a balloon. Only the wildest and wealthiest of the Victorian sportsmen would have anything to do with these horrible machines."

On reflection, I think this view was not quite correct. Although the brave men who set forth in devices like a Benz Velo of 1894 or a Panhard et Levassor of 1896 were certainly intrepid sportsmen, the cars they drove were not necessarily sports cars.

It was not until much later that cars appeared which could be handled with a certain verve, cars with accurate steering systems and good roadholding, with brakes (if only on two wheels) that could be applied with some measure of confidence, and with engines whose speed could be delicately varied by means of a throttle, and which had enough power to provide some exhilaration for the driver—for performance is always the chief characteristic of a sports car.

The first machines we might call sports cars today appeared many years ago—although the term "sports car" was not used until the nineteen-twenties. It wasn't until after World War II that the term gained real currency in the USA.

The granddaddy of all sports cars was the fabulous 1903 Mercedes Sixty. This 9¼-litre monster, whose inflexible engine ran at a mere 1,000 rpm, was in reality a racing car, fendered and headlighted for the pleasure of suicidal young millionaires. By 1907 there were other such semiracers: the Chadwick Fast Runabout and the Apperson Jack-Rabbit, for example. But cars more agile and more practical for ordinary use as well as

for racing were evolving. The 1911 Austro-Daimler and the 1912 Prince Henry Vauxhall have long been considered the first true sports cars. But certainly the Alfonso Hispano-Suiza of 1912, the 1911 Mercer Raceabout, and the 1913 Type 13 Bugatti deserve the appellation, too.

In our own time, when we say "sports car," we often think of a type which dates from the nineteen-twenties—the classic open machine which is only now disappearing. There is in my mind a picture of the typical, if perhaps idealized, sports car of the nineteen-thirties, when, it seems to me, sports machinery was at its classic best.

Such a car was an open two-seater, its bodywork light, narrow, and minimal, with little if any room for luggage. The doors were deeply cut away to give the driver and his passenger elbow room, although it was only necessary for the driver to be so accommodated; he was so close to the steering wheel he had to hold his arms akimbo. (The arm's-length style of steering-wheel manipulation is a fairly recent affectation.) The car's inmates looked out over a long, narrow hood, and the driver could see the tops of both sweeping front fenders. Turning his head, he could easily see either rear fender. Wire wheels with eared, knock-off hubs were mandatory.

Mechanically, the classic sports car usually had a ladder-type frame, stiff semielliptic springs, a solid front axle, ribbed drum brakes of great diameter, and a four- or six-cylinder engine of about 2 litres. More expensive cars' engines had overhead camshafts and were sometimes supercharged. Cheaper machines used other means to operate their valves. But in either case the aim was toward an engine whose revs would climb rapidly at a touch of the throttle. Gearboxes invariably had four speeds.

What joy to drive such a car. At idling speed the exhaust burbled happily. At speed the burble turned into a purposeful, rasping roar (silence was for more gentle machines). Double declutching up and down, it was sheer happiness to select just the right gear for each corner, each essay at high-speed passing on a two-lane road, each hill. Steering was quick as thought. A flick of your wrist and you were around a corner. And steering was dead accurate, too, with just a mite of oversteer. Unlike many present-day cars, a vintage sports car didn't

Preceding pages: 1932 Aston Martin International is classic, close-coupled, four-seated English sports car. Capable of about 80 mph, it has four-cylinder, 70-hp, overhead-cam engine. Front fenders are attached to brake drums and steer with the wheels.

S

Sporting 1908 Delage, left, and beautifully styled 1937 Delage, below, emphasize the tremendous advances in sports-car styling in less than thirty years. "Vutotal" *aerodynamique* Delage was designed by French genius, Henri Labourdette. Patented "Vutotal" system eliminated pillars at sides of windshield. Thick, load-bearing windshield glass was fastened to roof and cowl.

try to go straight on when you wanted to turn. In fact, it *wanted* to corner, perhaps just a wee bit more than the unsophisticated driver might anticipate. But this made for quick cornering without hard hauling at the steering wheel's rim. Not, I grant you, quite safe for Aunt Mildred.

Such cars did, in some people's view, have their shortcomings. Their friction shock absorbers were, in the imagined interest of roadholding, adjusted as tightly as possible. Their already stiff springs became as immobile as iron bars. Derrieres suffered. Protection from wind and rain was laughable. Heaters were nonexistent. After a longish trip in poor weather you might look and feel only slightly better than a topman of a square-rigger which had just rounded Cape Horn.

But such a vehicle was, if the owner tuned it a bit, admirably equipped for racing in club events on weekends. Even factories raced the selfsame sports machines they offered for public sale.

Such sports cars ranged through a wide spectrum of price and ferocity, from the cheap MG's and Amilcars to the costly Alfa Romeos and Bugattis. They might be as tiny as a 750-cc Austin Nippy or as vast as a pre-Rolls Bentley.

The years between the two World Wars were the heyday of the open sporting machines, and their habitat unfortunately no longer embraced North America. Of the great American sporting cars—Simplex, Mercer, Stutz, and the others —only Stutz survived, and that only until 1935. Even lesser marques like Kissel and Marmon, also with sporting traditions, ceased due to the Great Depression. England, France, Italy, and Germany built the world's sports cars and each inevitably imbued its machines with its own national characteristics, shaped by its geography and its social and economic system.

England was unique in having a large middle class which appreciated sports cars. On most of the Continent such

1926 Bignan was typical of many sports
cars built in small shops of a multitude of
French builders during the 1920's.
Bignan had a four-cylinder, 70-hp, ohc engine, and
once set record for twenty-four-hour run
at Le Mans. Odd braking system
used foot pedal to apply front brakes only.

machines were for the rich, except for those few young Frenchmen who could raise enough francs to buy inexpensive Amilcars and such.

British sports cars suited Britain's terrain. England has no high mountain passes, no great plains. Roads until recently followed ancient, winding packhorse trails. When I drove in England back in the mid-thirties, I was amazed by their wonderful smoothness. Most American highways of those days were comparatively rough.

England's sports cars fitted its roads. They were hard-sprung, since they had few bumps to absorb. Their steering was quick and positive, to cope with twisting and turning lanes. And mostly they were, by our standards, underpowered, since long, fast passages across prairies were not their role. Further, Britain's horsepower tax of those days kept engines small. The horsepower tax, due to the usual stupidity of officialdom, also favored small cylinder bores. So English engines then had longish strokes which limited revs.

Britain has built more makes of sporting car than any other country. Alvis, Aston Martin, Bentley, Frazer Nash, HRG, Invicta, Jaguar, Lagonda, Lea-Francis, Lotus, MG, Morgan, Riley, Singer, Squire, Triumph, Vauxhall do not exhaust the list. Some of these I'll deal with briefly, a few at greater length.

MG

The most popular of all English sports cars is the MG, whose prototype appeared some fifty years ago, when Cecil Kimber modified a stodgy Morris Cowley for competition in rallies and trials. Its successes led to production MG's, biggish cars with engines of about 2 litres. But it wasn't until 1929, when the MG Midget was born, that the MG became exactly the kind of sports car young Englishmen unencumbered by many pounds were looking for.

The first Midget was based partly on the Morris Minor, an economy car designed to compete with the Baby Austin. Like the little Morris it had a four-cylinder, 847-cc, single-overhead-camshaft engine. But the MG version had a little more go due to better manifolding and more sporting valve timing. Even so, it developed a mere 20 hp at 4,000 rpm. Sixty-five mph was possible.

The M-type was an instant success. It cost only $800 or so, it drank little petrol, and young Britishers thought its fabric-and-plywood, pointy-tailed body most dashing. Competition success helped, too. In 1930, five M's ran in the Double Twelve at Brooklands Track. Although fourteenth place was the best that one of them could achieve (at 60.23 mph), all five finished. The mere fact that the tiny machines could survive a twenty-four-hour run (in two twelve-hour bites) gave sales a filip. But it was the later, 750-cc Montlhéry Midget, built for racing, that gave the sports MG Midgets the wonderful businesslike look that endeared them to sports-car lovers for more than twenty years. The first slab-tanked, cutaway-doored model was the J2 of 1932, which developed 33 hp from its 847-cc ohc engine. After the J2 came the PA, the PB, and then the TA of 1936 which, to the distress of MG-ophiles, no longer had ohc, but a 1,272-cc push-rod engine. The TB's was slightly smaller at 1,250 cc. It was the next model, the now-revered TC, which first introduced Americans to sports cars and started the revulsion against Detroit's vulgarities that still continues.

The entrancingly spartan TC's gave way to the fattened-up and independently sprung TD's and TF's. By 1953 they, with their long, sweeping fenders and flat gas tanks, were superseded by a new kind of MG, no longer a "Midget" with a slab-sided body, but of a streamlined, "envelope" shape. This was the 1,489-cc-engined (later 1,622 cc) MGA, which sold very well, thank you: more than 100,000 in seven years. The MGB of today boasts an 88-hp, 1,798-cc engine, does c. 105 mph, and costs about $4,000.

There's still an MG Midget, too, with a 1,275-cc engine and 62 hp. It costs only $2,600, less in today's money than that 20-hp M-type of 1929.

RILEY

The delectable little sports Rileys never became as well known as the MG's in the US, for the obvious reason that they were no longer being built by the time Americans became sports-car conscious. Only the big 2½-litre touring Rileys of the late forties and fifties ever reached America in quantity. The best-known Riley sports models were the Brooklands, the Imp, the MPH, and the Sprite.

The Brooklands Riley which appeared in 1928 was

based on the Riley Nine, a likable little sedan with a sparkling performance, considering the size of its 1,100-cc engine. But Riley engines were unusual. Although their camshafts were not "overhead," they were mounted high up in the block and operated the inclined valves in hemispherical combustion chambers. J. G. Parry Thomas, who at the time held the Land Speed Record, was intrigued by the Riley Nine's engine and chassis, and started reworking one into a competition machine. Before he could finish, he was killed while having another go at the record. Reid Railton, who was then working at Thomson and Taylor, the famous firm of racing-engineers at Brooklands, then took over. He ended up with a highly desirable little sports-racing machine with a fantastic performance for an 1,100-cc car.

Its engine turned out 50 hp at 5,000 rpm and, owing to the light weight of its sketchy, long-tailed bodywork and small frontal area, it was capable of 90 mph and a zero-to-60 time of 15 seconds or so—great performance for 1,100 cc in 1928. One of these long-tailed little Rileys appeared in Zumbach's for servicing now and then during the mid-nineteen-thirties and its owner took me for a short run in Central Park. It was about eight years older than the MG TA another Zumbach habitue had demonstrated for me a few days earlier on the same roads. The Riley had it all over the MG in speed, pep, and lovely noises from its outside exhaust pipe. But it certainly was no car for a trip. The MG was far more civilized.

In 1928, a Brooklands Riley took the six-hour In-

Left: 1930 M-type MG sets off for
Monte Carlo Rally. M-type,
first MG Midget, had 847-cc, four-cylinder,
20-hp, ohc engine. Body was of wood
and fabric. Right: Famous TC MG was car
that helped start sports car
boom in America after World War II.

ternational record at 85.2 mph, and in 1930, among other racing successes, a Brooklands won the Irish Grand Prix.

The Brooklands wasn't really a production sports car; the factory made very few of them and they were mostly used for competition. It cost £420—more than $2,000 then.

It wasn't until 1934 that the four-cylinder, 1,100-cc Imp and the six-cylinder, 1,639-cc (later 1,726-cc) MPH sports Riley reached the showrooms. Bodied not unlike Zagato Alfa Romeos, but even better looking and more purposeful in shape, these had Wilson preselector gearboxes, large-diameter brakes, conventional half-elliptic suspensions, and a 90-inch wheelbase. Heavier than the old Brooklands, they hadn't quite the performance. But the hotter version of the Imp, the Ulster model,

was still quick enough. As late as 1950, in the hands of Mike Hawthorn, the first Britisher to win the Racing Driver's World Championship, it won its class at the Brighton Speed Trials. (Hawthorn won the first race of his great career in the same Ulster Imp.) An Imp cost £325 in 1935, the MPH slightly more.

In 1936, Riley brought out the lovely Sprite, which used a four-cylinder, 1,496-cc engine, the 12/4, first used in the company's bread-and-butter car in 1934. The Sprite also used the Wilson preselector gearbox. Weight was kept fairly low and the Sprite had a lively performance: 90 mph was possible. The only Sprite I ever saw in the US was one found wrecked, with its English driver dead, in the California desert in 1942. Several years later I got to know the man who bought the ruins, Robert

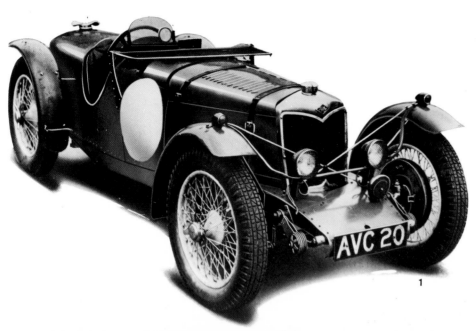

1

2

3

1. Brooklands Riley appeared in 1928,
had great success in 1,100-cc class.
2. 1934 Riley 9 Imp had
four-cylinder, 1,100-cc engine,
Wilson preselector gearbox.
3. Lotus Elan Sprint has fiberglass
body, twin-ohc, four-cylinder engine.
4. 1936 2-litre TT Aston Martin
at Brooklands Track.
5. 1932 International Aston Martin.
Note oil tank between front dumb irons.
6. 1973 Aston Martin has
5,340-cc, V-8 engine, air conditioning.

4

5

6

Cox. He had accomplished the difficult feat of rebuilding the Sprite in wartime with the long-distance advice of Riley's, who had, I'm sure, enough trouble themselves in 1942. Anyhow, that pretty little Sprite, rebuilt, was the only small sports car which felt almost as nice to handle as the 1,750-cc Alfa Romeo (*senza compressore*) I'd recently sold. But only almost.

ASTON MARTIN

The long list of British sports cars has today shrunk to some half-dozen names. One of these is Aston Martin, which goes back sixty years to 1913. In that year, Lionel Martin, a partner in the firm of Bamford and Martin, installed a four-cylinder Coventry-Simplex engine in a small Isotta Fraschini racing chassis and called it an Aston Martin (the Aston part of the name referred to the Aston Clinton Hill Climb venue, where Martin earlier had had some success with Singers.) Bamford and Martin had considerable competitive success with the cars which evolved from the marriage of the Isotta chassis and the Coventry-Simplex engine, but by 1926 only some fifty Aston Martin cars had been sold, and Bamford and Martin gave up.

It was Augustus Cesare Bertelli who for the next decade built the Aston Martins we remember most fondly. In 1926, with several associates including Lionel Martin, he set up a new company called Aston Martin Motors Ltd. The first of Bertelli's Astons to reach enthusiasts was the International (see accompanying photograph). This no-nonsense sports machine had a 1½-litre engine with a single chain-driven overhead camshaft, a unique "pent-roof" combustion chamber, and dry-sump lubrication. It developed 70 hp. But solid construction of the Astons tended to increase their weight, and not much over 80 mph was possible. Bertelli's Astons, however, were lovely machines to drive. Although it is more than thirty-five years since I last handled one, I still remember the wonderfully comfortable seating position (compared to the Alfa I had then) and the unique view of the front wheels *and* the axle permitted by the helmet-like front fenders which steered with the wheels. The stubby gear lever, which stuck up out of the four-speed gearbox mounted well behind the engine and separated from it by a short shaft, had a hard, positive feel. But shifting the gears in the nonsynchro gearbox did require a modicum of finesse. Acceleration was so-so, but somehow it didn't matter.

The Aston felt so nice to drive.

The International was followed in 1932 by the Le Mans model, then in 1935 by the Mark II. After that came the Ulster, more powerful (capable of 100 mph) but without quite the hand-built character of the earlier models. Bertelli was no longer in complete control. To save his company he had been forced to take in a joint managing director with money to invest. In 1936, the 15/98 model Aston Martin had a more powerful 2-litre engine, but dry-sump lubrication and the cycle fenders were gone, and the gearbox had synchromesh. A Speed Model, which retained the dry sump and eschewed synchronized gears, was available for tougher types; 100 mph was claimed for it.

After the war, Aston Martin became part of the David Brown tractor-and-gear empire. At first Astons used the pre-1939 2-litre engine. In 1950 the DB Aston Martins were powered by the twin-ohc 2.6-litre engine which W. O. Bentley designed for the Lagonda, another of Brown's acquisitions.

Since then Aston Martins have grown ever more potent and luxurious. During the nineteen-fifties and sixties they were notably successful in competition.

Today the Aston Martin—like the Maserati, certain Ferraris, and the Lamborghini—is a big, lush, hugely powerful road express for rich men. The current DBS is a four-seater powered with a V-8, twin-ohc, 5.4-litre engine churning out 360 hp. It weighs almost two tons and costs *c.* $20,000. I'd still rather have an International, which cost only $2,080 in 1932.

LOTUS

Of today's British sports cars there is one in particular whose character is not only much like those of the Great Past, but also embraces the many advances in suspension, steering, and aerodynamics that have been learned from recent grand-prix racing. This is the Lotus Elan Sprint and its sister cars designed by Colin Chapman, whose rear-engined racing machines have revolutionized the concept of the GP car. The Elan Sprint, +2S, and Europa are not hotted-up touring chassis, as are so many other sports cars, but have a much more desirable lineage: direct descent from racing machines. All of them have light, stiff-backbone chassis frames, independent suspension all around, and four-wheeled disc brakes. Twin-ohc, 1,558-cc engines are

Top: The winning Woolf Barnato-Glen Kidston
6½-litre Bentley being replenished
at Le Mans in 1930. It covered 1,821.06 miles
in twenty-four hours. Speed averaged
75.876 mph. Bottom: Ex-Leo Pavelle 8-litre
Bentley. This short, "sports-bodied" example had a
144-inch wheelbase. Only 100 8-litres were built.

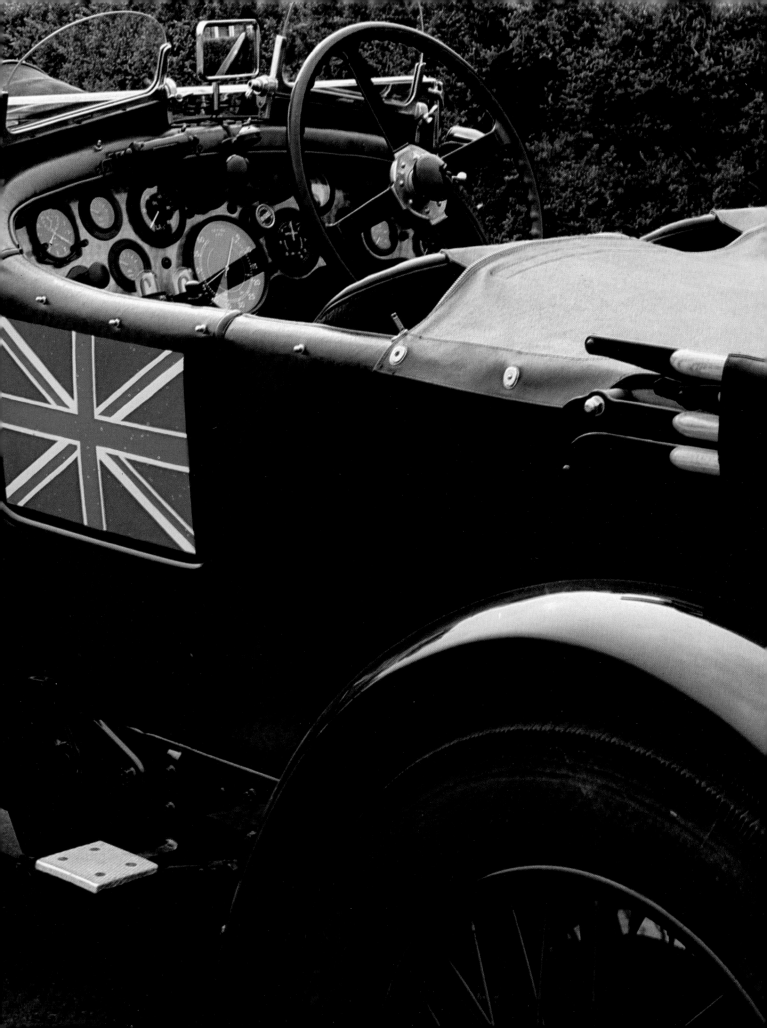

standard. Horsepower is 126 except in the US, where anti-pollution laws impose engine modifications that reduce power by some 15 hp. Still, because of their low weight, Loti in America have plenty of exciting urge. The 1,550-pound Elan Sprint moves from zero to 60 in about 9 seconds and is capable of 120 mph. But these numbers mean little. Examples of Detroit ironmongery might boast similar figures, but would be found inverted at the roadside if some bemused youth in, say, a Camaro, tried staying with an Elan on a curly bit of highway. For Elans must surely be the best road-huggers ever built.

There is, or was until recently, another Lotus: the Super 7, a stark, open two-seater, sold in kit form. Unlike the Elans, it had a space frame instead of the backbone. This lovely little brute, almost as open as a motorcycle, in the idiom of the nineteen-thirties, could be ordered powered with various engines; the latest option was the 1,600-cc engine which powered Ford's Pinto in America.

BENTLEY

More than forty years have gone by since an Englishman could buy a new Bentley—a real Bentley, not a modified Rolls-Royce bearing a Bentley badge. But those thunderous big machines still stand first in the hearts of tradition-loving Britishers. W. O. Bentley brought out his first car, the 3-litre model, in 1919, that euphoric year when a new era of peace and plenty seemed at hand. A nasty little slump followed almost immediately.

At a thousand guineas for a chassis, the Bentley was a car for the male offspring of the very rich, the county types, the kind of people Evelyn Waugh wrote about, and, of course, those few lucky ones who had found the war a bonanza.

There was nothing revolutionary about that first Bentley, nor, for that matter, about any subsequent model. It was merely carefully engineered and then meticulously constructed of the very best materials. But W. O. had a special genius for making the ordinary work in an extraordinary fashion —a fashion unusual enough to win the *Vingt-quatre Heures du Mans* five times: 1924, 1927, 1928, 1929, 1930.

That first 3-litre Red Label (for the color of the background on its radiator badge) had a 90-hp, four-cylinder, single-ohc engine with a nondetachable head, four valves per cylinder, twin carburetors (Smiths first, then SU's), and twin

magnetos mounted in a simple, ladder-type frame with semi-elliptic springs. The four-speed, close-ratio gearbox, although a lovely piece of work, was not too easy to manipulate—at least for me.

I sometimes drove such a "speed model" Bentley in the early thirties and, until I became acquainted with Alfa Romeos, thought it the greatest car I'd ever driven. The accuracy of its worm-and-wheel steering, its superb roadholding, and the stopping power of its brakes was a revelation to a youth used only to cheaper American machines. Its speed, too, was unusual for a day when 80 mph was considered very quick traveling, indeed. On a long straight that Bentley's speedometer would exceed 85.

No Bentley model exceeded the 3-litre in sales. Of the 3,061 sold between 1919 and 1931, when Rolls-Royce bought the company, 1,639 were 3-litre types.

The subsequent Bentley models, in order of appearance, were the 6½-litre Big Six in 1926, the four-cylinder, 4½-litre in 1927, and a hotter version of the Big Six, the Speed Six, in 1929. The huge and luxurious 8-litre came out in 1930. That awesome 156-inch-wheelbase giant was not meant to be a sports car, but in short-chassis form (a mere 144 inches) and with light, open coachwork there were few sports cars it would not leave in its wake. A finely tuned and modified version owned by the late Forrest Lycett covered the flying kilometer at 141.7 mph as recently as 1956. There were other, less desirable Bentleys, notably a 4-litre, push-rod-engined dullard which Bentley's directors, in spite of W. O. Bentley's warnings, insisted upon building to stave off disaster in 1931.

The Bentley was in production for only twelve years. Why then is it an artifact revered like HMS *Victory*, the Spitfire aeroplane, and Churchill's cigar?

Firstly, because the Bentley cars won at Le Mans during a period when the British were the Tail-end Charleys of motor racing. Secondly, perhaps, because the racing Bentleys were largely the province of a group of wealthy and elegant young men, the "Bentley Boys," who lent a certain glamour to the marque which still glows.

But, glamour or no, the Great Depression finished off the Bentley—that and the directors' decision to build fifty

Preceding pages: 1930 4½-litre "blower"
Bentley was rebuilt for Lord Montagu of Beaulieu.
Only fifty such supercharged Bentleys
were built. In spite of superb construction
and 105-mph speed, "blower" Bentleys
did not win races. Expense of manufacture helped
bankrupt the old Bentley company.

supercharged 4½-litre Bentleys (a type that never won a race) so that blown cars could be qualified for Le Mans, where a model was not considered a catalogued production model unless at least fifty had been built. Prototypes couldn't qualify in those days.

Rolls-Royce acquired the Bentley name in 1931.

VAUXHALL

It's sometimes argued whether the Austrian Prinz Heinrich Austro-Daimler or the British Prince Henry Vauxhall was the first sports car. I don't think either of them was; my vote goes to the 1903 Sixty Mercedes. Nor did either of the designers—Ferdinand Porsche and Laurence Pomeroy—worry about the point. The term "sports car" wasn't to become common coinage until the nineteen-twenties.

The Prince Henry Vauxhall was named after the 3-litre Vauxhall which entered the 1910 Prince Henry of Prussia tour. The Vauxhall did not win, an Austro-Daimler did. But when a 4-litre version of the Vauxhall was produced, it received the appellation "Prince Henry."

I had read about the Prince Henry Vauxhall for years and was impressed by its record. In 1913, when the first of what would be the postwar 30/98 E-types were already on the stocks, the Prince Henrys won thirty-two hill climbs and twenty-three firsts at Brooklands Track.

But when I first saw one in the metal, I was disappointed. The Prince Henry was so simple, its two-wheel brakes so puny, its side-valve engine so insignificant looking. My view changed when I was taken for a ride by its owner, Laurence Pomeroy, Jr., the late noted motoring writer.

The Vauxhall was no truck-like brute, as were so many pre-World War I cars with sporting pretensions. Pom handled it delicately, easily, although he drove it with verve and even a mite too much speed for my nerves. Much of its easy handling was due to its low unsprung weight. Its light wheels, sans front brakes, and its thin tires were aids toward this virtue.

The engine seemed to be doing no work. At 60 mph it was turning at a mere 2,000 rpm. Top speed was 75 mph. The outside hand lever applied the two-wheel brakes, and a foot pedal controlled a brake at the rear of the four-speed gearbox.

Neither of these did much retarding.

The E-type Velox appeared in 1919. It still had an L-head engine, but now with more power—98 hp instead of the Prince Henry's 75 hp.

In 1923 the E-type was replaced by a car which was to become one of the most renowned British sports cars—the OE 30/98 Vauxhall. With overhead valves and twin S.U. carburetors, the OE engine put out 120 hp in its latter days. Front-wheel brakes on early OE's were an afterthought, but later models had quite good hydraulic brakes.

In 1926, General Motors bought out Vauxhall and the cars built after that date deteriorated to GM standards.

ALVIS

The first Alvis I ever saw was the only really unconventional car the conservative British firm of Alvis ever built.

It was being driven, on a Saturday in 1935, by that early entrepreneur of exotic foreign cars, Ray Gilhooley, who stored his peculiar wares in the Liberty Storage Warehouse on West 64th Street and then tried to sell them in a showroom he operated around the corner on Broadway. He was bringing the Alvis to the showroom to demonstrate it to me. Gilhooley, an ex-Indianapolis driver of Isotta Fraschinis, always drove as if he were trying to qualify for the 500. As the Alvis came partly sideways toward me, its front end flapped oddly; its wheels pointed in a direction quite different from that in which I knew Gilhooley wanted to go. Still, Gilhooley made it around the corner successfully.

The Alvis's acrobatics put me off and Gilhooley didn't sell it to me. I wish now that he had.

That Alvis was a front-wheel-drive, all-independently-sprung, eight-cylinder model built in 1929. In 1928 there had been a similar four-cylinder version. Both machines had 1½-litre, ohc engines. A Roots blower was optional. Despite my reservations, the roadholding of these low-slung cars was very good. In 1928, a pair of them came in sixth and ninth at Le Mans. In 1930 only blown eights were sold. Production of front-wheel-drive models ended that year.

The first sports Alvis appeared in 1923 (Alvis had by then been in business for only two years). This was the famous 12/50 "Duck's-back" model with a 1½-litre, push-rod,

1935 Squire was built by Adrian Squire's tiny English company. Fewer than fifteen Squire cars were ever manufactured. Supercharged 1,500-cc, twin-ohc engine developed 110 hp. Zero to 60 mph in 11 seconds and 110-mph speed compared favorably with performance of continental sports cars with which Squire hoped to compete.

ohv engine. (There had been an earlier "Duck's-back," the 12/40 without ohv. "Back" is a polite euphemism for the shape of the car's derriere.) The 12/50's engine, which turned at 4,000 rpm, was capable of pushing the little Alvis along at 76 mph, a fine speed in 1923. The 12/50 was a very sturdy, good-handling machine, and was guaranteed for three years. It is still a favorite of vintagents, who now manage to exceed 80 mph in carefully tuned versions. The 12/50 was fairly costly at *circa* $3,000 (£600) but worth it. It was built until 1929, when it was superseded by a six.

Alvis, between 1930 and 1939, produced both bread-and-butter models (albeit very high quality b-and-b) and also a pair of highly exciting sporting machines—the Speed Twenty-Five and the 4.3-litre. The Speed Twenty-Five appeared in 1936. It had a 3½-litre, pushrod engine and was easily capable of 95 mph. The 4.3, especially in short-chassis form and fitted

with a delectable close-coupled, four-seater touring body, is to my mind the very epitome of sporting open car. The 4.3-litre, ohv, three-carburetor engine produced 125 real horsepower and would propel the solidly built car at better than 105 mph. Zero to 70 took about 16 seconds. The 4.3 was superbly finished, had independent front suspension, automatic chassis lubrication, built-in jacks—the works. It cost about $5,000 (£995), a lot of money in 1938.

In 1940, the *Luftwaffe* completely destroyed the Alvis works in Coventry. After the war, Alvis built a series of excellent cars, notably the TC 21/100 with which Sir Alec Issigonis was involved. Later models—the TE 20, the TE 21 with horsepower up to 130 bhp, and some cars with svelte Swiss coachwork by Graber—had disc brakes and automatic transmissions. But none of these had the exciting look and feel of those old Speed Twenty-Fives or 4.3's.

Left: 1939 4.3-litre Alvis.
Right: E Type V-12 Jaguar has 5.3-litre
engine. Its 241 hp gives Jaguar
over 140-mph capability. The Jaguar was at
one time called the "poor man's Bentley."
This one is more like a "poor man's Ferrari,"
even though it costs $10,500.

Alvis, now part of British Leyland Motors, hasn't built passenger cars since 1967.

LAGONDA

The Lagonda was, somehow, always overshadowed by the Bentley. Perhaps this was because the Bentley created a mystique for itself by doing so well at Le Mans—something Lagonda didn't manage until it won that race in 1935, after the old pre-Rolls Bentley was gone. The Lagonda was, in its own right, a very fine sports car, in spite of seeming to ape the Bentley with a similar radiator shell.

The first Lagondas built at the turn of the century were not cars but two- and three-wheeled devices meticulously constructed by an American immigrant to England, Wilbur Gunn from Lagonda Creek, Ohio. Hence the Latin-sounding name. (Lagonda is supposed to be an American Indian word for "smooth-running stream.")

Gunn's first four-wheelers didn't appear until 1910, when he turned out a series of utilitarian four- and six-cylinder models tough enough to do well in Government-run tests over the nonroads of czarist Russia. For a time, almost every Lagonda built went to the Russians.

Gunn died in 1920, and an entirely new kind of Lagonda—the first sports model—made its debut in 1926. This car had a 2-litre, four-cylinder, twin-ohc engine mounted in a quite conventional chassis frame. The car was of notably high quality, the frame being made of a special Vickers steel which, according to the factory, could "be tied in a knot" and still be restraightened. Quick and accurate Marles steering was fitted as well as four-wheel brakes adjustable from the driver's seat. Eighty miles per hour was possible—fast for the nineteen-twenties. In supercharged form, 90 mph was reachable.

The twin overhead camshafts of the four were not

161

only complex—they were expensive to make, and a push-rod-engine six, still of 2 litres, was brought out. This 16/65 model was now underslung and capable of as high a speed as the ohc model.

In 1930 engine size went up to 3 litres. This engine was built by Meadows and had twin SU carburetors, a hefty seven-bearing crankshaft and ignition by either coil or Scintilla magneto.

It was on one of these models that the wildly complicated German Maybach gearbox was offered. This monstrosity could be manipulated to provide no fewer than eight speeds forward and four in *reverse*!

The 3-litre Lagonda, spidery and with cycle-type fenders, was, in 1931, my idea of what a sports tourer ought to look like. In 1931 I wrote away to the factory for more information than I could find in *The Autocar*. A thick parcel of catalogues duly arrived. With them came a letter offering me the American agency for the marque and also offering to sell me any Lagonda at a forty percent discount. But a 3-litre Lagonda cost about $5,000 in that Depression year. Even $3,000 was too rich for my blood. I *do* wish I'd saved those catalogues, however.

In about 1934, Lagonda built a delightful small sports car, the Lagonda Rapier, with a twin-ohc 1,100-cc engine and a preselector gearbox. But Lagonda had luxury on its mind and sold the rights to build the car to another company, Rapier Cars Ltd.

In 1935, under new management, a new, more luxurious, but bulkier Lagonda was brought out, a 4½-litre six. Its

Left: 1913 Prince Henry Vauxhall
has 4-litre, 75-hp engine, will better 75 mph.
One of the first sports cars, it was
given the name "Prince Henry" after an
earlier 3-litre version which
competed in the German "Prinz Heinrich" trials.
Right: 1930 3-litre Lagonda.

engine was the big, rough Meadows engine that had powered the Invicta until its demise in 1934. But Lagonda improved this engine by, among other things, fitting twin Scintilla magnetos; this heavier car was faster than the lighter "100 MPH" Invicta had been. (I had never been able to make my Invicta exceed 94 mph.)

The 4½-litre Lagonda was soon greatly improved by W. O. Bentley, who came to the company after quitting Rolls-Royce, where he had been since their purchase of the old Bentley assets. Under Bentley, various better versions of the 4½-litre six were brought out, including the M45R Rapide and the LG-6.

The LG-6 was the greatest of these. With independent front suspension, a wonderfully rigid chassis, and huge brakes, it felt safe and solid at 108 mph, its top speed. Its chassis, more sophisticated than those on the early sixes, was really designed in preparation for the new V-12 W. O. was designing.

There were a fair number of V-12 Lagondas imported into the United States after the car's debut in 1937. And, naturally, Zumbach's was the place they were brought for service. And I well remember Jacques Schaerley grumbling about their fiendish complexity. Once I listened as Werner Maeder tried to give Gary Cooper step-by-step instructions for tuning his V-12 over the telephone to Hollywood. Considering Maeder's Swiss accent and Cooper's mechanical noncomprehension, I've often wondered if that Lagonda ever ran again.

The V-12 had other faults. Its power curve was such that it had little torque at low revs. It was necessary,

1

2

therefore, to shift it like a small-engined sports car to keep the revs up. Still, it was a very quick motor car. Stripped, a Lagonda V-12 lapped Brooklands Track at 128 mph and, in 1939, against hot stuff like blown Alfas and Bugattis, a V-12 Lagonda managed a very creditable third place.

The production of that great V-12 Lagonda ended when Britain went to war. After the war the David Brown companies took over Lagonda and for a time built both 2.6- and 3-litre, all-independently-sprung models. They're gone now, but if you check the name of the outfit that now builds Aston Martins, you'll note that it calls itself "Aston Martin Lagonda Ltd."

SQUIRE

I submit that one British sports car, the Squire, should get a little more space than some of the others I've mentioned. Not because it was a howling success. It wasn't. Yet it could have been, had it been further developed. My excuse is that the Squire has fascinated me ever since I first saw it announced in London's *Autocar*.

Schoolboys love to make drawings of the visions of sports cars that dance in their heads. Today such sketches might look like the carapaces of insects with engines in their tails. Some decades ago such schoolboy dream machines had impossibly long hoods, madly sweeping fenders, and bellies that scraped along the ground.

One English schoolboy, Adrian Squire, was able to turn such visions and sketches into reality. In 1926, at sixteen, he had not only made drawings of his heart's desire but had also composed a catalogue of his "1½-litre Squire two-seater," which was to have a 1,496-cc engine and an extremely low center of gravity which "ensures maximum stability in cornering." He wrote of "an exhaust with a deep mellow rhythmical boom" and added finally that "no attempt has been missed to make the Squire car the owner-driver's ideal."

Eight years later the delectable little Squire car, amazingly like the youthful catalogue writer's specification, was in production. During those eight years Adrian Squire single-mindedly prepared himself for his chosen role as a producer of the perfect sports car. At seventeen and a half he quit his public school to study electrical engineering at Faraday House in London. Then he became an apprentice at Bentley Motors. After that he worked as an engineer for MG.

In 1931, Squire at last set up Squire Motors Ltd. at Remenham Hill, near Henley-on-Thames. He was twenty-one. Two other directors of the company were a twenty-year-old, G. F. A. Manby-Colegrave, and Reginald Slay, called "uncle"

1. 1937 AC Ace had 2-litre, six-cylinder, 70-hp, ohc, three-carburetor engine, and 85-mph speed.
2. Current AC 428 has 7-litre Ford V-8, Frua body. Automatic transmission is optional.
3. 1932 Type 55 Bugatti. Its 2.3-litre, twin-ohc, supercharged engine was similar to that in Type 51 Grand Prix car.

1
2

1. Type 35B 2.3-litre supercharged Bugatti was most successful grand-prix machine ever built.
2. Well-filled instrument panel of 35B. Note magneto protruding from panel.
3. Frontal aspect of Type 41 Bugatti Royale.
4. The Royale had the longest wheelbase of any production car ever built—169 inches. Its 13-litre engine was 4 feet, 7 inches long.

3

4

by his confreres because he was an elderly twenty-six.

At first these youths ran Squire Motors as a filling station and repair shop for sports cars. Inevitably, other car-crazy youngsters were attracted to the noisy establishment, which for a time seems to have busied itself largely with working on cars in which Manby-Colegrave went racing. Among these was a low-chassis, 4½-litre Invicta to which the Squire cars, when they at last appeared, bore a striking resemblance, although they were considerably smaller, lighter, and more efficient. Invictas' chassis were underslung aft, however, while the first few Squires were conventionally overslung. Later Squires were, like the Invicta, underslung.

The first prototype Squire car appeared in 1934, some months after the incorporation of a new company, the Squire Car Manufacturing Co., which was capitalized for the munificent sum of £6,000.

Over the years many fine cars have been put into production and then fizzled out, forgotten. The Squire, somehow, is unique. Very few were built and yet the memory of the marque remains green. People who have never seen a Squire speak of it with awe and regret. Why? I think it is due mostly to the Squire's look—its long, low lines, its length of hood, the lovely shape of its radiator. Adrian Squire's schoolboy notion of how a sports car ought to be built lives on in many of us.

The Squire had a very conventional ladder-type chassis frame with a half-elliptic spring at each corner. Brakes were hydraulically actuated and of such tremendous diameter —15 inches—that they filled the inside diameters of the knock-off wire wheels. The drums were of manganese alloy, the brake shoes of electron. Sometimes the brakes (which could stop the car in less than 25 feet from 30 mph) had *too* much muscle and cracked the chassis frame near the front spring shackles.

Squire did not build his own engines. He bought R 1 Anzani engines from the British Anzani Co. and modified them slightly. These engines had twin overhead camshafts and a capacity of 1,496 cc. Since the camshafts were driven both by chains *and* a train of gears, and the valves had huge clearances (exhaust: forty-thousandths of an inch; inlet: thirty-thousandths), the engine was hardly a quiet one. Adding to the racket was a Roots-type blower driver off the nose of the crankshaft. The power developed was about 110 bhp. The supercharger added some 35 hp to the power of the stock Anzani engine but caused problems—mostly blown gaskets. This was solved by carefully lapping the head to the block (a two-day job). Squire didn't like to admit he hadn't built the engines; cast into the inlet manifold was his "S."

The gearbox was a Wilson preselector—a type I've always thought perfect for sporting use. To shift you move a lever on a numbered quadrant near the steering wheel to the gear you want. To actually change gear you merely kick down a floor pedal (it looks like a clutch pedal) and—zing!—you're in that gear. You can choose the gear you're going to use long before you actually shift. Hence "preselector."

The handsomest design element in the Squire's ensemble was its radiator shell surmounted by a Squire-built quick-filler cap (the fuel tank had one, too). Although of large size and fed by two water pumps, the radiator was handicapped owing to the Anzani engine's lack of a fan. Squires boiled over in summer traffic.

This bare description of the Squire's anatomy gives no insight into the way the cars were constructed. Adrian Squire was satisfied only with perfection and the few cars he built showed it. And they performed that way, too. Each new owner was presented with a BARC certificate stating that the car he had bought had bettered 100 mph on Brooklands Track. Acceleration was outstanding for 1935—zero to 60 in 13 seconds. Cornering power was phenomenal, and surprisingly for such a low-built car it didn't get into the wild slides ultralow cars like Invictas were notorious for. (I once owned such a sliding Invicta.)

Alas, the Squire didn't sell. At first the price was £1,250 for the short-chassis, Vanden Plas-bodied two-seater and £25 more for a four-seater. Later the price was reduced to £1,000 with coachwork by less exalted *carrossiers*. Still hardly any sales.

Adrian Squire must have been blinded by his own enthusiasm if he thought that he could compete in roughly the same price class against the blown 2,300-cc Type 55 Bugatti or the Gran Sport 1750 Alfa Romeo. An Aston Martin cost about half as much as a Squire in 1935.

To spur sales Squire tried to gain publicity from racing. A single-seater with a specially tuned engine was entered several times in Brooklands races. The driver was Luis Fontes. But the Squire was unlucky, once breaking its crankshaft and then splitting its fuel tank. The only time the single-seat Squire placed in a race was when it took third position at 70.8 mph in a minor handicap race at Brooklands Track.

Although the Squire Car Manufacturing Co. was liquidated in July, 1936, it wasn't quite the end of the story. A Squire customer, Val Zethrin, bought some of the spare parts and tried valiantly to continue production. He built three cars. Altogether Adrian Squire had built seven machines.

After his company failed, he joined the great W. O. Bentley at Lagonda. During the war he went to work for the Bristol Aeroplane Co. But he was still hopeful that he could someday again build his lovely little cars. This was not to be. He was only thirty when he was killed by a German bomb dropped on Bristol in 1940.

The French are nonconformists—at least when it comes to machinery—and the cars they build have reflected this. Unlike the British, the French during the great vintage years of the sports car had no very large middle class; Bugattis were for the rich. Although big cars like Delage, Delahaye, Talbot-Lago, and Hispano-Suiza attracted wealthy sporting drivers, they were really *voitures de grand luxe.*

Except for the Amilcar, cars for the enthusiastic and less pecunious driver were built in tiny numbers by many small constructors and very few were exported. Who now remembers their names: BNC, Bignan, Chenard et Walcker, Derby, Georges Irat, Lombard, Salmson, Sénéchal, Tracta?

Today the Matra seems to be the only French sports car to carry on the tradition.

BUGATTI

Ettore Bugatti, during thirty-odd years of productivity, manufactured some 9,000 cars bearing his name. Though comparatively few, these cars had, and still have, an incalculable influence on the world of automobilism. Every sports car built during the twenties and thirties was inevitably compared with the Bugatti. Only the Alfa Romeo ever has equalled it, and even today some Bugattiste, upon viewing the impressive machinery of, say, a modern Ferrari, is likely to murmur, "It isn't exactly a Bugatti, is it?" For no other car ever built has had that aesthetically exciting look to its mechanical parts: its polished front axle carved with the exactitude of a nautical instrument, its gearbox like a jewel casket, its engine a sharp-edged block of light alloy scraped and fettled like the base plate of a high-precision lathe.

I regret that I have owned but one Bugatti, a Grand Prix Type 51, and even that was in partnership with a friend. But I have driven and been driven in many types, from a four-cylinder Type 23 Brescia of the mid-nineteen-twenties to an eight-cylinder supercharged 57SC of 1938. All of them had the taut, lively, nervous feel and the adrenalin-pumping sound that only a Bugatti has.

Recently I had a chance to ride in that *voiture de grand luxe,* that car for princes, the vast and arrogant Type 41, the Royale, "The Golden Bug." I thought, as I ensconced myself in its luxury, "Here is the one car that M. Bugatti constructed that cannot possibly remind one of a racing machine."

I was wrong. There was no mistaking the blood lines of the Royale. It is pure Bugatti in the way its radiator (surmounted by a silver elephant) danced on its stiffish front suspension. For, in spite of having *coupé de ville* coachwork topside, the Royale underneath has the same kind of chassis you'd find in a racing Bugatti: polished tubular front axle, quarter-elliptical springs aft, and the rest. There was none of the mushy softness you might expect in a fancy limousine.

Despite its tremendous proportions—169-inch wheelbase, 5-feet, 6-inch track, over 7,000-pound weight, and 24-inch wheels (7.50 x 24 tires!)—William Harrah's driver whipped it through traffic like a sports car (except that he refrained from performing any fancy manipulations with the gear lever). The Royale, with its eight-cylinder, 13-litre engine, has so much torque and power (over 300 hp at 1,700 rpm) that a gearbox is almost redundant. Still, M. Bugatti did supply a three-speed transmission in the rear axle with a low gear for starting on steep grades, a second speed which was direct (3.6 to 1), and an overdrive gear (2.66 to 1) for high-speed cruising at up to

1926 series CGSS Amilcar
had simple four-cylinder, L-head,
1,100-cc engine. Light and
spidery, its 35 hp propelled it
at 70 mph. Good brakes and
quick steering made it known as
the "poor man's Bugatti."
The name "Amilcar" was said to be
an anagram of the name of the
company's president, Emil Akar.
The Amilcar was built
under license in several
other countries besides France.
In Italy it was called the
Amilcar-Italiana. Bottom picture
is similar but taller CGS.

125 mph.

It was Bugatti's hope that the Royale chassis he offered for $30,000 would attract royal buyers. But none such crowned head ever bought one from him, even in 1927 when quite a few crowns still existed. Only six Royales ever were built and two of them are now in the Harrah Automobile Collection in Reno.

Ettore Bugatti was an Italian who built the greatest of French cars in the then German town of Molsheim (for Alsace was German at the time he first established himself there).

Bugatti was born in 1881 in Milan. The family tradition was artistic, not mechanical. But Ettore Bugatti, fascinated by that new mechanism, the automobile, was both. He built artistic motor cars. His first car, built when he was eighteen, was an original, different from anything anybody else was building, and his last designs of 1947, when he was near the end of his life, still were uniquely Bugatti.

By 1902, before he was twenty-one, Bugatti already had made a name for himself as a racing driver and a talented designer. In that year the great old Alsatian firm of De Dietrich, which had been involved with metallurgy since 1684, decided to build Bugatti-designed cars under license. Bugatti's father had to sign the contract because Ettore was still a minor.

Bugatti left De Dietrich in 1904 and other famous car manufacturers—Mathis, Peugeot, and Deutz—used his talents. At last, in 1909, Bugatti had had enough of working for others. It was in Molsheim that he set up the fantastic fiefdom that was to be his home, factory, vineyard, aviary, museum, hotel, and horse farm for some thirty years, except for the four years of World War I.

Bugatti built cars for two kinds of customers: real racing drivers and rich would-be race drivers who could enjoy the sounds and smells and road manners of a *pur-sang* Bugatti without risking the dangers of the racing circuit. Such a man could be thought quite dashing by the unknowledgeable. If Monsieur DuPont, the stock broker, bought himself a modestly powered through princely tourer, the Type 44 "Molsheim Buick" perhaps, his friends, to DuPont's delight, certainly said, "What a devilish fellow is that DuPont. He has bought himself a racing car in which to drive to his office." And DuPont might wear a white cloth racing helmet and goggles on his way to work, too. (I am ashamed to admit to such helmet-wearing *gaucherie* myself in a 1750 Alfa Romeo forty years ago.)

The jewel-like racing machines Bugatti built were the most successful of all time. In 1925 and 1926 they won more than a thousand victories. These wins were by no means all factory victories by Molsheim-prepared teams. Many, if not most, of them were by private individuals who bought themselves, say, a Type 35 and went racing. For unlike the cars of other builders then and now (try buying a current grand-prix Ferrari for yourself), racing Bugattis were freely available to drivers willing to pay for them.

That Type 35 is well worth examining. From horseshoe radiator to wedge tail, it is visually and functionally the quintessence of all Bugattis, both racing and touring. A 35's chassis seems impossibly delicate—less than an inch thick forward. But it gets much thicker aft—close to 7 inches thick under the dash where you can't see it because it's hidden by a louvered undershield. The short, flat, front springs, gripped by a multiplicity of clips, penetrate the tubular axle through square apertures. The axle and steering connections are of polished steel, not merely for looks, but because any dangerous cracks in them will be visible. (Modern restorers who chrome-plate these parts defeat Ettore's purpose.) The rear springs are short, thick, reversed quarter-elliptics. The wheels are of cast light alloy with eight flat spokes. Brake drums are cast into the wheels. When such a wheel was changed during a race, the worn brake drum came with it and the brake linings were instantly exposed for adjustment.

All Types 35 had straight-eight engines, perhaps the loveliest looking power plants ever to reside under the hood of a motor car. They were built in five versions:

The *Type 35* Grand Prix was unsupercharged and had a cubic capacity of 1,990 cc (60 x 80 mm). It developed 90 hp and had a top speed of 110 mph.

Type 35A, the "*course imitation*," was just that—an imitation of the GP car. British Bugattistes disdainfully call this a "boy's racer" despite its 100-mph speed. Unlike other Types 35, which had five-roller-bearing crankshafts and rods, the 35A had three roller bearings on its crankshaft and plain bearings on its connecting rods. It was considerably cheaper.

Type 35C Grand Prix was similar to the 2-litre Type 35, but was fitted with a Roots-type supercharger. Its 130-hp engine enabled it to reach 125 mph.

Type 35T Grand Prix was similar to the unblown Type 35, but had a longer stroke (60 x 100 mm) which gave it a 2.3-litre capacity.

Type 35B Grand Prix was the ultimate development of the Type 35, the great classic "supercharged Bug." With 140 hp it could better 130 mph.

Remarkably, even the most puissant of the Types 35, the blown 2.3 35B could be driven on the public highway, as some few lucky owners of 35B's joyously still do. I even drove the Type 51 (I partly owned) in New York traffic. Windshield-less and fenderless and without lights, it was not quite the mount to use in the rain or at night, and I avoided such an environment. The only embarrassment I recollect was stalling the engine on Fifth Avenue and having to jump out in order to use the hand crank while cab drivers jeered. I should point out that the Type 51, which came out in 1931, was almost identical to a Type 35B, except for having a twin-overhead-camshaft engine instead of the single-ohc of the 35B. Many 35B's today have been embellished with fenders, lights, and even windshields. It was possible at one time to buy from Molsheim an electric starter and a cradle-like device for fitting it to the car.

But this was the hard (if more exciting) way of tasting the pleasures of a 35B as a touring car. In 1927, the easy way—if you could afford $7,500 or so (with import duty)—was to buy a Type 43 supercharged Grand Sport. When I first saw one in 1931, I almost expired with desire for the boat-tailed, cycle-fendered beauty I was offered for $1,500. But, alas, even that price was too much for a twenty-one-year-old in the early days of the Great Depression. I never drove a 43 with a boattail body—the standard Bugatti coachwork. I did, however, drive one, a Type 43A, with a rather ugly roadster body complete with rumble seat. I still remember it as the most delightfully violent car I've ever driven, no doubt because it was my first experience of such a machine.

The Type 43 was powered with the same blown single-ohc engine as the Type 35B Grand Sport, except for a slightly lower compression. It provided 115 hp. The engine in the 43A was slightly further detuned to 100 hp. By modern standards these ratings seem pedestrian. But forty-odd years ago a sporting car capable of 110 mph and zero to 60 in about 12 seconds was well-nigh miraculous.

Of course, the wonderful noises, the howl of straight-toothed gears, the whine of the blower, added to the exhilaration. But what I remember best from those days of two-lane roads, when continual passing, pulling out of line, and judging the speed of oncoming cars was necessary, was the way you could almost ignore other traffic. In a Type 43 you were so much faster, and accelerated so much more quickly, that other cars could be treated as stationary objects through which you pursued a slightly snaking course. And the Bugatti steered so quickly and positively, had such good brakes (although they required heavy pressure), that you felt supremely confident and secure.

The Type 55 was, like the Type 43, a sports version of the twin-ohc Type 51 grand-prix car. Imagine a car of 1932 which would do 120 mph, accelerate from zero to 60 in under 10 seconds, and hit 100 mph in third gear!

Why, then, if Bugattis were so wonderful (which they were!) did I become an Alfisto rather than a Bugattiste? First, perhaps, but least important was the fact that in 1932, when I bought my first Alfa Romeo, Alfa was knocking the spots off Bugatti in racing. This must have impressed a novice. More important was the fact that a 1,750-cc, twin-cam, blown Alfa Romeo would do everything a Type 55 Bug could do (although it was slightly slower), and you didn't have to devote your life and fortune to keeping it running correctly. A 1750 Alfa would start no matter how cold it was; a Bugatti, unless it was coddled in a warm garage (as M. Bugatti suggested), could stubbornly resist commencing. Some present-day Bugattistes seem almost proud of the religious rites they go through—warming the oil and water on the kitchen range, checking each sparkplug, turning the engine over with the hand crank before even trying to start the engine.

Admittedly a Bugatti engine's nondetachable head precluded head-gasket trouble, but who wanted to pull the engine block out in order to attend to the valves? On models with gearboxes in their rear axles it was necessary first to detach the axle from the rear springs in order to do a valve job. In the case of the Type 41 Royale, your mechanics had to remove the huge 220-pound crankshaft before the cylinder block could come out for attention. But I suppose that if you were rich enough to buy such a regal conveyance you also were rich enough to support squads of *mécaniciens*.

The Type 57 and its derivatives—the wonderful 57S, 57C, and 57SC—which were made until World War II, were no longer semiracing cars with touring coachwork. Although still *voitures de pur sang* there was great consideration for luxury and silence. Their straight-eight, 3.3-litre, twin-ohc engines were not only exciting to look at, but gave an exciting performance, especially in the 57C or 57SC versions. The 57SC (*sport-compresseur*), with its 200-hp engine was capable of 135 mph with touring coachwork. As far back as 1936, a 57S (the unblown *sport* model) driven by Robert Benoist put 135.4 miles into an hour's run on the Montlhéry Track near Paris. Even the 57 with its unblown *normale* 130-hp engine was capable of close to 100 mph.

The Types 57 were surprisingly cheap to buy. A 57 *normale* was delivered in New York for about $7,500, less than the $8,500 asked for a 3½-litre Bentley, to my mind a far less desirable machine. And that ultimate Bugatti, the 57SC, cost only £1,015 in chassis form in London just before World War II.

I admired the 57's but didn't really lust after one, even though George Rand, who, with the brothers Collier, ran the small Bugatti agency in New York, took me on a hair-raising foray into Central Park in a 57C. Perversely, I thought that the easier-to-take-care-of 57 was now not Bugatti-ish enough, that it was too big, and that it just didn't sound like a Bugatti anymore.

Who bought Bugattis? Few Americans did. I don't believe Rand and his confreres sold more than two a year. Earlier, before the Depression, a few reached the United States, but I doubt whether there were twenty-five Bugattis between the Atlantic and Pacific during the nineteen-thirties. In 1936 I went to Paris expecting to hear the streets ringing with Bugatti exhausts. Except for two very tatty specimens, the only ones I saw were in the Bugatti showrooms on the Avenue Montaigne. I did get to ride in a Bugatti railcar (powered with four Royale engines) on my way to the Grand Prix de Deauville. There I did see Bugattis in the street. The first one I saw, a closed Type 55 two-seater, bouncing and roaring on the *pavé* in front of the casino, was being driven by a uniformed chauffeur with the car's stout, pink-faced, white-mustached owner in the passenger's seat! It carried a GB plate. The other Bugs, too, were almost all British. "That's where Bugattis go," I thought. "England!"

I still don't know if I was right. But there's no doubt that the British have always been wildly in love with Bugattis. Their Bugatti Owners Club has been celebrating *le pur sang* since 1929. The club magazine, *Bugantics*, is the bible of Bugattistes around the world. Since 1937 the club has owned an estate, Prescott, devoted to hill-climbing competitions. There they have erected an imposing wrought-iron gate, a memorial to Ettore Bugatti and his son Jean, who had driven at Prescott before his death in 1939.

Bugattis today are not merely highly desirable motor cars. They have become the venerated objects of cultists. They are rebuilt not just to new condition but to a degree of perfection far beyond even Ettore Bugatti's high standards. They are so polished and plated and engine-turned and greaseless that only a brute would subject them to the dirty realities of the highway. Some Bugattiphiles, not satisfied with owning just a few Bugattis, go to extremes. One of them, in Alsace, hoards hundreds of Bugattis in ecstatic privacy where no one may look at them. A few years ago a string of flatcars rolled across the US loaded with a collection of Bugs this collector had bought in California.

What's a Bugatti worth today? At least several times its cost when new and sometimes much more. It is hard to put a price on a work of art.

AMILCAR

In the early nineteen-thirties, when my brother and I wandered about among junkyards and used-car lots with the vague aim of finding sports cars we could afford, we ran into some very unusual machinery. I remember a Fiat which had been "rebodied" into a racer. Its most remarkable feature was a long, pointed tail which looked oddly limp. Upon close inspection we found it to have been sewn up out of imitation leather, a

1

2

1. 1,750-cc Gran Sport Alfa Romeo had six-cylinder, twin-ohc, supercharged engine.
2. 1933 2.6-litre "Mille Miglia" Alfa has twin-ohc, supercharged engine.
3. Modern Alfa Romeo Montreal. It lacks anti-smog devices required for US sale.
4. This 1933 8C 2300 Alfa Romeo was driven into second place at Le Mans by Heldé and Stoffel in 1935. British champion, the late Mike Hawthorn, owned it for a time. Bodywork by Touring of Milan.

3

4

FGC 409

material often used in those days as the outer skin of cars—Vanden Plas Bentleys and Weymann-bodied Stutzes, for example. But those had wood skeletons underneath; the Fiat's tail was as boneless as an octopus. Some genius had stuffed it (with feathers?). It could be pushed around like a pillow.

Most of the few sports cars which could be bought cheaply in those days were gruesome devices like that poor old Fiat. There was, however, one make of car, the Amilcar, which we came across from time to time. A few years earlier, before I knew anything at all about cars, I had thought the Amilcar the most desirable in the world. But those we now saw were near ruins, the victims of many previous and callous owners. Rusted, dirty, and dented, they still might have attracted us at the prices asked for them; none cost more than $50. Yet they seemed much too fragile and spidery in design to repay the effort necessary to revivify them. Further, the view under their hoods was disappointing; their tiny engines did not even half fill the space allowed. I have for years regretted our decision not to buy one of those Amilcars, for, as I discovered later, they could be delicious little machines.

The Amilcar was the archetype of not-too-dissimilar sporting voiturettes made by dozens of Parisian makers who rushed into building sports cars immediately after the First World War. Many were *garagistes* who assembled their machines from bits and pieces bought from outside suppliers. They built the cars one at a time and had little need for fancy machinery, assembly lines, sales departments, or advertising. A few sets of wrenches, a clear space in which a couple of mechanics could work, and a deal with a fellow down the street who could pound out a simple, open, two-seated body, made a man a car manufacturer. Surprisingly, the cars they built were, albeit a bit coarse, great fun to drive, due mostly to their reliable and peppy little engines, light weight, and quick steering.

The Amilcar, built in the Gallic idiom, was far more successful than any of those built in the makeshift *usines*. It, at least, was built in a proper factory and almost entirely from parts, including the engine, made in its own works.

In 1920, that happy postwar year when anything seemed possible, two engineers, Edmond Moyet and André Morel, who had worked for the builders of the defunct Le Zèbre car, were bitten by the manufacturing bug. They got the financing to do this from a couple of money men, Emile Akar and Joseph Lamy, and gave their new project the resounding name *Société Nouvelle pour l'Automobile Amilcar*. Akar and Lamy were the bosses (Amilcar was an anagram of their names), Moyet was chief engineer, and Morel the chief race driver.

The Amilcar was originally designed as a small economy car, but in 1921 Morel produced a sports version, the Type CC, which was instantly such a success that it eclipsed the utility car. Its specification sounds impossible: a wee L-head, 903-cc, four-cylinder, 18-hp engine, a three-speed gearbox, a decidedly unrobust ladder-type frame with quarter-elliptic leaf springs, and a rear axle without differential. Brakes were on the rear wheels only. Wheelbase was 92 inches. As if this wasn't primitive enough, the engine, which had no water pump but depended on the thermosyphon system, had no pressurized lubrication, either. A peculiar method was used: There was no oil pump; the engine flywheel had "buckets" cast in it, and these dipped into the oil and threw it into ducts leading to the parts requiring lubrication. The clutch ran in the same oil bath. If the oil level was too low for the buckets to reach it, there were frightful consequences. This first Amilcar had a top speed of about 50 mph, not too bad for a flea-powered car in 1921. But it weighed only 1,000 pounds.

The CC Amilcar was, in the hands of Morel, immediately successful in racing. In the June, 1922, Bol d'Or twenty-four-hour race, Morel covered more than 900 miles to win. Later that summer at Le Mans, in the Grand Prix des Cyclecars, two of the three 903-cc models came in third and fourth, beaten only by the bigger 1,100-cc, overhead-camshaft-engined Salmsons. Although Amilcars did poorly in the early twenty-four-hour races at Le Mans, they fared particularly well in lesser races and in hill climbs. The factory claimed that Amilcars won more than a hundred such events in 1924.

By then the 903-cc model had given way to the Grand Sports CGS model, a far better machine. The new 1,074-cc engine, still with an L head, now had a proper pressure lubrication system and developed about 30 hp at 3,600 rpm (early CGS types with flywheel buckets had thrown their oil everyplace but where it was needed at high revs and during fast cornering). The new model now had front-wheel brakes and outboard half-elliptic springs forward. The chassis was beefed up, too. Speed was up to 75 mph.

A friend bought one of those used-car-lot Amilcars I had disdained. He did a quick job of rebuilding it (people didn't go to great lengths of restoration before World War II) and proudly showed up at my house in it early one Sunday morning.

He couldn't have done much work on the exhaust system, for mine was but one of many heads that were stuck out of apartment-house windows when what sounded like strings of especially loud Chinese firecrackers woke up the neighborhood. I remember that from above the pointy-tailed Amilcar looked as narrow as a canoe.

When I arrived downstairs, that spindly narrowness, exaggerated by tall, skinny wheels and high-mounted, channel-shaped strips bent into a combination of running boards and fenders, gave the impression that the Amilcar was in danger of capsizing while standing still. I bravely climbed over the side into the passenger's seat, which was, due to the narrowness of the body, set slightly to the rear of the driver's seat. This staggering allowed the passenger to rest his right arm on the body behind the driver.

Visibility forward through the tiny windshield was amazing. Fenders spaced away from the body permitted a view of the insides of the front wheels. The small-diameter instruments would have done justice to a Bugatti (indeed, the Amilcar was called the poor man's Bugatti). I am sorry to say, however, that the upholstery was imitation leather. We screeched off down the long city block, with me trying to put my feet through the floorboards as we approached the corner. My intrepid friend did not brake. He accelerated. That impossibly narrow-tracked (43-inch) Amilcar went around that corner impeccably and fast. I was fearful that he might take the next corner faster. Which he did. We remained right side up. We did not slide. Once on the West Side Highway (40-mph speed limit), my conductor felt it necessary to show off his car's speed. He curvetted in and out of the Nashes and Hupmobiles as he quickly gained speed. Acceleration was surprisingly good. But 70-odd in that Amilcar was a bit much—for me, at least. We weaved. The engine screamed. Seventy seemed much faster than 120 mph in a modern sports

car. When my friend let me drive, I didn't get above 50. I remember most how nice and quick and precise the steering was, and how bumpy the ride was, too.

An Amilcar in the mid-twenties, owing to high import duty, cost about $2,000 in the US, £285 in England, and much less in France. A fair number was sold in America to the offspring of the rich, and those were the ones available in the thirties after Papa went broke in the Crash. Amilcars sold beautifully until the bad years arrived. In 1927 and 1928 almost forty Amilcars a day were driven out of the doors of the big, 1,200-man factory on the Boulevard Anatole France.

An improved version of the CGS, the famous CGSS Surbaisse model appeared in 1926. It was called the Surbaisse because it was slightly lower, but this model had more power, too —about 40 bhp at 4,500 rpm. It was claimed to be capable of 80 mph. It was a supercharged Surbaisse Amilcar which won the Monte Carlo Rally in 1927. Afterward it was possible to order factory jobs so equipped. In this form 50 bhp was developed.

It is hard to realize how very popular these simple but tough little sports cars were in their day. It is estimated that some 10,000 of them were built during the nineteen-twenties. They were built not only in France but also in Germany, Austria, and Italy. The German version was called the Pluto, the Austrians called theirs the Grofri (because an outfit called Grosse and Friedmann were the builders). In Italy the car was named the Amilcar-Italiana.

Amilcar also built racing machines. Some of these were based on the CGS and CGSS, but it was the 1926 1,100-cc Type C6 which was the most successful of these. These superbly built machines had six-cylinder, twin-overhead-camshaft engines with big Roots blowers. The head was not detachable and the crankshaft machined from a solid billet ran on seven roller bearings. As early as 1927 one of these marvelous little racing voiturettes lapped the Montlhéry track at 118 mph. The Type C6 heaped laurels on the name Amilcar year after year.

After 1929 the classic Amilcar sports cars went out of production. During the twenties the company had also built various stodgy bread-and-butter cars and these were made until the late thirties, when Amilcar finally succumbed under the competition of mass-producing giants like Citroën. In its later years

Left & below: Maserati Ghibli is a luxurious gran-turismo road express with a 5-litre, ohc, V-8, 335-hp engine. It is claimed to achieve 174 mph, despite 3,640-pound weight. Right & bottom: Maserati Bora is super-sports bomb, with 4.7-litre, ohc, 335-hp V-8 engine that pushes it at 175 mph.

Amilcar was controlled by Hotchkiss, the French car builders.

 I know of only a few Amilcars still existing in the US. There is, however, a thriving Amilcar register in Britain. What is an Amilcar, say, a Surbaisse, worth today? I can't say exactly. Not too long ago, a man I know spent some $10,000 restoring one.

 Italy is where the great sports cars come from: Maserati, Alfa Romeo, Ferrari, Lamborghini. Even the Bugatti from France was built by an Italian, Ettore Bugatti.

 Surprisingly, Italy built such sports cars, notably the Alfa Romeo, more than forty years ago, when Italy had practically no middle class which could afford them and when its wealthy car fanciers were a very tiny group.

 But Italians, even the poorest, have always been wildly enthusiastic about motor sport. Their excitement over the Sicilian Targa Florio and the now-defunct Mille Miglia was perhaps greater than that generated by any other people over any other sporting event in the world.

 The Italian sports car has a wild, tough temperament like that of the Italian driver and the roads over which he drives with such *brio*. Italy's mountain roads with their many hairpin bends and steep grades made superaccurate steering and su-

perb brakes imperative if her impetuous drivers were to stay alive. Although today's Italian autostradas may forgive cars with American-style controllability, Italians learned long ago how a car ought to steer and respond, and they are not about to settle for less. Precision and beauty in mechanism and coachwork have been traditional in northern Italy since medieval times, when Italians fashioned the most handsome and practical armor in all Europe.

ALFA ROMEO

As I've more than indicated elsewhere, Alfa Romeos were for a long time my pampered darlings. These were mostly machines of the nineteen-twenties and thirties. And even today, if I were to buy a new sports car, it would be an Alfa. Not because I consider it superior to a Ferrari, Maserati, or Lamborghini. Not at all. An Alfa, at $5,000, not only suits my purse rather more easily than those other supercars, it is also smaller and lighter, more my idea of what a sports car should be—agile, handy, and nervous.

 Alfa started building Darracqs under license as far back as 1909. But it wasn't until 1925 that a really sporting Alfa Romeo, the 22/90 RLSS, appeared. This had a 3-litre, six-cylinder, push-rod engine, with twin Zenith carburetors and magneto ignition, that developed 85 hp. The chassis was of ladder type with semielliptic springs, friction shocks, and not-too-effective

Maserati Mistral is handier, shorter gran-turismo machine than the Ghibli. It had a 4-litre, six-cylinder, ohc, 255-hp engine (or a 3.7-litre, 245-hp engine) and a five-speed gearbox. Factory claimed 158 mph from the larger engine. Unlike the Ghibli and Bora, it was available with open "spyder" coachwork.

four-wheel brakes. A four-speed gearbox was fitted. Sound fairly stodgy? Yet I found the one I bought in 1932 the most exciting thing on wheels! Capable of some 85 mph, it outaccelerated, outsteered, and even outbraked every four-wheeled implement that Detroit, to my knowledge, had produced. (I seldom encountered such exotica as Duesenbergs in those days!) I must admit that, although a joy in the country, it was a tiring, heavy machine in city driving. When, in 1936, I discovered a 1929, 1,750-cc *senza compressore* (without blower) two-seater for sale, I quickly advertised the big 22/90 in *The New York Times* Sunday edition.

We think there was little interest in foreign sports cars forty years ago, but we mustn't forget the inevitable core of enthusiasts. The telephone woke me up before 7 o'clock that Sunday morning. A breathless character insisted upon seeing the Alfa "right now." By 8 o'clock I had sold the car to him. I still regret not taking the 1922, 28/95 sporting Mercedes the young man offered as a trade-in. The telephone kept ringing all day and during the following week I received thirty-odd letters and calls anent the Alfa. Perhaps all that action was due to the low price I had asked in the ad: $400. Sadly, to this day I have not seen or heard a word about that 22/90 Alfa, which now would be a much-desired vintage piece worth bags of money.

Then began my happy, decades-long involvement with 1750 Alfas.

The 6C 1750 was directly descended from six-cylinder, 1,500-cc models which had first appeared in 1925. At first, these had single overhead camshafts; later types had twin ohc. These 1500's acquitted themselves wonderfully in competition. In fact, the first time a supercharged, twin-cam 1500 raced (in June, 1927, at Modena) it took first place. The driver was a young man named Enzo Ferrari. In 1928, a similar machine driven by Ramponi and Campari won the Italian Mille Miglia.

These 1500's were a complete break from the comparatively ponderous 22/90's. Designed by the great Vittorio Jano, they were small, low, light machines, artistically contrived sisters of Alfa Romeo's successful GP racing machines, the P2's. The quality of their workmanship, especially of their foundry work, has seldom been equaled by anyone, except perhaps in Bugattis, which had a minimum of castings in their construction, in any case.

I have for a long time sung paeans of praise to 1750 Alfa Romeos, and I beg the indulgence of readers who catch me repeating myself.

The 6C 1750 that first appeared in 1929 differed little from the 1500. Its cylinders were merely bored out by another 3 mm, which added 250 cc of capacity. "Handling" is the word most applicable to a 1750. No car, not even the later Alfas, ever gave the driver such supreme confidence that it would do exactly as he wished. You didn't consciously steer a 1750 around a corner, any more than you consciously steer your body when walking around one. A 1750 went where your brain, assisted by a mere suggestion from your wrist, thought it ought to point. And *exactly*—to the inch. But you paid a little for such prescience on the part of the steering. It refused to be bullied. Try, with an iron grip, to keep it pointed exactly ahead on a straight stretch and you find yourself being taken on a swerving course. The secret is to relax your grip and let the 1750 find its own way. It will go straight on.

Engine response was instantaneous. A touch on the accelerator (which lived, unusually, between the brake and clutch pedal) and the revs screamed up. I remember learning to be careful about where to place my foot when climbing out of my Gran Sport Alfa with the engine running. A careless touch

Ferrari Dino (above), with engine aft, has 2½-litre V-6 engine capable of 140 mph, zero to 60 in 7½ seconds. Center section of roof is detachable. Left: 1949 Ferrari Type 166/MM was known as Barchetta (little boat). It has a V-12, 2-litre, 140-hp engine and a top speed of 137 mph. In 1949, similar car won at Le Mans. Right: Ferrari 365 GTB/4 Daytona has V-12, 4½-litre engine, 175-mph top speed. Stock model is capable of racing at Le Mans.

would send the rev-counter needle sweeping around its dial. But such response made double-clutching a joy.

Don't imagine that a 1750 Alfa Romeo was a fussy little beast to maintain. If you fed it gasoline and oil and lubricated it (Tecalemit slide-on fittings), it required no special nursing. In at least one way it was easier to service than a modern Alfa; its valves could be adjusted much more easily. A present-day Alfa requires shims under its valve caps when adjustment time comes. And you have to remove the camshafts first. Old Alfas had toothed steel mushrooms fitted to the valve stems. A tool which came with each car had teeth which fitted the mushroom's teeth. You merely fitted the end of the tool into one of the little sockets cast into the engine's head and turned to the correct clearance.

The 1750 Alfa had a simple, ladder-type chassis frame, with a cart spring at each corner. Hartford-type friction shocks controlled their oscillations. Somehow those Italians knew something about spring length which no one else ever seemed to learn. The springing was far from supple but it had none of the bone-jarring harshness which lesser sports cars display. No matter how fast a 1750 might be driven over pot holes, the chassis never bottomed. My wife's 1968 Plymouth Barracuda S with "sports" springing bangs its chassis down on its rear axle on every bump, even with new shocks. After thirty-five years of having Alfas around to copy, Detroit still doesn't know how.

A 1750's mechanical brakes, however, were not up to modern standards. It was only in that department that a 1963 Alfa Romeo Giulia I owned for a time outdid its grandfather. But we mustn't be too critical of present-day Alfas. They're much cheaper. A Gran Sport 1750 Alfa Romeo in the early thirties cost some $7,000—close to $30,000 in Nixon dollars. A modern Alfa Romeo Spyder costs about one-sixth of that.

Mentioning modern Alfas reminds me of how easy a Gran Sport 1750 Alfa was to start. The modern Giulia I owned hated to start in cold weather. The six-cylinder 1750 would scream into action at one press of the starter button, no matter how cold it was. If it had been standing for a few weeks in its unheated garage, I'd tickle the pin on the double-choke Memini

Ferrari Boxer has a startling new configuration by Pininfarina. Its engine, as the Italian catalogue says, is placed *"posteriore centrale"*—aft. Unlike previous Ferrari engines, this one is horizontally opposed—hence "boxer." Its flat, twelve-cylinder, four-ohc, 4,390-cc engine puts out 360 hp and top speed (claimed) of 187 mph.

carburetor before pressing the button (which was also the ignition light) on the Bosch switch panel.

The six-cylinder 1750 put up a sparkling competition record. In 1929, Campari and Ramponi again won the Italian Mille Miglia and in July of that year, Benoist and Marinoni took first place in the Belgian twenty-four-hour race at Spa. On handicap (and not too long a handicap, either), 1750 Alfas often ran away with top honors when racing huge Bentleys and Mercedes'. In 1929, Boris Ivanowski, a Russian émigré who raced in England, was handed a four-seater Alfa 1750 which F. W. Stiles, the British Alfa agent, had just sold to a customer; Ivanowski was asked to race it in the Irish Grand Prix. He won at 76.4 mph against Glen Kidston, who was second in a Big Six Bentley at 79.8 mph; Sir Henry Birkin came in third in his 4½-litre "blower" Bentley. And in 1930, Nuvolari, Campari, and Varzi won the Tourist Trophy on the Ards circuit against such heavy metal as Malcolm Campbell's 38/250 SS Mercedes and Birkin's "blower" Bentley.

The nadir of the Depression might not have been a felicitous time to bring out an expensive new car. But in 1931

Alfa Romeo announced a successor to the 1750, the 8C 2300, a car that for years was to make Alfa Romeo dominant in competition. The 8C 2300 had eight cylinders of the same size as those in the 6C 1750—65 x 88 mm. The cylinders were in two banks of four each, but the aluminum, twin-ohc head was in one piece. The supercharger lay alongside the engine and was driven by a gear from the crankshaft which, like the cylinders, also was split in half, with the gear at its midpoint. The hollow camshafts, similarly split, also were driven from the same gear through a train of gears. In standard form, a 2.3 Alfa put out some 135 bhp.

The 2.3 Alfa Romeo with which I am currently most familiar isn't a 2.3 at all. Like many 2.3's (including many raced by the factory), it has been bored out to 2.6 litres.

Oddly enough, this 1933 car has been owned in succession by three friends of mine. Before they got hold of it, it had been famous as the "Guy Templar Mille Miglia Alfa." Much of its status was achieved during a well-publicized race at Brooklands Track in 1939 to decide Britain's "Fastest Road Car." Sadly, Templar's Alfa wasn't; a stripped-down Delahaye beat it. This Alfa, however, is no slouch, having lapped Brooklands at 116 mph, with a speed of 121 down that now-derelict track's "Railway Straight." In 1946 it was Fastest Road Car at the Brighton Speed Trials, doing the standing kilometer at 70.34 mph.

I first saw the Templar Alfa in 1953, when George Dartt proudly drove it to my house on Long Island, directly after having extracted it from the ship which transported it from England. Dartt had paid a mere $2,400 for it and was justly proud of its puissance. Too proud, perhaps. Because a few months later, at Bridgehampton, Long Island, during a vintage-car race, he overrevved and put a connecting rod out of business. The Alfa then languished for years while a mechanic put it to rights. Surprisingly, he did a fine job. The next owner, in 1955, was Charles Addams, the cartoonist. Addams coveted a Bugatti owned by my neighbor Ed Bond, of Old Saybrook, Connecticut. A trade was arranged and in 1959 Ed became the owner of the Templar Alfa. Ed loved this Alfa but succumbed to a weighty offer (about four times as much as Dartt had paid), and the car left his bed and board. The new owner then sold it to an Englishman and the car went back to Britain. Bond pined and grieved, flew to England and, after paying its weight in gold

sovereigns, retrieved his Alfa Romeo. It's now in Connecticut again, where he sometimes lets me drive it.

It's a fine, brutal beast of a machine, but I don't like it as much as those 1750's I once owned. Certainly it's faster and makes more horribly pleasing noises. But it doesn't have that delicate precision of a 6C 1750. Yet, after a 1750, I'd rather own it than almost any other car on earth, including all your modern Maseratis, Ferraris, or whatever.

You might imagine that a blown, twin-ohc-engined, forty-year-old machine might tend to fussiness. Bond's Alfa certainly does not. You switch on and the engine explodes into a sudden staccato roar. Then you let it idle for a time—a longish time—for the oil to warm. Idling does not oil its cold, near-racing-range sparkplugs. Then, with its elegantly thin but not whippy gear lever in the low-gear notch of its gate (which sits on top of an aluminum extension from the gearbox—almost ex-exactly like that of a 1750), you let in the clutch. And it's no tricky life-or-death affair, but easy and smooth.

One thing you notice immediately. You're not down inside the car, you're on it. You stick out. The top of your head is above the top of the windshield. You can see both front fenders; but you cannot see the instrument panel owing to the way the cowl extends above the instrument panel on the Castagna body (Zagato bodies have the same vice). You have to duck your head to see the dials. Bond's Alfa has a soup-plate-sized English rev-counter hitched to the steering column.

There's no particular trick to driving the Alfa. You don't even have to keep the revs up. In top gear you can let them drop below 1,000 without feeling that you're mistreating the engine. It will actually pick up cleanly from that speed and go right on up to 5,000 rpm without a stumble. But you don't, obviously, drive like that. You use all of the gears and enjoy the lovely rising and falling sounds as you shift from ratio to ratio.

The first time I drove Bond's Alfa I started to handle it with the careless abandon with which I'd driven my 1750. I got it a bit sideways on a fast corner before I realized it wasn't quite as forgiving as the smaller car. Possibly this feeling of slightly lesser controllability is caused by the heavier 2.6 engine. I'm not sure, either, that the increased power of a 2.6, which also meant an increase in weight and complication, made it a much more desirable car than a blown 1750.

The 8C 2300's and their variations (the 2.6's and 2.9's) crushed all opposition in the first half of the nineteen-thirties. In grand-prix racing, first the two-seater Monzas and then the Monoposto single-seater P3's ended the long reign of the Bugattis. And they were almost unbeatable in sports-car racing. The Targa Florio, Le Mans, the Mille Miglia, all became rapid processions inevitably led by Alfa Romeos.

In 1934, Alfa Romeo produced several versions of six-cylinder machines, the 6C 2300 and the 6C 2300 B, and at the end of the thirties the first of the 6C 2500's. These were production-type cars of no great interest, and certainly not in the great idiom of the 6C 1750 or 8C 2300. It should be noted, too, that present-day Alfa Romeos are really descended from these lesser cars.

There was, however, one more great sports Alfa produced before World War II. This was the 8C 2900 B. (The 8C 2900 A's never reached the market, being prototypes used only in factory-entered races.) Thirty 8C 2900 B's were built, and these, it is said, were constructed to use up the thirty supercharged grand-prix engines sitting idly in the Alfa storerooms after the racing team had turned to twelve-cylinder machines. Detuned, the engines were installed in independently suspended chassis, which invariably were clothed in superb two-seater coachwork.

I was lucky enough, in 1939, to get a ride in one of these magnificent machines—the one Maclure Halley, after much importunity and after paying some $11,000, succeeded in prying out of the Alfa factory in Milan. Its 180-hp engine looked much like that in an 8C 2300, but the rest of the car no longer had that "lean and hungry" look of the more functional machines of a decade earlier. You sat in, not on, the Superleggera body—too deeply in, I felt. It was almost annoyingly comfortable and lush. But it did go—zero to 60 in about 9 seconds—about as quick as Ed Bond's 2.6, if less nervously.

After the war, the first sports Alfa to appear was a revamped version of the prewar 6C 2500. Expensive and with plush bodywork, it sold in limited numbers in this country to well-heeled Italophiles—night-club impresari and such. It was a quite boring motor car.

Preceding pages: Lamborghini Jarama
catches the eye of a hot-dog
vendor on New York's 10th Avenue. Jarama
400 GT 2+2 has 4-litre, V-12,
350-hp engine, 162 mph claimed top speed.
Other Lamborghinis are four-place
Espada and 200-mph, rear-engined Countach.

In 1951, what was really the first of the modern Alfas appeared. This was the 1900, which had a four-cylinder, chain-driven, twin-overhead-camshaft engine very much like those in the current models. Also, like the present-day Alfa Romeos—the 2000 series—it had an integral body-chassis, coil-sprung front suspension, and a coil-sprung, rigid rear axle. Expectedly, the newest Alfas are very much better machines with their superb five-speed gearboxes, disc brakes, and other lovely amenities. In both open Spyder form and with various closed bodies (the Giulietta of 1955, the subsequent Giulia, the all-new 1750, and the present 2000), these four-cylinder models have been the most successful of all Alfas. The six-cylinder 2600, which first appeared in 1962, has been superseded by the V-8 Montreal, which is largely based on the successful Type 33 sports-racing Alfa Romeo. Unfortunately, this exciting machine will most likely be unavailable to Americans. It seems Alfa doesn't think it worthwhile to go through the smog/safety brouhaha required for US certification.

MASERATI

The Maserati brothers, Alfieri, Bindo, Carlo, Ettore, Ernesto, and Mario, were not sports-car builders. (In any case, Mario was an artist.) Starting in the nineteen-twenties, they built race cars. The few sports Maseratis that took the road before World War II were violent and intractable racing machines to which cycle-type fenders and minimal lights were fastened almost as an afterthought. For years I sought one particular specimen which was rumored to have found its way to the USA. This was based on a *Sedici Cilindri* (sixteen-cylinder) racing car built in 1929. It was powered by two 2-litre straight-eight engines stuffed side-by-side under its wide hood. In 1929, in racing form and driven by Borzacchini, this 300-bhp model was timed at 152.9 mph on Cremona's ten-kilometer straight stretch, setting an International class record. I hope it still exists somewhere.

The Maserati brothers (Ernesto, Bindo, and Ettore were the only ones still involved; Alfieri had died in 1932) sold their company to the Orsi family of Modena in 1937 and contracted to run things for ten years. At the termination of the contract in 1947, the Maserati brothers left to form a new car-building operation—OSCA.

It was under the Orsis that the first modern, non-racing sports and GT cars emerged. A small, sohc, 1500-cc-engined car with Pininfarina coachwork appeared in 1948. But with only 65 hp (later increased to 2 litres and 100 hp), it had no great success. It wasn't until 1953, when the A6GCS sports-racing car, powered by a twin-ohc 2-litre engine developed from grand-prix racing was bodied by Pininfarina into a GT coupe, that Maserati was started on its course toward its present position as a leader in building great, luxury grand tourers. The first such GT machine offered for sale in any considerable number was the lovely A6G-2000 of 1955–56. Bodied by Zagato, Allemano and Frua, it was a worthy ancestor of today's delicious-looking productions.

The particulars of the first "Maser" I ever drove are shrouded in the mists of thirty years past. All I remember is that it was red, had fenders and lights, and that it terrified me. Its sadistic (for hoping to see me suffer) and foolish owner (foolish for letting me get behind its wheel) offered me a drive in the midst of New York's traffic. I remember that it steered quickly and beautifully. But I had no experience of its gearbox; I never got it out of first speed, for even in low gear it moved too quickly for the city traffic and I found myself slipping the clutch to go slowly enough. I was happy, not only to shift seats with the brutish Maserati's grinning owner, but also to see that he had almost as much trouble driving it in traffic as I.

Recently I went for a ride in a new Maserati Bora. There couldn't have been a greater contrast between two devices designed to move on four wheels. For the Bora certainly must be the most sophisticated sporting GT car of all time.

The Bora is a midengined, all-independently-sprung two-seater, powered by a 4.7-litre, 335-hp V-8 with four overhead camshafts and a five-speed ZF all-synchro gearbox. It is clothed in superb coachwork designed by young Giorgetto Giugiaro, who also styled the Maserati Ghibli. Although these bare specifications are by no means prosaic, their sum is greater than its parts.

I went aboard the Bora with Bob Grossman, the successful racing driver (Le Mans, Sebring, etc.) and American distributor for Maserati; he sells several hundred each year. He demonstrated that not only were the seats and steering wheel hydraulically movable in many directions, but also that the pedals magically moved in and out hydraulically to compensate for variations in leg length. A boy-sized driver can sit high and well back for a good view of the road and still reach the pedals comfortably. Nor will a six-footer lack headroom. We set forth. Grossman inserted the Bora into the heavy traffic outside his premises and immediately treated all other cars like near-stationary objects cluttering up the road—and with no feeling of derring-do. The Bora moved smoothly, quietly. Even though the engine was inches from the backs of our heads, we talked in normal tones—mostly in praise of the Bora. Grossman attacked several miles of hill upon which the highway designers seemed to have drawn the curliest road of which their drafting instruments were capable. Dozens of 20-mph-limit signs embellished the roadside. Grossman went up to about 80. The fat-tired Bora took the turns without slide or squeal. Only the forces acting upon our viscera and the pressure of our hips against the sides of the amazingly good seats told us how the Bora was defying lateral G. Grossman descended in the same manner, using his brakes at times now—remarkably consistent brakes with Citroën hydraulic circuitry (Citroën owns a big piece of Maserati). How fast is the Bora? About 175 mph. This is the one to buy if you have about $25,000 with which to indulge yourself.

There are other luscious Maseratis: the four-place Indy, the two-seated Ghibli, both front-engined with 5-litre, quadruple-camshaft engines similar to that in the Bora. Also *circa* $25,000.

FERRARI

In spite of competition from its Italian confreres—Maserati and Lamborghini—Ferrari is still *the* magic name to the high-income-tax-bracket types who care about creating a sporting image for themselves as they reach middle age. Even though many of the rich doctors, dentists, and book publishers are quite clueless as to how such a machine can and should be driven, that's not *Commendatore* Enzo Ferrari's fault, for today's Ferraris are eminently capable of rewarding their drivers with tremendous speed and racing-car acceleration allied to precise handling. And they are mechanically reliable.

Fifteen or twenty years ago, Ferraris were a mite fussy. I remember an acquaintance's contretemps. He had just acquired a near-new one, driven it from the dealer's showroom, and stopped for a traffic light a few hundred feet down the street. A "chopped and channeled" Ford containing a duck-tail-haired youth drew up noisily beside him. The Ferrariste felt taunted, especially since he had a young lady passenger. When the light changed, he revved his engine and let in the clutch less than gently. The Ferrari engine screamed, but the car just stood there as the Ford disappeared down the street. It wasn't the first suspect, the Ferrari's clutch, that had failed. It was its differential. The pinion gear had not only lost some teeth, it had been wiped clean of them. It was no longer a gear but a neat, truncated cone.

Not that Ferrari clutches in those days were so all-fired perfect. I recall an incident in the nineteen-fifties at a foreign-car repair shop which I patronized. The foreman of the establishment told his son and apprentice to drive in a Ferrari which a customer had parked outside the shop. The son revved the Ferrari's engine (although not nearly as exuberantly as do public garage car-jockeys), let in the clutch a bit brusquely, and stopped. "Dummkopf!" screamed Papa. "You haff the clutch schpoiled." He needn't have excited himself. That Ferrari's owner was used to buying new clutches.

Ferraris today no longer display the weaknesses of their forebears of the nineteen-fifties. In those days, the chief emphasis was on their great twelve-cylinder engines. Chassis construction was almost an afterthought. Gearboxes, clutches, differentials were secondary. In the very early days, although Ferrari wouldn't admit it, they were sometimes parts brought from Fiat.

My friend John Cuccio is the most intense Ferrari-phile I know. He has owned an impressive string of Ferrari cars and now drives a GTB 4, as nervous and potent a carriage as is practical on the public ways. He is emphatically scornful, in his polite way, of those doom-oriented types who darkly warn people away from Ferraris lest they be driven crackers by unreliability and frightful expenses.

"Isn't there some pain mixed with the pleasure, John?" I asked.

"No pain, no problems, only traffic tickets," he said. "There used to be one thing that was a nuisance—wet plugs. Choking the engine to start from cold would wet the plugs with

Above: 1919 Kissel Gold Bug had six-cylinder, 61-hp engine. Note extra seat which pulled out from body like a drawer. Left: 1929 Kissel White Eagle speedster had straight-eight, L-head, 126-hp engine. A claimed speed of 100 mph was not compatible with steering and roadholding of the car. Golf-bag carriers were a standard feature.

raw gasoline. They'd take forever to clear and sometimes the only remedy would be a plug change. That problem is solved now. Marchal, in France, makes a twelve-plug kit for Ferraris. A little wetting bothers them not at all."

"What about the extra-fancy tuning and service at crazy high prices?"

"The prices at the Ferrari dealership are not all that rough and, anyhow, I find I don't need any fussy tune-ups. The garage across from my office changes the oil and greases it. That's all it seems to need."

I noted that Cuccio's Ferrari was bumperless. "Why did you take the bumpers off?" I asked.

"Oh, it's much cheaper to fix the body than to buy new bumpers," said he. Perhaps Ferrari parts *are* expensive.

Enzo Ferrari's first street machine, the Type 166 Inter, appeared in 1948. (The numbers defining Ferrari models indicate the cubic capacity of each of the twelve cylinders in the V-12 engines. Thus 166.2 x 12 equals 1,995 cc.) It was a somewhat detuned version of the 2-litre, 166 Mille Miglia sports car which, driven by Biondetti, won the Mille Miglia in 1948. Its V-8 engine had the low compression ratio of 7.5 to 1 and only a single Weber carburetor; 110 bhp was developed. Known as the Barchetta (little boat), its body by Superleggera Touring, it was the archetypal sports car for years afterward.

In the twenty-odd years since the birth of the Type 166, there has been a mind-reeling number of models of sports Ferraris, all of them with V-12 engines in dizzying variations. Today's Ferraris—not the racing sports cars—but the great distance-eating GT machines in which one can approach 175 mph and yet quietly trickle through traffic without drama, are the Ferrari 365 GTB 4—the Daytona—and the 365 GTC 4, which is only slightly less potent.

Luigi Chinetti, the car's importer, let me take out the Daytona I photographed. I cannot imagine what developments in the future of automobilism can possibly make a motor car any better than this unbelievable machine. (I know, of course, that inevitably even better cars will evolve.) At 90 mph, the Daytona felt as if it were merely ambling, which it was. Accelerating (zero to 60 in about 7 seconds) was a joy, with none of the feeling that we might at any moment go sideways. (A tendency I'd noticed

in my son's Detroit muscle-car). Yes, the ride below 75 mph was noticeably firm, but it was a reassuring firmness which told me that at 150 mph (which we did *not* reach in the purlieus of Greenwich, Connecticut) there would be no worries about roadholding. The Daytona is perhaps the only machine in existence which in stock form is capable of going racing at venues like Le Mans or Sebring.

Another Ferrari-built car (which nowhere bears the name Ferrari) is the delectable Dino 246 GT. Like the Maserati Bora, the Lamborghini Miura, and the De Tomaso Pantera, the Dino carries its engine amidships. (It's athwartships, too.) Unlike other Ferraris' engines, the Dino's is a 2,418-cc V-6, a wonderfully snarling, howling mechanism which has a stimulating effect on the driver's blood circulation, since all the noisy mechanical excitement—the workings of the overhead camshafts, the loud breathing of the Weber carburetors, and other unidentifiable tintinnabulations—is but inches behind his ears. A five-speed box aft of the engine stirs the gears around, but, like other remotely controlled transmissions required by aft-mounted engines, it's a bit notchy to shift.

On the road a Dino is marvelously responsive. Steering is ultraquick, solid, and millimetrically accurate. Zero to 60 takes 7½ seconds. Top speed is 140. Discs—all around, of course—are without peer. At 60 mph the Dino took but 140 feet to come to a stop. Mr. Chinetti's price of $14,900 for one of

these little paragons is not in the least unreasonable.

There is only one American sports car in production today—Chevrolet's Corvette. Its mechanical features, overseen by that excellent engineer, Zora Arkus-Duntov, are admirable. Its sharp, middle-American styling is, in my view, deplorable.

The Stutz Bearcat, the Mercer Raceabout, the Simplex Speed Car were indisputably sports cars in their day—although no one called them that. I have elsewhere written profusely about them. There was, however, another marque, the Kissel, which was at one time a much-desired American sports car and which is worth brief notice.

KISSEL

I didn't get a chance to drive a Kissel—a 1929 White Eagle Speedster—until the mid-thirties, when Kissel cars had already disappeared from the market.

The Kissel White Eagle was then as sporty looking a machine as any American builder had ever put together. Long and low, with crowned fenders, cutaway doors, a top which folded like a horseshoe behind the contoured seats, and even a golf bag resting against a rear fender—it looked sensational.

Its mechanical specifications were impressive, too: a 126-hp, straight-eight, L-head Lycoming engine of 298.6 cu. in. (4.7 litres), hydraulic brakes, and a 132-in. wheelbase. A top speed of 100 mph was claimed. A White Eagle cost $3,275 (£655) in 1929.

When the friend who owned it offered to let me drive, I remember being more than slightly frightened by the Kissel soon after I took the wheel. We were then in New Jersey on some fairly empty roads, and I must admit that in my youthful ignorance, I immediately tried to show off a bit. I foolishly tried to drive it as if it were a real sports car, of which I had had some little experience.

I lost that Kissel on the first corner. Luckily, I didn't hit anything when I left the road backward after trying to prevail in a desperate contest with the slow steering. The owner, no longer my friend, instantly changed seats with me and managed to extricate us from the sand into which I had put his pretty car.

Happily, when we were in the Holland Tunnel on our way back to New York, my ex-friend had a spot of trouble, too. The hydraulic brakes failed. Using only the hand brake, he crawled back to his garage. I never saw that pretty White Eagle Kissel again.

An earlier Kissel sports car, the Gold Bug, which first appeared in 1919, was more famous in its day than the White Eagle. It got its name from its chrome yellow color similar to that in which Mercer Raceabouts were painted. The Kissel Gold Bugs had L-head, six-cylinder engines of up to

This 1953 Z-102B Pegaso was called "El Dominicano" in honor of Dominican dictator Rafael Trujillo, for whom it was especially built at a purported cost of $30,000. Ahead of its time in body design, it had a plastic bubble roof aft.

482 cu. in. (4.7 litres). Their two-seater bodies were ultra-sporting for their day and had an ingenious extra seat which slid out like a drawer.

The Kissel, which at first was called the Kissel Kar, was built in Hartford, Wisconsin, starting in 1906. Most Kissels were sturdy, unsporting tourers and sedans and, unlike many makes of limited production, they were not "assembled cars." Kissel made almost every part in its own factory, even bodies.

In 1931 Kissel joined Moon to form New Era Motors for the production of the front-wheel drive Ruxton, which, sadly, was not a success.

PEGASO: The Spanish Sports Car
I have in front of me an instruction book for the Z-102 Pegaso.

Bound in red morocco, stamped in gold, and encased in a box made of cloth and watered and gilded paper, it must be the fanciest book ever destined to receive a mechanic's greasy fingerprints. This book was, I suspect, given to me as a sort of prize for surviving a demonstration run in the company of a Pegaso factory test and racing driver named Señor Palacio.

In 1953 a car dealer on Long Island was struck with the idea that he could sell the then astronomically expensive, excruciatingly complex, albeit wonderfully constructed sports car, the Spanish Pegaso. After importing some half-dozen of the exotic machines, he set up a very odd establishment for their sale. A suave, Spanish-speaking sales manager headed a staff of spectacular young women. These ladies, dressed to the nines and

1955 Pegaso Berlina Model Z-102B had
remarkably intricate and beautifully constructed
chassis. Its engine—2.8-litre,
four-ohc, V-8, 170-hp—gave the Z-102 model
125-mph speed. Other Pegasos, some
of them supercharged, had engines of up to
350 hp. Coachwork above is by Saoutchik.

made up like chorus girls, were the sales force.

One of them took me out for a ride in a coupe and suggested that I drive. I handled the car rather gingerly at first; it seemed such a fierce brute. But after a few miles I began to enjoy it. Steering was quick and to-the-inch. The five-speed gearbox, although devoid of synchromesh, was wonderfully forgiving to my ham-handedness. The revs screamed up at a mere touch on the throttle. The engine made all the right hard noises —perhaps a mite too much noise for a closed car. In a way, the car was a delightful anachronism. It felt more like a harsh racing sports car of the tough twenties or thirties than the softer machines we were already used to in 1953. One thing bothered me a bit—the brakes. Nothing much seemed to happen in that department unless I applied inordinate pressure, this owing to typical sports-racing practice—the use of hard brake linings to obviate fade.

I got the impression that the lady demonstrator felt that I had not fully tested the abilities of the Pegaso. "I'll call Señor Palacio," she said. "He'll show you what it can do."

Indeed, he did. The good señor had no English, I had no Spanish. After screeching out of the agency forecourt onto a narrow country road, he pointed to the gear lever and showed me that he could shift up and down through all the gears without touching a toe to the clutch. Then in third speed at about 80 he twitched the steering wheel and put the right wheels into the ditch. He twitched the steering again, laughed heartily, and shot out of the ditch still at about 6,000 rpm in third. Nodding and smiling with satisfaction, he rattled away at me in Catalan (he was from Barcelona). He was, I think, demonstrating the Pegaso's superb stability. He charged down the road in and out of suburban traffic at something over 100 mph and then demonstrated cornering. The car negotiated the corners far better than my nerves did. Now came the *coup de grâce*. We very rapidly approached a Y junction, just before which there was considerable sand in the road. Palacio jammed on the hand brake, twisted the steering wheel, and spun on the sand. At the instant the tail of the car pointed up one leg of the "Y," Palacio shifted into reverse and went down the road backward for a bit, then stopped, engaged a forward gear and shot away. I found out later that this fancy way of changing direction was part of Palacio's demonstration repertoire. The devil knew the sand was there and had obviously practiced his maneuver. I earned that deluxe instruction book.

The Pegaso was built in Barcelona in what had been the old Hispano-Suiza factory. A new management, ENASA (*Empresa Nacional de Autocamiónes S.A.*), first showed the Pegaso at the Paris *Salon* in 1951. Every superb bit of the car, except for the Bosch electrical items, was made right there in the factory in the great tradition of Hispano. In fact, many of the workmen and technicians were from the great old days of Hispano-Suiza.

The Pegaso was designed by Wilfredo Ricart who had been with Alfa Romeo in the nineteen-thirties. There he had been responsible for the Model 512, a disastrous rear-engined machine in which Alfa's great test driver, Marinoni, was killed. There, too, he acquired Enzo Ferrari's hatred; Ferrari is downright vicious about him in his memoirs. There have been stories, too, about Ricart's enthusiasm for Mussolini's fascism, which perhaps explains his reappearance in Spain. Nonetheless, in the Pegaso, he produced a brilliant car.

The Z-102 incorporated almost every design element which was considered advanced in 1951. It had a V-8, 2.8-litre engine with four overhead camshafts which delivered 188 bhp at 6,500 rpm. The camshafts were driven by a train of gears, true racing-car practice but noisy. It was available with either a single Weber carburetor or with four of them. In 1954 a larger 3.2-litre engine with a supercharger developed 225 bhp. The cylinder blocks, crankcase, and gears were of aluminum alloys; cylinder liners of nitralloy were screwed into the block in Hispano-Suiza fashion.

The five-speed gearbox, differential, de Dion axle, and rear brakes (with giant, finned, ventilated drums) were all part of a single magnificently constructed and finished unit. The steering gear was of remarkable configuration: The steering shaft was geared to a vertical shaft in a tower-like casting; this vertical shaft was then coupled to more-or-less conventional steering rods. It was well-nigh impossible for the steering shaft and wheel to be forced rearward in a collision.

Bodies were welded to a platform-type chassis. Most coachwork—and it was of a very high order—was built in the factory, although a few were built by Touring in Italy and Saoutchik in France.

A catalogue I have quotes a top speed of 142 mph for an *unblown*, open Z-102 and claims that the supercharged model was even faster. I doubt it.

The Pegaso was horribly expensive. A simple-bodied roadster was $15,000. A ridiculous confection with a plexiglass tail, built-in bar, and various other conceits, purportedly built for the Santo Domingan dictator Trujillo, was said to cost $30,000. Ricart and ENASA had hoped that rich Americans would buy the Z-102. But the Americans kept their hands in their pockets.

As usual, it was thought that racing successes would lend glamour to the marque. Several races—the 1951 Spanish Grand Prix, the Carrera Panamericana, and the 1953 Le Mans—were entered, but the Pegasos failed to reach the starting line. The closest the cars came to actually racing was at Le Mans. But there my friend Palacio had brake trouble in practice and his teammate, Jover, had a frightful accident. In 1953, however, a Z-102 broke production-car records at Jabbeke in Belgium at 151 mph for the flying kilometer. (An XK-120 Jaguar again broke the record at 172.41 mph a few days later.) In 1954 Palacio started in the race through Mexico, the Carrera Panamericana, but retired soon after the start.

Ricart, still trying to increase sales, produced models with bigger engines of 4 and 4½ litres with up to 300 bhp. He even tried offering a cheaper push-rod model. But to no avail.

Porsche 911 with "Targa" semiconvertible
body. 911-series Porsches are
available in three degrees of fierceness:
the 911 T with 134 hp, the 911 E
with 157 hp, and the 911 S with 181 hp.
All have horizontally opposed
six-cylinder, rear-mounted engines.

By the time the Pegaso went out of production in 1959 only a few hundred had been sold.

ENASA, of course, is still in business—big business, producing some of the best trucks and buses anywhere.

Germany, was, before World War II, never much of a sports-car country. Although a handful of upper-class types roared around in gigantic Mercedes-Benzes, there were very few small, moderately-priced sports cars. There were, in fact, hardly any middle-class young men who could have bought them. During the nineteen-thirties, when young men in other countries were enjoying themselves in cars like MG's and Amilcars, German young men were involved with more martial enthusiasms.

The Adler and the Hansa are hardly remembered, but the BMW of the nineteen-thirties stands forth as an exception. Since BMW today builds not out-and-out sports cars but touring machines of the highest type, it is covered in another chapter. Today, the remarkably successful Porsche is the German sports car *par excellence*.

PORSCHE

I freely confess that I was not impressed by the first Porsche I ever drove. Had anyone told me then that the Porsche would become one of the very great sports cars of all time, I would have hooted at him.

It must have been .in 1949 that I drove the first Porsche to be brought to the USA. Max Hoffman had just taken on the distributorship, and he allowed me to take that early 356 model for a run in Central Park. I found that it oversteered so badly that I almost lost it on every corner. I didn't like the difficult nonsynchro gearbox at all. I did admire the Porsche's uniquely slippery shape.

But Porsches then, as today, went through a continual and rapid process of development and improvement. The 356 Porsche was an aristocratic descendant of the Volkswagen designed by Dr. Ferdinand Porsche. It was, however, Porsche's son, Ferry, who masterminded the new sports car. Like the VW, it had a horizontally opposed, 1,100-cc, four-cylinder, air-cooled rear engine. In its early days, each Porsche engine was painstakingly assembled by one man who signed his work by stamping his initials into the crankcase. Bodywork was built by outside suppliers, mostly Reutter, a firm which has since been absorbed by Porsche. In 1951, engine size went up to 1,300 cc and then to 1,500 cc. Horsepower kept climbing. By 1952, the 1,500 cc Super, which had a roller-bearing crankshaft, put out a healthy 70 hp; 105 mph was possible.

By the time the 356 was superseded by the current formidable 911 series in 1965, a 356 C had a 95-hp, 1,600-cc engine. By then, too, the skittery tail-end characteristics had mostly been developed out, although not to the extent that a driver could entirely forget that he had a fair bit of weight out back.

In look, the 911-series Porsche is not too dissimilar from its ancestors of almost a quarter century ago. And it's still a two-seater plus. The plus being a pair of minimal seats behind the driver and passenger.

The 911 is offered in three versions: the 911 T, the 911 E, and the 911 S. All have 2,341-cc, horizontally opposed, dry-sump, six-cylinder engines. The 911 S is the hot member of the family, having an engine which puts out no less than 181 hp at 6,500 rpm. A top speed of 143 mph and a zero-to-60 time of under 7 seconds is promised.

I had a run in a friend's 911 E, which is slightly less puissant than the S. It was fabulous. True, the revs had to be kept up to get the kind of performance you'd get out of, say, a Ferrari Daytona. But a Daytona's engine is some fifty percent larger (and a Daytona costs twice as much). But shifting up and down to stay at optimum revs was hardly a chore. I've never handled a better gearbox. Steering was delightfully precise and light. And that old bugaboo of oversteer is gone—at least at the cornering speeds I attempted.

911 Porsches are not economy cars (although they are economical of fuel). A 911 S coupe with a five-speed box costs $10,225 in the US. But a 911 T with a four-speed transmission is only $7,960. The midengined 914 coupe with a 1.7-litre engine costs $4,499.

Since its earliest days, the Porsche factory has enthusiastically competed with a great variety of models in every kind f motor sport. And it has won more races, hill climbs, rallies (you name it, they've done it) than I could list in a couple of chapters.

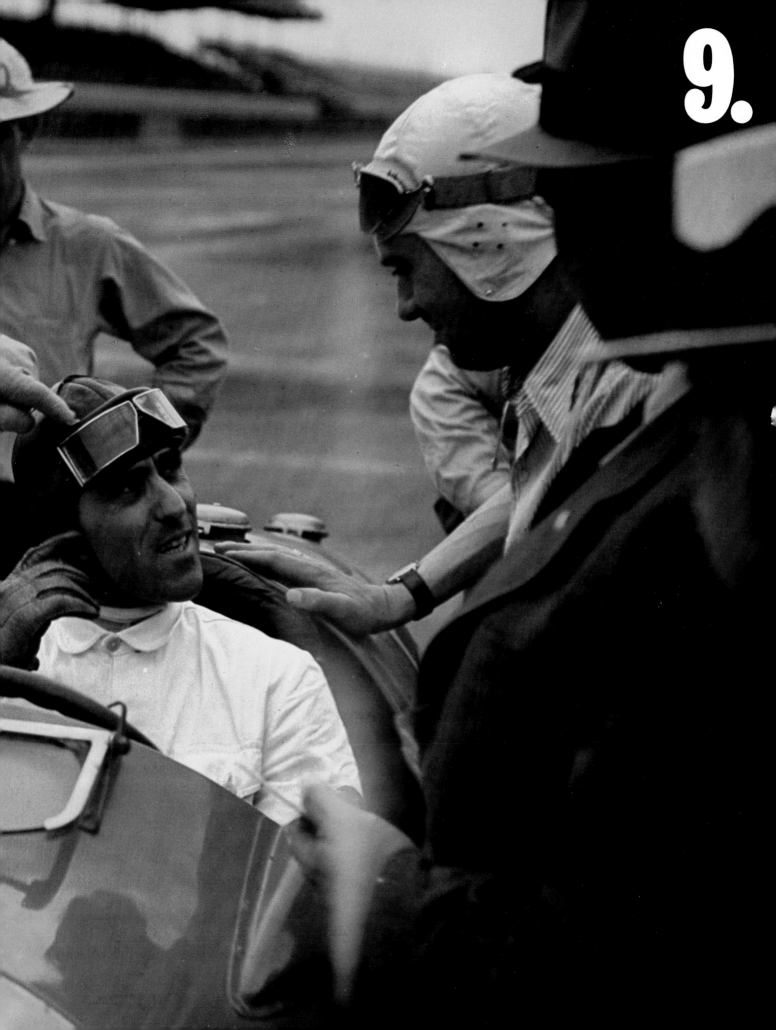

COMPETITION

When the automobile was very young racing was a simple thing. Cars started here and went there as fast as they could. The car that got there first won. There were no categories of cars, no special kinds of races. Today the proliferation of narrowly special types of cars for Grands Prix, Le Mans, Stock-Car Racing, Formula A, Formula B, Indianapolis, Demolition Derbies, Formula V, Sports-Car Racing, Drag Racing, Can-Am is dizzying and getting dizzier.

In the very early races of the eighteen-nineties it was not usually speed that decided the winner. The winning car was often the one that covered the longest distance before disintegrating. Within a half-dozen years, however, the painfully crawling gas buggies—like Levassor's Panhard of 1895 and the Duryea brothers' machine (which had won the Chicago *Times-Herald* race in 1895)—evolved into lethally fast racing monsters. Entered mostly by wild upper-class young men eager to prove their careless disdain of dying, the races of the dozen years before Haig, Ludendorff, and Joffre put an end to a brave generation were as insanely glorious as any the world has since seen.

It is hard for us to imagine what it must have been like to drive a brutish racing machine of the early nineteen-hundreds in one of the great country-to-country races of those days: Paris–Berlin, Paris–Vienna, Paris–Madrid (Paris was still the center of the world).

The cars which thundered across Europe from about 1902 onward were much improved over the primitive machines which had struggled so painfully over the roads of France in the last few years of the nineteenth century. Those ancients—short and high, with vague and wobbly tiller steering which could be yanked out of the driver's hand by a stone or a rut, with horse-carriage brakes which bore against the outside of their spaghetti-thin tires—had been dangerous even at bicycle speeds.

The cars which embarked on the cross-country races were perhaps even less roadworthy, for their huge engines permitted tremendous speeds—as high as 70 mph by 1902. Big-wheeled with fragile pneumatic tires, their weak, high-off-the-ground chassis drilled with holes for lightness, without either shock absorbers or castor action in their over-quick steering, they were appallingly dangerous.

Their crews—gentleman driver plus paid *mécanicien*

—perched in the open atop the bodyless chassis frames, the driver in a bucket seat, the mechanic sideways on the floorboards. The latter's job was mostly to diddle with the rows of brass drip-feed lubricators on the dashboard and to help with the frequent tire changes.

The roads over which these bearded, leather-clad men raced were as suicidal to drive over as the cars were to drive. Their powdery surfaces rose in opaque dust clouds which trailed the cars. Passing was an insane plunge into the unknown. Many a time the road turned while the blinded passer bore straight on. The trick of following telegraph lines visible above the dust didn't always work. Sometimes the wires went directly across-country while the road curved. The local citizenry and their pigs, goats, and other livestock, long used to considering the public highway a place of assembly, had no conception of the speed of a racing car and moved out of its way no more rapidly than if it were a farm cart drawn by oxen. Near towns, idiotic spectators formed a solid wall. Charles Jarrott wrote in his *Ten Years of Motors and Motor Racing:* "It seemed impossible that my swaying, bounding car could miss the reckless spectators. A wedge-shaped space opened out in the crowd as I approached, and so fine was the calculation made that at times it seemed impossible for the car not to overtake the apex of the human triangle and deal death and destruction. I tried slowing down, but quickly realized that the danger was as great at forty miles an hour as at eighty."

The primitive pneumatic tires of those days were devils to be constantly fought. If a driver was lucky, he could wait to change them at one of the repair-and-replenishment depots his firm set up along the road. There the tire fitters would slice away the worn tires with knives before installing new ones. But usually the unlucky driver and his mechanic had continual tire trouble, which meant that the crew had to pry off the tire (demountable rims and wheels came later), rip out the tube, patch it or replace it, and then pump it up. A mile or two farther on they might have to go through the same deadly drill again with fingers already torn and bleeding. And like the surgeon who leaves scissors and rolls of bandage inside his client's abdominal cavity, it was not unknown for exhausted drivers to leave tire irons between tubes and tires.

Preceding pages: Ernst Von Delius
and Rudolf Caracciola heckle Tazio Nuvolari
about his peculiarly shaped
goggles during practice for Vanderbilt Cup Race
at Roosevelt Raceway, Long Island,
in 1937. Nuvolari is in twelve-cylinder
Alfa Romeo which broke down during race.

At first the great races were country-to-country—Paris–Berlin, Paris–Vienna. But in 1903 the disasters of Paris–Madrid put an end to such noble contests. Although exaggerated in its day (the sensational British press called it "The Race to Death") and enlarged upon since, in retrospect the debacle of Paris–Madrid seemed inevitable. The flimsy cars carrying overpowerful engines, the ridiculously high speeds over highways hardly suitable for post chaises (Louis Renault in the light-car class was timed at some 90 mph as he approached Chartres!) were invitations to trouble. Worst of all were the wildly excited and uncontrollable masses of French spectators—millions of them who had no conception of speed. The few regiments of French foot and light cavalry had little effect on the onlookers' self-destructive antics. No one knows how many were maimed. But Marcel Renault was killed, Barrow was killed, his De Dietrich smashed to bits. Stead's De Dietrich collided with Salleron's Mors and then crashed. Mayhew smashed his Napier against a tree. Porter overturned his Wolseley, which burned. Tourand charged the crowd, etc., etc.

The shocked authorities ended the race at Bordeaux. Gabriel, *averaging* 65 mph, was first on his big Mors. Salleron, despite his collision with Stead, took second place, and Jarrott on a De Dietrich finished third.

And that was pretty much the end of town-to-town racing. I can't think of any such races until the Carrera Panamericana of the nineteen-fifties—the wild and woolly road races in which Mercedes-Benzes and Lincolns and others charged furiously across the mountains of northern Mexico.

Another contest, a battle for the Gordon Bennett Trophy offered by that flamboyant proprietor of the New York *Herald*, James Gordon Bennett, had been engaged in by some of the competitors in the town-to-town races. This cup went to the automobile club of the country which won—not to the manufacturer. It was a sort of war of car nationalities. Each country could enter three machines of which every tiny bit—every tire, sparkplug, or cotter pin—had to be made within its boundaries.

After Paris–Madrid, the Gordon Bennett race—held on a closed course under the rules of the country that had won the previous year—became the important contest. In 1904, Théry (called "*Le Chronomètre*" because of the regularity of his lap times) won on a Richard Brasier for France. He did it again in 1905, this time using the then-new shock absorbers which did much to curtail the bounding and dancing which was still such a dreadful characteristic of the big, over-engined racing cars.

In 1906 the French made trouble. They fumed that, as the leading automotive country, it was patently unfair for them to be limited to only three cars when semibarbarians like the Germans, with a comparatively small car industry, could also field three machines. This in spite of the fact that the Mephistophelean, red-bearded Camille Jenatzy had trounced them on a Mercedes in 1903.

So the Gordon Bennett was replaced by a new race without the old strictures, the great French Grand Prix, first run near Le Mans. In 1906 François Szisz on a Renault won at 66.8 mph on a fearfully hot day. Some of the car crews (no one but the driver and mechanic were allowed to touch the car) had to go through the hell of changing tires twelve or more times. But the Renault's wheels had been fitted that day with demountable rims. Although changing a demountable rim is rather more time-consuming than changing a center-lock wheel (a means still in the future), it's a lot quicker and easier than struggling to remove a flat tire from a rim that doesn't come off the wheel. The new rims undoubtedly ensured Szisz's win.

The French Grand Prix was run again in 1907, this time at Dieppe. But the French were no longer unbeatable. The days when Panhards won everything were over. Nor did the Brasiers, which had won the Gordon Bennett twice, ever win again. A FIAT driven by Felice Nazzaro was the victor in 1907. In 1908 it was Lautenschlager with his Mercedes.

Although the Grand Prix—there was then no Grand Prix except the French Grand Prix—was the top race, there were other important races. The Kaiserpreis of Germany was one, and the Targa Florio in Sicily another. And above all we must not forget that peculiarly and particularly American brannigan, the Vanderbilt Cup Race.

Long Island, that dismal monument to real-estate speculators, was not always encrusted with scrofulous growths of development houses and shopping malls. Seventy years ago it was open country upon whose northern edges the superrich built their baronies in imitation of French chateaux and British castles.

Michelin Tire Depot in London, built in 1912, has representations of early races built into its outer walls. Their multicolored tiles have stood London's weather for more than sixty years, and look as bright as when they were cemented into place. They make those desperate contests look almost serene.

In 1904 William K. Vanderbilt, one of the more visible money barons, who had long toyed with fast motor cars and was a sometime entrant in European motor races, offered a cup for the winner of a closed-circuit race on Long Island. The distance varied each year, anything from 250 to 500 miles, and the result was a series of scenes of carnage, confusion, and excitement not equaled until the present-day Long Island Expressway was opened to traffic.

The American crowds and the small-town cops had not learned any of the lessons of Paris–Madrid. They'd never even heard of Paris–Madrid. Crowd control was ridiculous during all the years in which the race was run—1904, 1905, 1906, 1908, 1909, 1910. After 1910 the Vanderbilt went bush league. It ran in Milwaukee, Savannah, Santa Monica, San Francisco, and lost its éclat.

The first Vanderbilt was won by George Heath on a 90-hp Panhard. Another French machine, an 80-hp Darracq driven by Victor Héméry, won in 1905. In 1906 the winning car was again a Darracq driven by Louis Wagner.

Vanderbilt had said that one of his aims was the development of American racing machines. During the first few years of the Vanderbilt Cup many American makes had been entered—Simplex, Royal-Tourist, Pope-Toledo, Locomobile, Christie, among others. But it was not until 1908 that an American machine, a 120-hp Locomobile, driven by George Robertson, won. Both the 1909 and 1910 races were won by an American car, an Alco driven by Harry Grant. So Willie Vanderbilt did after all succeed in what he said was his purpose.

Certainly, the Vanderbilt Races, according to graybeards who've reminisced to me about them, were wonderful to watch. Seeing and hearing those monstrous, bellowing Darracqs and Locomobiles charging along, trailing dust clouds, on the narrow dirt roads of Roslyn and Manhasset (now chokablock with Pontiacs and cardboard houses), is something I'm sorry to have missed. But the oldsters tell about other things besides the actual racing: the thousands of acetylene-lamped cars crawling across the Brooklyn Bridge during the night before the race; the tented depots in which mechanics struggled to prepare the racing cars; the cheap all-night saloons near the racecourse jammed with roistering citizens, some armed with wire cutters to snip the fences around the course; the rich young bloods, fresh from Reisenweber's and Rector's and Jack's (those posh turn-of-the-century eating and drinking emporia), arriving at the course at dawn with their veiled doxies beside them and their Mercedes' or Simplexes' tonneaus overflowing with champagne and lobster. (And having to pay a potato farmer $10 to park and $1 for the use of his privy.)

Grand-prix racing cars still depended on giant engines. But a new generation of lighter, smaller machines was in the wings. Voiturette races for the Coupe de l'Auto sponsored by the French sporting paper L'Auto, had shown what quick, handy cars like Hispano-Suiza, Delage, and Peugeot could accomplish. In 1912, at Dieppe, a team of "light" Peugeots came out to do battle with the old-style giants. Cars such as David Bruce-Brown's gargantuan 15-litre Fiat and the equally huge-engined Lorraine-Dietrich were now opposed by 7.6-litre Peugeots. Seven-litre engines are still very big by our standards today, but in 1912 the twin-ohc, hemispherically headed, inclined-valve engines designed by the Swiss, Ernest Henry, were sensational. Even more sensational was George Boillot's win at 68.45 mph. In 1913 and 1914 Henry Peugeots won the French Grand Prix again. In 1913 Jules Goux took one to America to win the Indianapolis 500. That Peugeot had a 5.65-litre engine. In 1914 the Peugeot driven by Boillot to second place at Indy had a mere 3-litre cubic capacity. That year the winner was René Thomas on a Delage.

Mercedes rarely races when there is a chance that someone may beat them. That was as true in 1914 as it is today. But Gottlieb Daimler's son Paul had designed a new single-ohc engine which the Germans were sure would take the measure of the Peugeots. The Germans, itching for war on the battlefield, brought their xenophobic outlook with them to the racecourse. They prepared their cars with military secrecy at a village away from the Lyons circuit. They worked out a strategy which assigned one of the Mercedes' as a decoy to force the French cars to overrev. They practiced pit work and signals to Prussian military standards. (This was the first time that pit signals were used.) The French revanchist outlook was quite as bad. To them George Boillot was not merely a great racing driver, but a symbol who would help redress the shame of Sedan in 1870. The

Germans won and nobody cheered, nobody played "Deutschland Über Alles." (Boillot lost again in 1916, when his fighter plane was brought down by a German pilot.)

Despite great expectations that new techniques—especially those developed from military aviation—would revolutionize the automobile, there were few basic changes in the designs of competition machines after the war. True, new light alloys came into greater use. Engines became smaller, were supercharged, and revved faster. Body shapes did not push as much air ahead of them as had the bluffer shapes of the past. Basically, however, the racing cars of the twenties and much of the thirties were not too unlike Henry's great Peugeot of 1912.

New names came to the fore. Bugatti. Then Alfa Romeo and Maserati and finally Auto Union. Briefly, Delage was great—especially with the remarkable 1½-litre V-8, which astounded the racing world in 1927.

I don't know why the racing of those years between the wars seems somehow to have been more important than the racing we have today, why the drivers—Nuvolari, Achille Varzi, Rudolf Caracciola, and the others—seem larger than life. Everyone everywhere knew the name Tazio Nuvolari. Who recognizes the name Emerson Fittipaldi? Perhaps it is because racing has become so fragmented. In the twenties and thirties grand-prix racing was king. No other kind of racing really counted, neither the annual sports-car race at Le Mans nor that peculiarly ingrown American phenomenon, the Indianapolis 500. Nor were the 1,500-cc class races in Europe, or the dirt-track and board-track events in America, exciting and entertaining as they might have been, of very great import.

One reason for the popular interest in earlier grand-prix racing was the fact that, although the machines involved usually were built especially for racing and were quite unlike those the manufacturers offered for sale, they did bear the names of the great factories that entered them. You too could be the owner of a Bugatti, an Alfa Romeo, a Mercedes-Benz. Today Ferrari, Lotus, and Matra are perhaps the only big names identifiable among the very many specialist cars on the grand-prix circuits.

There was another way a race-goer could identify with the machines screaming around the Avus or Montlhéry.

He could dream of buying an old Type 35 Bugatti or a Monza Alfa Romeo, fitting it with lights and fenders, and terrifying the neighbors. No one would have any such purpose in mind with one of the winged vacuum cleaners raced today.

There doesn't seem to be anything nationalistic about grand-prix racing nowadays. Maybe it's because the British, who dominate it, are too civilized for such idiocy. During the nineteen-thirties, however, when Mussolini and Hitler were trying to frighten people into thinking that Italians and Germans could do anything better than anybody, they latched on to motor racing, the most important sport in Europe, as a fine way to prove it. First Alfa Romeo, Government-controlled then as now, succeeded in blowing everybody else off the circuits. Bugatti had dominated grand-prix racing in the nineteen-twenties. But Alfa, starting in 1931 with the Type 8C, the 2.3 blown eight-cylinder Monza, and then the Type B-2600 P3 Monoposto single-seater, won everything in sight. In 1932, for example, P3's won the French, German, Italian, and Monza Grands Prix.

Mussolini's pals to the north weren't about to allow mere *Italiener* to get away with anything like that. When a new formula for 1934–1937 was announced by the *Association International des Automobile Clubs Reconnus* (AIACR), the body which controlled racing, the Germans goose-stepped to their drawing boards to get a crack at the 500,000 Reichmarks that *der Führer* was offering as a prize for the most successful German racing machine.

There were two contenders: Mercedes-Benz, whose chief stockholder had been a heavy contributor to the Nazi party, and Auto Union, whose designer Ferdinand Porsche was one of Hitler's pets and the chief architect of the Volkswagen. Both the Mercedes-Benz and the Auto Union were so brilliantly conceived, so forward in design, that they made every other racing car in existence look as if it ought to be in a museum alongside Levassor's Panhard. The first of the new generation of racing machines built by Mercedes-Benz was the M25. It had a 3.3-litre, straight-eight, twin-ohc, supercharged engine which in its first 1934 version put out over 350 bhp. Further, its light, independently sprung chassis, built with the precision of a chronometer, and the clean lines of its wind-cheating aluminum body, frightened many into thinking, "Maybe those Germans *can* do

1. Lorraine Barrow in the De Dietrich car in which he died after hitting a dog during the 1903 Paris–Madrid.
2. Louis Renault drove this 30-hp Renault while competing in the light-car class in the Paris–Madrid.
3. Luttgen in a Mercedes in the 1908 Vanderbilt Cup Race.
4. George Boillot at Boulogne in his Peugeot in 1913.
5. Ray Harroun won the 1911 Indianapolis 500 in this Marmon.

1

3

4

5

2

things better." The far-out design of the Auto Union reinforced that dread thought. Porsche's tour de force, the P-Wagen, had its 4.9-litre, single-ohc, V-16 engine mounted in its tail. Some 380 bhp was realized at 6,000 rpm. Its chassis was of light tubes. In the earliest examples coolant circulated through the tubes, but leaks gave rise to second thoughts, as they had in some nineteenth-century Peugeots which had a similar plumbing arrangement.

After overcoming a few early contretemps in 1934 (Alfa Romeo trounced the Germans handily at that year's French Grand Prix), the Germans remained unbeatable until the war. It became almost monotonous to watch Caracciola, Manfred von Brauchitsch, and Luigi Fagioli win for Mercedes, except when Bernd Rosemeyer and Hans Stuck beat them in Auto Unions.

The P-Wagens and the Mercedes-Benzes, despite their superiority, were continually improved. The most puissant Mercedes-Benz was the W125, which had a 5.6-litre engine developing a shattering 646 bhp. The W125's chassis was quite different from that of the M25. With a tubular chassis, torsion-bar suspension, de Dion rear end, and a lower, sleeker body, it handled as it had to in order to stay on the road at its 193-mph speed in road-racing trim.

The Auto Union, too, had increased its horsepower to 600—from 5.6-litres. Further, its partially fabric body, like that of a light airplane, soon became paneled in aluminum. Although today's rear-engined racing machines handle very well, Herr Porsche had not quite mastered the dynamics of the rear-engined car. Few race drivers liked driving the skittery Auto Union at speed, even such masters as Nuvolari and Varzi. Only Bernd Rosemeyer ever became a virtuoso of the tail-heavy bombs.

The Italians, overwhelmed, didn't give up. Alfa Romeo increased its horsepower. By 1936 it had a twelve-cylinder machine of 400 bhp. Maserati tried with a 4.6-litre V-8 car. Nothing helped.

In 1938, under a new AIACR formula, engines were limited to 3 litres blown (4½ litres unblown). Mercedes-Benz and Auto Union both came up with remarkable machines, Mercedes with a 500-hp, blown V-12, Auto Union with a triple-cam-shaft, blown V-12. Alfa tried various engine configurations: a straight-eight, a V-12, and a V-16. Maserati showed up with a blown straight-eight. The Germans remained almost invincible—almost. For the French had developed the 4½-litre Delahayes and Talbots to meet the regulations for unblown machines. With low fuel consumption as compared to such thirsty cars as the Mercedes, which drank a gallon of fuel every 2½ miles, they could save time on pit stops. On a 4½-litre Delahaye that smooth French virtuoso René Dreyfus outdrove Hermann Lang and Rudolf Caracciola on their Mercedes-Benzes to win the Grand Prix of Pau in 1938.

Alfa Romeo turned toward 1½-litre racing with a new supercharged straight-eight which produced a thumping 205 bhp at 7,000 rpm—tremendous for those days. This was the famous Type 158, which was redeveloped after the war to produce almost twice the horsepower. Mercedes-Benz retaliated with a 1,500-cc, 260-bhp V-8 and beat its Axis partner at Tripoli in 1939.

If the cars of those distant pre-World War II days were as different from those of today as the giants of Paris–Madrid were from them (the time in years is about the same), the drivers of those times seem a different breed, too. Although they were not all "gentlemen drivers," as those of the early nineteen-hundreds had been (there had been rather a fuss because the flamboyant Mercedes driver, Camille Jenatzy, was not to the manner born), some of the tradition held, especially in England. The Earl Howe, the Honorable Brian Lewis (now Lord Essendon), the Duke of Richmond and Gordon were among the better-known British drivers in the nineteen-thirties. On the Continent, too, such types were not uncommon. Von Brauchitsch, the Mercedes driver, is one example. Purses and starting money were pittances compared to what modern drivers earn from a deluge of cigarette, camera, even perfume advertisements. The Marlboro cigarette people alone put more than $1 million into racing in 1973.

Many drivers had private incomes. Only superdrivers like Nuvolari and Caracciola made enough money to survive. Their life styles were vastly different from the high-pressure, jet-transported existence of the long-haired mod types who conduct today's grand-prix projectiles. Drivers seldom left Europe

1. Bernd Rosemeyer and Auto Union before 1937 Vanderbilt Cup.
2. Mechanic replenishes Auto Union as Ferdinand Porsche watches.
3. Auto Unions at Vanderbilt Cup used sixteen sparkplugs.
4. Rear engine of Auto Union. Note swastika at far right.
5. American Rex Mays surprisingly took third place
at Vanderbilt Cup in outdated eight-cylinder Alfa Romeo.
6. 1936 Grand Prix Maserati Type 6CM had blown 1½-litre engine.

1

2

3

4

5

6

Top: René Dreyfus
discusses problems with
his teammate in 4½-litre,
twelve-cylinder
grand-prix Type 145
Delahaye racing car which
has been converted to
"sports car" by addition
of lights and mudguards.
Right: Rudolf Caracciola in
1937 W 125 Mercedes-Benz
grand-prix car. This
5.6-litre Mercedes
developed a fantastic
646 hp, had tubular chassis,
torsion-bar suspension.

to race. Getting to a race in America meant a week each way on a ship; now it takes just hours for both car and driver in a jet airplane.

In 1936 and 1937 some of the European cracks journeyed to Long Island to drive on the road-racing circuit at Roosevelt Raceway. Compared to the flamboyant characters in trick hats who race today these seemed quiet and unsophisticated. Nuvolari, for example, although famous as the world's greatest driver, was unknowledgeable in the ways of American press agents. A flack for a Broadway show brought along a cutie he wanted to pose with the little Mantuan. As Nuvolari sat in his Alfa Romeo, the press agent sat the lady on the edge of the Alfa's cockpit and photographers aimed their cameras. Nuvolari made a grab for her and tried to pull her into the car, grinning and saying "*Grazie, grazie.*" I still think he thought she was some kind of unusual American present.

If Nuvolari was unsophisticated in the ways of publicity men, he certainly knew his way around a racecourse. At Roosevelt that year he took his Alfa around the peculiarly pretzel-shaped circuit in seeming boredom but still quicker than anyone else. On corners he seemed not to be trying at all, yet he whistled past drivers squealing their tires and desperately sawing away at their steering wheels.

Many of those outclassed drivers in completely unsuitable cars were Americans used to dirt tracks and to Indianapolis, who had before the race been ridiculously confident of their superiority. Jean-Pierre Wimille in a 4.7-litre Bugatti took second place behind Nuvolari, Antonio Brivio in an Alfa Romeo, third. Sportingly, the British had brought a group of 1,500-cc ERA's to Roosevelt Raceway. They knew that they hadn't a chance against the heavy metal—the Alfas and the Bugattis. But they were pleasantly surprised to find that not a single American machine came in ahead of them.

The Germans—Auto Unions and Mercedes-Benzes—came in full panoply the following year, with tire experts, spark-plug experts, and various other boffins, including Dr. Ferdinand Porsche himself. (An interesting sidelight is the fact that every German machine had a swastika painted upon its flank. Examine photographs of these same Mercedes-Benzes and Auto Unions which their respective press departments issue today and you'll find no such embellishments. They've been retouched out.)

Everything rumored about the Germans was true. Their mechanical finish, their pit work, their organization were unlike any ever seen previously in the United States. And when the Mercedes-Benzes and Auto Unions ran, spectators were stunned, shaken, made breathless by their groundshaking, screaming speed. They won, of course. Bernd Rosemeyer was first in his Auto Union, Richard Seaman in a Mercedes, second. But miracle of miracles, Rex Mays, the American Indianapolis driver, in something called a Bowes Seal-Fast Special squeezed in between a couple of Germans to take third place. That Bowes Seal-Fast Special was really a tired old Alfa Romeo sold to Mays by the Scuderia Ferrari, which handled Alfa's racing team in those days.

It wasn't until almost a decade later, after the war, that grand-prix racing became interesting again. Ettore Bugatti was dead. No Bugatti would make that fine sound of tearing calico on any grand-prix circuit again. Maserati and Alfa Romeo were ready to continue as before. Talbot-Lago was bestirring itself. ERA was still alive. The Germans were still in quod. But there was a great new name to reckon with. Ferrari.

Ferrari, as I've said elsewhere, did not really exist as a manufacturer until after the war. His first grand-prix cars, the 1½-litre Type 125's, first came out for the Italian Grand Prix in 1948. But for the next ten years or more Ferrari's cars were the most important in racing. For a time Alfa Romeo with its potent 1½-litre Type 159, developed from the prewar Type 158, held Ferrari off. When Alfa quit grand-prix racing in 1951, Ferrari had his own way until 1954 when Mercedes-Benz again took to the circuits. Ferrari amazed the racing world by the dazzling proliferation of models he produced to meet varying conditions and regulations, and in 1954 when the grand-prix formula required 2½-litre unsupercharged engines (or 750 cc with a blower) Ferrari was ready. But so were Maserati, Mercedes-Benz, and, of all makers, Lancia. All three gave Ferrari a bad time for a while. Mercedes had a wonderful new car, the 2½-litre Type W196 with desmodromic valve gear (the valves were pushed shut as well as opened by the camshafts). Lancia had a team of V-8 quadruple-camshaft machines with fuel tanks in sponsons on their flanks, and Maserati had its new space-framed 250F.

1

1. "Funny car" with its fiberglass body hinged back. Driver sits in rear behind big supercharged engine. Note elaborate transporter in rear.
2. Tires burn as "funny car" makes run to break them in. Rear wheels are much larger than those in front.
3. Open-wheeled Formula F car undressed for tuning before race.
4. Amateur Sports Car Club of America drivers line up before race at Thompson, Connecticut.
5. Race-readying a home-built dragster.
6. 1908 poster for Bosch magnetos.

Despite this formidable opposition, and drivers like Stirling Moss in the Mercedes and Fangio in the Maserati in 1957 (when he won the driver's championship), Ferrari managed to stay mostly on top until the end of the nineteen-fifties. For Mercedes had quit GP racing in 1955, and Lancia had not only quit but had presented its cars to Ferrari.

Looking back, the *grandes épreuves* of the fifties seem to have been a continuation of a kind of racing which relates more to the thirties than to our time. The cars still had their engines up front, drum brakes were still the norm, and the cars were in most cases the productions of factories which built passenger cars for sale to the public. It was in the fifties, however, that racing became a mass sport, not only on the European Continent but also in Britain and the United States.

It was the not-so-stodgy British who, as the fifties waned, changed the world of grand-prix racing. They ended the day of the big, front-engined machine and made tiny, ultralight, 1,200-pound, chassisless, winged insects the kings of racing. Even Ferrari almost immediately copied the British. And, amazingly, the roughneck drivers and hard-eyed middle-Americans who run

the Indianapolis "brick-yard" had to give up their long-beloved Offenhauser-engined roadsters for the "funny cars," after the late Jimmy Clark came in second in 1963 in his Lotus. As I write this, in March, 1973, the Indy drivers in their Offenhauser-rear-engined funny cars (not to be confused with funny-car drag-sters) are doing test laps at Indianapolis at very close to 200 mph.

A few years ago one of my sons, then about eighteen years old, became the ecstatic owner of a deplorable motor car, a tired and very large 1961 Chevrolet Impala. No sooner had he acquired this jewel than he started improving it. I arrived home one evening to find him and his friends dismembering the Chevy's engine in our not too sanitary driveway. "Let them play," I thought. "They'll never get things together again and that revolting Chevrolet will, happily, go to the junkyard."

But the boys did get the Impala running again, as evidenced by loud noises from its defective exhaust system one Saturday night. The next morning, my son asked if he might drive to the local dragway. "Go ahead," I said, "but don't race

that bomb." He mumbled something and left, paying no attention to my feeble joke.

Late that afternoon, I heard the Chevy's stumbling exhaust note in the driveway again. The boy was back. And he was bearing an atrocious-looking trophy, all imitation marble, plastic eagles, and gilt pot metal. His old Chevy had won its class in a drag race.

How was it possible for such a miserable machine to win anything? Here's how drag racing works. You show up at the dragway with a car, pay a fee—about $5—and you're assigned to a class. The strip is a quarter mile long, plus enough added distance to allow 200-mph cars (with parachutes to aid their brakes) to come to a stop. You always race side by side against one other car in your class, the two of you being called to the starting line at the same time. In front of you is a "Christmas tree" of lights vertically arranged. You watch intently with your engine revving as the lights go on in turn until the green one which means GO is lit. Then you pop the clutch and GO! The car which cuts the electronic beam at the end of the quarter mile wins its heat. The reason my kid's Impala won his class was be-

cause the cars he ran against were, perhaps, even worse than his.

But the "funny cars" and the "slingshot" dragsters, or "rails," which are the stars of drag racing are another matter. These are beautifully constructed. Often they have supercharged engines of 800 hp or more that produce blinding speeds—under 6 seconds for the quarter mile and over 200 mph by the end of the 440-yard run, when braking parachutes are released.

The "slingshots," those long, skinny devices with bicycle-type front wheels, whose drivers sit so far aft that their legs are over the differential gears, now seem to be eclipsed by the "funny cars," which are shortened "slingshots" with more normal front wheels. They wear what appear to be ordinary Detroit bodies that are really light fiberglass replicas which hinge up in one piece to permit engine maintenance and driver ingress.

Famous drivers of these exotic machines do not merely compete for the trophies; some go from drag strip to drag strip, with their machines on elaborate transporters, in order to collect appearance money—often as much as $1,000 for one time.

Stock-car racing is another peculiarly American type

Left: Lancia competing in Press-on-Regardless Rally in northern Michigan. Run at night over back roads and logging trails, this is most rugged American rally.
Right: British "mini" throws snow on Alpine turn in Monte Carlo Rally. Drivers cover 2,000 miles of European roads in January, across the Alps.

Top: Mark Donohue waves as
he wins 1972 Indianapolis 500 at
161.987 mph. Ultralight,
monocoque-bodied race cars like
those universally run in international
grand-prix racing have replaced
the heavy roadsters at Indianapolis.
Many Indy cars still use Offenhauser
engines. Above: Sam Posey
leading through a turn. Rear wing
increases adhesion by creating
down-pressure on tail of car.

of competition. If anyone still believes that these mechanisms are "stock," he will also believe that the car he buys from his Friendly Ford Dealer is capable of 200 mph. Certainly the cars look like Dodges, Chevrolets, Plymouths, and the rest—but only to the beer drinkers in the grandstand. A racing stock car has its doors welded shut. There is no glass in the side windows and the driver is strapped into a cage of strong steel tubing. Engines, clutches, gearboxes, driveshafts, and almost every other component have all been strengthened to racing specifications.

After all, Cale Yarborough *did* average 162.162 mph for 500 miles at the Charlotte, North Carolina, Speedway in 1969, and in a "stock" Ford.

Stock-car racing is as southern as Tennessee sour-mash whiskey. And its T-shirted spectators flock to it by the hundreds of thousands, more than to any other kind of car racing in the US. It's supposed to have been an outgrowth of the kind of racing backwoods southern boys, hauling bootleg whiskey, engaged in when fleeing "revenooers." But it would certainly not have achieved its success without the strong efforts of

promoter Bill France, czar of NASCAR (National Association for Stock Car Auto Racing), who has recently relinquished his throne to his son, Bill, Jr.

Stock-car racing is big business. In 1971, in 1,000 events, total prize money was $5,230,179. Four drivers each won more than $100,000, and Driver Richard Petty won $309,000 (more than £120,000).

The Sports Car Club of America, organized in 1944, was in its early days a club for those Americans who had just discovered the joys of driving MG's and XK120 Jaguars. It organized rallies and nonprofessional races and was a very gentlemanly outfit. Today, as Del Owens, public relations director of the SCCA, says, "We're a multimillion-dollar business—no longer a country-club organization."

The Sports Car Club of America conducts the big-money Can-Am (the Canadian-American Challenge Cup Series), sports-car races in which such international stars as Mark Donohue, George Follmer, and Denis Hulme are involved, the L & M Championship Formula 5000 races for single-seat, open-wheel

cars, where purses range up to $75,000 and attract famous drivers like Graham McRae of New Zealand and England's David Hobbs, and the Trans-Am races for touring and grand-touring machines like Porsches, BMW's, Mustangs, and Corvettes.

But the SCCA still runs club races where the impecunious amateur can enjoy charging around road courses and tracks in a great variety of machines—from Volkswagen-powered, Formula Vee open-wheelers, to the cheapest of sports cars, such as the little bug-eyed Austin-Healey Sprites, Austin mini sedans, and hotted-up Saabs. He must, however, attend SCCA-conducted drivers' schools, where he gets at least six hours of instruction before he can appear on a starting line.

If grand-prix and sports-car racing have become so perverted as to make it difficult to tell just what makes of automobile are racing against each other, this is certainly not true in that rough kind of competition—the rally. For the big international rallies, like the Monte Carlo, the East African Safari, the Acropolis, and various other such car-bashing events, are much used by manufacturers to publicize the virtues of their

passenger cars.

The Monte Carlo is the granddaddy of rallies, having started in 1911, when twenty-two cars made the run. In 1973, there were 298 starters. Only fifty-one cars finished, which should give you some idea of how rugged a thing is the "Monte." It is run in January, when the days are gray and short and the roads snowbound when they're not coated with ice. The cars start from cities all over Europe—Lisbon, Glasgow, Warsaw, Palermo, Stavanger—and head for sunny Monte Carlo over set routes fiendishly calculated to send them some 2,000 miles along the wintry roads of the Continent, and then across the slippery, zigzag arctic passes of the Alps. All this is done against the clock. Cars must reach controls within time limits or lose points, and the navigator must keep his wits about him as he struggles with fearsome mathematical calculations despite sleepless nights, sheer terror, or hate engendered by his partner's personal peculiarities.

So many cars come through this frigid travail that eliminating tests are necessary to narrow down the field to find a winner. In some years this consisted of a sort of "Grand Prix" race run through the streets of Monte Carlo.

In 1973, the "Monte" was run in three parts, the first being the run down to Monte Carlo, the second a twenty-eight-hour run with "special stages" over a road circuit through the rugged terrain from Monaco to Grenoble (the "special stages" are timed sections which demand racing speeds and tough-guy racing tactics). The third part was a test for the sixty crews which had the best times over the second leg. This was an even wilder twelve-hour affair in the mountains behind Monte Carlo with seven "special stages" over three mountain passes. In this last stage there was a loop near the village of Burzet which became blocked with snow after fifty competitors got through. Instead of eliminating the loop, the organizers kept on sending cars in. Chaos resulted. Some excitable crews, angered, went on strike and blocked the road back to Monte Carlo, so no one could finish. One driver, the Finn Timo Mäkinen, wasn't about to let such a small thing as a roadblock hurt his chances. He backed up his little Ford Escort, took a run right at the barrier, and at the last minute swerved and mounted the high bank at the side of the road and went around the blockers. Other drivers went around in other ways—across ditches and through fields, while striking

drivers homicidally pursued them to head them off. In the end, a French crew, J. C. Andruet and a handsome young lady with the *nom de guerre* of "Biche," won in an Alpine Renault.

Although problems with striking, roadblocking drivers are something new, the "Monte" has always posed difficulties for its entrants. Before the war, crews coming from Athens reported that they had been impeded by Balkan peasants who had been breaking up the wooden bridges across rivers for firewood. They had had to work their way down the high, snow-covered banks and cross on the ice. In 1931, Donald Healey, driving an Invicta, skidded on glare ice near his starting point in Norway, struck a telegraph pole, and knocked his rear axle askew. This locked his rear brakes. Healey disconnected the brakes, drove across Europe and the Alps without rear brakes, and won the "Monte" outright.

I have twice been in Monte Carlo to witness the end of the great rally. During one of these visits, a Finnish driver on the team of Plymouth Valiants which ran that year took me for a ride up the old hill-climb route which runs from Monte Carlo to La Turbie. I learned then that the crack someone made about Finnish rally drivers was correct. "These Finns," he said, "get a car sideways on the ice when they leave Helsinki and don't straighten up until they're in Monte Carlo."

American rallies (except for the tough professional Press-On-Regardless Rally run over 2,000 miles of logging trails and back roads in Michigan) are tea parties compared to violent and dangerous rallies like the Monte Carlo. Organized by sports-car clubs, they are weekend jaunts for owners of sports cars who are looking for something less dangerous than racing and more purposefully automotive than merely driving out to the beach. Any kind of car, including the most housewifely American sedan, is suitable, for all speed limits are observed. These rallies are really more like scavenger hunts against the clock than automotive competitions. The winners are usually computer operators or other time-distance mavens who know how to work slide rules, stopwatches, surveying odometers, portable calculators, and similar boring hardware. The last time I became involved in such a rally, the winning team consisted of an engineer and a tax estimator who won a 523-mile run by being only 74 seconds off schedule.

Sports cars for professional racing
are artificial machines unusable on highway.
Top: 1,000-kilometer KLM race. In front
are Clay Regazzoni of Italy, Jacky Ickx
of Belgium, and Tim Schenken of Australia.
Bottom: A pair of French Matra-Simcas
come in first and second at Le Mans.

10

AUTO SHOWS

London held its first "International Exhibition of Motors" in May, 1896. Surprisingly, Paris, which led the world in automobilism, didn't have such an exhibition until a year later. Even then the cars were shown not in an exhibition of their own but in a corner of the *Salon du Cycle*. Bicycles were still far more important than motor cars. The great *Salons de l'Automobile* didn't get started until 1900.

It was also at bicycle shows that American cars were first exhibited. And it was at these shows that the big American bicycle manufacturers first felt the chill winds that in a few years would blow the two-wheelers into limbo. For the crowds that showed up at the cycle shows clustered around the automobiles. The bicycle stands attracted practically no one. Some bicycle builders, however, were canny enough to smell future profits. The names Winton, Pierce, Peerless, Pope, Rambler, among others, would soon move from the steering heads of bicycles to the radiators of cars. (I wouldn't be too surprised, however, to see names like Ford and Chevrolet on some bicycles soon. The bicycle has come back; in 1972, almost as many light two-wheelers were sold in the US as were cars.)

The first automobile exhibition sans bicycles was held in Chicago in September, 1900. Dreamed up by the promotion manager of a Chicago paper, the *Inter-Ocean*, it had a middle-American flavor all its own. Beating the drum for its show, the *Inter-Ocean* promised:

"On the opening day there will be a general parade of nearly five hundred vehicles, with standing and moving exhibitions, when the general public will be allowed to examine the vehicles in and out of the buildings, and ride in them in the parks." All kinds of "tests," "manipulations," "races both forward and backward," and a "ladies' day" were promised.

Twenty vehicles showed up for this outdoor show in Washington Park. And it rained all week.

The first real automobile show was staged indoors in New York's Madison Square Garden a month after the damp debacle in Chicago. Fearful that their show, too, might be less than a resounding success, the promoters, the Automobile Club of America, decided that a mere exhibit of cars might be boring. They thought that it should be proved that the cars could actually go. To this end they built an oval track in the auditorium upon which the machines showed that they not only ran but could be steered around obstacles and stopped when necessary.

The most exciting exhibit was that of John Brisbane Walker, who built Mobile steamers. The flamboyant Mr. Walker showed his car, not in the main hall, but on the roof. There, at great expense, he had built a steep board track which soared up the side of the old Madison Square Garden tower in dizzying curves. Every half hour or so one of his death-defying young drivers zipped the little Mobile steam buggy up into the blue, let it teeter there for a moment and, to prove that it could be braked rearward down a declivity, ran it backward, stopping now and then, down the incline.

Winton, Duryea, Knox, Haynes-Apperson, Locomobile, Pope-Hartford, National, Riker, Packard were among the names at that 1900 show. All are gone now. All.

But the auto shows aren't gone. They're just a little different. The potted palms which decorated the shows until World War II are gone, having given way to architectural abominations of pink plastic and aluminum extrusion. The European shows seem to have retained a decent quiet in which a man can contemplate the machine he wishes he could afford. But such admirable silence is almost universally shattered at American car shows. Slinkily dressed and impossibly curvy young women equipped with microphones parrot the inanities of ad copy writers as they slowly revolve on turntables that bear also the latest styling exercises of the crazed youths who seem to staff the design "studios" of Detroit. The poor girls repeat their litanies over and over, fearfully amplified into the higher reaches of the decibel scale. Happily, they tend to drown each other out.

Another, quieter, ploy of Detroit's marketing geniuses is the bugged car, which is supposed to record the comments of the multitude as it presses close to admire the cars on display. A Detroit minion once complained to me that much of the material on the tapes referred to the gravity-defying bosoms of the young ladies. But this was some years ago, when such attributes were more stylish.

The British give employment to very pretty ladies, too. But this is done only on Press Day—the day before the show opens, when only journalists and press photographers are supposed to be admitted. Recently, I attended such a soirée with

1. View of 1973 New York International Automobile Show.
2. Pretty girl was used as ploy in poster
advertising 1903 de Dion-Bouton car.
3. Straight-laced Russians were the only ones to
use semidressed young ladies to attract
attention to their cars at 1973 New York show. The
girls in the fur bikinis were plugging the new Lada.
4. Tired old party takes rest at auto show.

1

2

4

3

1

2

Exhibitors at London's
"57th Annual Motor Exhibition"
vied with each other to
attract photographers on Press
Day—the day before the
public is admitted to the show.
1. A pair of Oriental cuties
stuffed into the luggage
space of Reliant Scimitar.
2. Mod young lady on a Jaguar.
3. Antique Michelin Tire
Company bus brought a bevy
of leggy girls.
4. Topless miss promoted sunroof.

3

4

my camera. The girls at Jaguar, Lamborghini, Michelin, even at staid iron-curtain Skoda cooperated most admirably in allowing me to pose them in, I must admit, rather trite attitudes. I had less luck at the stand where a removable-top manufacturer was perspicaciously displaying a young woman who had removed *her* top. Large numbers of conservative British photographers were so intent on recording this innovation in coachwork that I had great difficulty getting close enough.

Still, I suppose this artistic approach is better than the zoological one that was tried in New York a few years ago, when some public relations boys laid on a lion to pose with a model, whom it immediately tried to eat.

This embarrassment was perhaps more serious than one I suffered at an earlier New York auto show. This was one of the shows for foreign cars organized by the late Herb Shriner at the time when such machines were still considered peculiar and exotic. I had been asked to appear as a sort of judge to pick the outstanding cars and to award some kind of prize—a cup or

medal—I disremember just what.

I decided to do things in style. At that time I owned the Rolls-Royce I have earlier described, a Springfield P-I with a Brewster Riviera body, a *coupé de ville* in which the chauffeur and footman sat outdoors and the passengers sat in an excruciatingly fancy but ridiculously tiny compartment aft. This passenger section had a lushly upholstered rear seat, accommodating two people, and two minuscle folding jumpseats. This grand equipage was sedately painted primrose yellow and light gray.

I engaged a liveried chauffeur to drive to the show at Grand Central Palace (a footman was beyond my financial abilities) and invited Mr. and Mrs. Austin Clark to accompany my wife and me. Bravely, Clark accepted. We first drove to dinner where we consumed much wine. The chauffeur, standing at attention as he held the door of the yellow Royce open for us after dinner, created a sensation on Second Avenue. The women sat on the rear seat and Clark and I perched on the jumpseats—Clark's facing forward, mine facing sideways so that my back was wedged against the right-hand door.

We arrived at Grand Central Palace in a blinding blaze of lights for the television cameras. A much amplified voice announced, "Mr. and Mrs. Henry Austin Clark and Mr. and Mrs. Ralph Stein in Mr. Stein's Rolls-Royce." A major-domo opened the car door behind me and I rolled out backward and inverted into the gum wrappers and cigarette butts of Lexington Avenue. Some style!

The prize-giving was hardly more successful. Rolls-Royce had just let it be known that their new Bentley Continental would be sold only to people of Superior Social Status. Low types like me could not buy such lordly machines. Would I award a cup to such snobs? I certainly would not. The new four-cylinder Austin-Healey got the prize. Two nabobs from RR who had journeyed from England to New York in full expectation of receiving the cup, empurpled with righteous rage and using very low-class words, told the show's management what they thought of them, of me, and of the thirteen colonies.

The chicken-hearted management immediately found a cup (how they got hold of one at 11 o'clock at night is still a mystery) and awarded the Bentley a *special* prize. And I slunk out to my *American* Rolls-Royce.

11

COLLECTORS

Automobiles are built to go. But there are an awful lot of people who don't think so. To them a motor car is an object to look at, revere, polish, write about, take apart, reassemble, auction, photograph, invest in, collect. But drive one? Hardly ever. At one time we would have called this kind of collector's automobile an antique car. But like almost everything else, things have become more complicated. There are now Classic Cars, Special-Interest Cars, Brass-Age Cars, Vintage Sports Cars, Post-Vintage Thoroughbreds, Replicars, and Historic Commercial Vehicles (a very fancy name indeed for old trucks).

Before World War II, only a very few people—attracted by the lovely look, hand craftsmanship, and shiny brasswork of early cars—bought, refurbished, and drove the old-timers, which then cost little. Those enamored of such early machinery often had the mechanical ability to get the cars into running order. Nor did a prewar automobile seem terribly old in the nineteen-thirties. In 1938 I was offered a very pretty 1914 Panhard-Levassor touring car for $60—not as an antique collector's piece but as a car to use. The man who offered it to me drove it every day in New York. I did not need another car, and although much tempted by the white paint, leather, and brass radiator of the Panhard I commended it to a friend who needed such a multiseated conveyance. Two days after he bought it he transported his wife and many children to Toledo in it.

Sadly, many fine old cars, unsalable even at ridiculously low prices, found untimely ends on the scrap heap. And automotive scrap heaps are almost as old as the automobile. Cars of the eighteen-nineties—Lanchesters, Benzes, and other such automotive incunabula—were ruthlessly junked in the early nineteen-hundreds.

There was, however, a pioneer collector, Edmund Dangerfield, editor of England's *Motor* magazine, who, despite the ridicule of some of his contemporaries, believed that historic early cars ought to be preserved. In 1912, when some of the very first cars were barely twenty-five years old, he founded the world's first car museum on Oxford Street in London. The dislocations caused by World War I brought about the dispersal of the exhibits. Some, luckily, found their way to other museums, but many of the cars, stored out-of-doors, were destroyed.

In 1927 the London *Sunday Graphic* sponsored the first reenactment of the 1896 "Emancipation Run" from London to Brighton. Then called the "old crocks race," it was a bit of a circus, with dressed-up participants, cute names painted on the cars, and other such vulgarities which would cause present-day London–Brighton drivers to blanch with shame. The London–Brighton became respectable in 1930 when the Royal Automobile Club took over its sponsorship.

Also in 1930 three enthusiasts sitting in the saloon bar of the Old Ship Hotel in Brighton organized the Veteran Car Club, the first of its kind in the world. Within a few years similar clubs were formed in the United States. Antique-car collecting was no longer an aberration practiced by a few cracked characters. It was now a respectable and organized pursuit. The clubs held antique-car meets, gave out prizes, and published magazines which not only disseminated information (and some misinformation) about antique motor cars but also carried advertisements of cars and, perhaps equally important, columns of ads offering parts. Other advertisements were piteous appeals for parts needed for restoration.

After World War II the antique-car movement boomed. Car collectors avidly combed the countryside for early machines. In those days—the nineteen-forties—it was still possible to unearth treasures hidden in barns or mouldering in fields. Or even in carriage houses on estates where ancient Rolls-Royces and Pierce-Arrows had been laid to rest under dust covers and forgotten. One pair of collectors friendly with the rich in a fancy East Coast watering place hauled away such treasures as pre-World War I Panhards and Napiers, in many cases merely for the asking.

In the early fifties, a friend of mine, a well-heeled man I'll call Scrivener, with an insatiable desire to own every old car in the world, once invited me along on one of his forays in search of treasure. For such a trip he would doff his Savile Row lounge suit in favor of a pair of greasy coveralls, and hitch a trailer to a disreputable car he kept for the purpose of seeming poor. I joined him on his Westchester County estate and with the trailer clanking behind, we set forth.

Scrivener had a set purpose that day. He was going to revisit places where he had found old machines which for various reasons he had been unable to pry from the clutches of

Preceding pages & right: Early-morning start in Hyde Park of England's annual London to Brighton run for cars built until 1904. More than 200 early cars make the run each year while hundreds of thousands of spectators line the route to watch.

their owners. The first place we visited was in a decayed area of small, wooden row-houses in the Bronx. We stopped in front of one of them and Scrivener knocked on its door. An incredibly frowzy old fellow opened the door and greeted Scrivener with great warmth. In turn, Scrivener greeted him with even more warmth, shaking hands and smiling toothily.

We were invited in. The interior was as I feared. Chairs piled with old clothes, empty bottles on the floor, un-washed dishes here and there.

"How about some wine," said Scrivener's pal, "I made it myself." I demurred. Scrivener accepted and insisted that I do, too. Scrivener not only drank his with relish but praised the awful stuff. (He had a notable cellar at home.) After this cere-mony, the old fellow said, "I guess you want to show your friend my car." Scrivener bounded out of the derelict overstuffed chair he had shared with a pair of old overalls as if one of the chair's loose springs had wounded him.

The old man led us out to his unpainted backyard garage. Scrivener helped pull open the sagging doors. It was dim inside but I was surprised to see that it was not stuffed with trash. Confronting me was a huge car with a towering limousine body.

"What is it?" I asked Scrivener.

"A Simplex," he whispered. "A 1912 Simplex."

I could understand now why Scrivener had been so disgustingly cordial to its owner, why he had drunk that ex-ecrable wine. For Scrivener was not only crazy about old cars, he was positively insane when it came to Simplexes. He already owned two of them but was slavering for more.

I examined the Simplex. It was dirty and the paint was alligatored. The brasswork—huge headlamps, sidelamps, ra-diator—was almost black from oxidation. I opened one of the tall doors to the passenger compartment. The seats, the tapestry trim were covered with mold. I looked at the date of a newspaper covering the floor—1919.

Under the hood lay a four-cylinder engine, big as a couple of tombstones. Foul with grease and dirt, it hissed malevo-lently through its open priming cups when Scrivener's friend turned its crank. "She's nice an' free," he said proudly.

Suddenly he turned to Scrivener. "Mr. Scrivener," he said, "you been coming here for a coupla years to see me and my

1908 60-hp Napier is property of British
automotive journalist Ronald Barker.
Unlike many collectors of antique cars,
Barker does not coddle his
machine. He enters his big Napier in races
and rallies for antique cars,
and roars around the countryside in it.

Famous car restorer Ralph Buckley
about to start 1899 Panhard et Levassor on
which he had been working for more than
a year. Car was almost completed, but he had
not previously tried to start the
engine, which had not been run for sixty
years. It started after two turns of crank.

Simplex. You've made me a nice offer for it. Until now I've kept my promise to my old boss who left the car to me in his will, where it said that I should turn over the motor once a month."

He cranked for a couple of revolutions and went on. "Mr. Scrivener, I just got my New York City tax bill. I need the money. The car is yours."

I expected Scrivener to start writing in his checkbook, but that wasn't his method. Instead he whipped out cash—hundred-dollar bills—and a blank bill of sale. In minutes the Simplex was legally, solidly, incontrovertibly Scrivener's.

After we'd winched the big machine aboard the trailer, we headed back toward Westchester. Remarkably, Scrivener's warm friendship toward the ex-owner of the Simplex had cooled to the extent that he had barely murmured good-bye when we left. All he talked about were the unusual attributes of the Simplex behind us and the low price he'd paid for it. "Imagine, a 50-hp Simplex for one thousand bucks," he gurgled.

"That dough?" I asked. "Why'd you give him cash?"

"So that he couldn't change his mind. If I'd given him a check he might have decided not to cash it and I might not legally own the car. I never give one of these people a chance to back out. I never try to hold a car with a deposit. The only safe way is to pay cash and remove the car immediately."

I didn't see Scrivener or his Simplex again for a year or more. I was then aimlessly following the judges around as they made their very serious examinations of the entries at that greatest of all antique-car meets, at Hershey, Pennsylvania.

Had Scrivener not been so eagerly in evidence near his Simplex, I might not have recognized it. It looked, as could be expected, newer and glossier than it had when it was first delivered in 1912. (I'm not really sure that it looked glossier. In 1912, automobile bodies were varnished over many coats of rubbed-down coach paint. That varnish was shinier than modern finishes but, alas, had a short life. Fancy people had their cars revarnished yearly.)

The judges, delve as they might, found very little to pick on and the Simplex lost few marks. Later in the day I heard that it had won first place in its class.

That's the way things were some twenty years ago. Scrivener had spent $1,000 for his Simplex. Since it was in quite good condition, with no vital bits missing, its restoration by a good professional restorer (of whom there were very few then) had not cost the earth, although Scrivener was a perfectionist.

Unlike some other car collectors, Scrivener had insisted on complete dismantling of the Simplex. The tall body had been lifted off the chassis. Its upholstery had been redone—leather in the chauffeur's quarters and the correct cloth aft. The restorer had even found the right kind of tapestry trim in the stock of an old carriage-supply house. With the upholstery removed, a few rotted places in the wood framing of the body had been discovered. The offending pieces of framework had been removed and used as patterns for new members.

Chassis, engine, transmission, wheels, radiator, lamps, and a hundred other things each received its own treatment, cleaning, polishing, and adjustment. In spite of the Simplex's originally good condition it still took some 1,500 hours of finicking labor to make it a prizewinner. In the early nineteen-fifties such work cost under $4 an hour. Added to this were the outlays for materials: leather, wood, bolts, brass polish, paint, floor mats, a thousand little items. By the time he was ready to drive his Simplex to the Hershey meet, Scrivener had almost $12,000 invested in his gem.

Things are quite different in the nineteen-seventies. The chances of Scrivener finding such a Simplex stashed away in a Bronx garage are almost nil. Nor would anyone sell him one for $1,000. Today everyone has wildly inflated ideas of the worth of even such trash as 1950 DeSotos, let alone such lordly things as Simplexes.

If you're rich and *must* have an early car, the chances are that you'll have to go to a dealer in such vehicles—or, if you're adventurous, to an auction run by one of those great old houses that used to look down their patrician noses at anything but Gainsboroughs, or Georgian silver, or perhaps wooden things by Mr. Chippendale. Sotheby's, Christie's, and Parke-Bernet, plus a dozen others auction Rolls-Royces as well as Rembrandts these days.

A few years ago at such an auction I came early and got a seat. While a rather boring Packard was on the block I noticed a friend, the late, great automotive writer Ken Purdy, standing on the sidelines. I waved a pencil at him. "Sixteen thou-

Acres and acres of cars at Hershey, Pennsylvania,
during world's biggest antique-car
meet. Classic cars now far outnumber brass-age
cars. Right: Huge area is covered by
flea-market where hundreds of vendors haggle with
customers over headlights, speedometers,
radiator shells, and other such valuable junk.

sand dollars from the man in the fourth row," said the auctioneer. Purdy grinned but I was appalled at the prospect of owning that Packard at that frightful price.

Happily, the car went to $18,000-odd and I breathed easier. The point is that if I *had* been saddled with that Packard I could today get twice $16,000 for it.

A year or two ago a Connecticut doctor paid $59,000 for a Type 57 SC Bugatti. It's worth more now. How much? Well, Duesenbergs have touched the $100,000 mark, a 1929 Boat-tail Packard $51,000, and recently a man bought for exhibit one of the numerous Mercedes-Benzes attributed to Adolf Hitler's ownership and paid $153,000 for it.

You'll note that none of these machines is an "antique." They are "classics" of the nineteen-thirties. Oddly, the pre-1914, beautiful, rare, brassbound, gas-lighted cars seem less in demand than the semi-mass-produced classics of pre-World War II. This perhaps is due to the simple fact that there are fewer of the older cars around to *be* in demand; the best of them repose in big collections or in museums.

The machinations of dealers have, I fear, something to do with prices, too. These gentry have managed to inflate artificially the prices of some pretty dull mass-built automobiles by selling them as "investments." Surprisingly, some of these huge Packard and Cadillac touring cars of the twenties and thirties have done better than most common stocks.

I can see one reason why a thirties "classic" may be preferable to a pre-1914 car. It can be driven on the public highway, since it has four-wheel brakes and is capable of keeping up with modern traffic.

Some brave types, notably members of the tiny Pioneer Automobile Touring Club in the US, sometimes take to the road in archaic two-wheel-braked cars, but most owners of such machines haul them around on trailers. In 1953 Scrivener drove his 1912 Simplex to Hershey. Such a trip in such a car from Westchester County to central Pennsylvania would be unthinkable today. Even owners of big classics—1935 Lincolns, 1939 Rolls-Royces—transport their "investments" on trailers. I'm convinced that some of these people would garage their cars in safe-deposit boxes if they could find some big enough.

Dealers have found another sales gimmick. For some years now judges at big meets have scored cars on a 100-maximum point system: so many points off for a dirty speedometer glass, so many off for the wrong kind of floor mat, etc. No car can possibly get 100 points. A score of 95 means that a car is a confection of almost unbelievable perfection, a machine which looks as if it never has had contact with anything so dirty as a human being, and certainly never has had messy things like lubricating oil and grease poured into it. The ideal car for winning points is not a car at all, but a full-sized model of a car.

The gentlemen who deal in antique and classic cars (remember, they're still used-car dealers) talk less about the mechanisms, the ingenuities, the designs of the cars they buy and sell, than about the number of points a car has gained at the last meet. I get the impression that a great clunker of a 1928 Pierce-Arrow with 95 points is more desirable to them than a 1928 Hispano-Suiza with a mere 85 points. Ridiculous!

The point system is one reason why many collectors' cars are so seldom started up, let alone driven. If dirtying up its engine or scuffing up its pedals will take 10 points off a $90,000 Duesenberg's 90 score, it may mean a drop of $10,000 in value for the car. Better keep it jacked up and under cover in an air-conditioned garage and show it only to cocktail-party guests. That way it will be worth more next year.

Not only the rich love great old automobiles. Postwar collectors who couldn't see spending $10,000 or more on some fine old aristocrat—an early Lozier, say, or a Bentley, turned toward Model T and Model A Fords. They were lovely to look at, easy to restore, and not too expensive to buy. But today a restored 1931 Model A Ford Roadster may cost $6,000—a bit much, even if you're the leading plumber in town.

This expensive situation has caused a turn toward American cars mass-produced in the forties and fifties. Buicks, Chevrolets, even Hudsons and Nashes go for high prices. These Detroit clunkers are dignified by the all-embracing name of "Special Interest Cars," and there even exists a magazine which, with deadly seriousness, runs road tests and historical articles about these tired old appliances.

Still, thousands of people labor mightily at restoring such vehicles for which they have paid surprisingly high prices. (I have in front of me a Sunday *New York Times* which offers a

Top left: This display at Hershey flea market
consists entirely of old brass side lamps. A good pair
is now worth several hundred dollars.
Top right: One man's trash is another man's treasure.
Bottom: Judges peer at every hidden
part of 1903 Oldsmobile before deciding if it
has enough points to win a prize.

Upper left: Interior of cylindrical building which houses collection of antique cars at Heritage Plantation of Sandwich, Massachusetts. Lower left: Exterior of reproduction of Shaker barn built to contain Heritage Plantation cars. Below: William Harrah looks down on a tiny part of Harrah's Automobile Collection in Reno, Nevada. More than 1,100 cars comprise world's largest exhibit of antique, classic, and sports cars. Speedboats and airplanes are also on show. About 150 people restore and care for the cars.

"Buick, 1941, Sedanette, $1,395.) These stamped-out conveyances are not easy to restore either—not nearly so easy as cars of sixty years ago.

To really restore a car it is necessary, in my view, to completely disassemble it into its component parts, make each part like new again, and then put all the bits back together. This usually results in a new old car. Such a course, albeit time-consuming, presents no great difficulties in early cars, or even in many of the high-quality hand-assembled cars built in Britain and Europe until fairly recently. Cars as sophisticated as Type 57 Bugattis, P-II Rolls-Royces, or even twelve-cylinder Hispano-Suizas, are amenable to thoughtful and careful unbolting and unscrewing of their corpuses. Really ancient machines, once their fastenings are freed from the grip of rust or corrosion, come apart with amazing ease and rapidity.

This simplicity of disassembly can sometimes lead to trouble. A neighbor of mine once hauled home a small 1910 Pope-Hartford. It was in not too bad condition, all of it being there. Even its headlamps were *in situ*. He asked a few friends, including me, to help him dismantle the car on the following weekend. Meanwhile, following my advice, he liberally anointed every nut, bolt, and screw he could reach with Liquid Wrench.

On the appointed day three of us helped the Pope's owner attack the poor little machine. The lamps, naturally, came off first, were carefully wrapped up (in pillow cases, to my friend's wife's dismay), and brought into the house. Other parts which interfered with the removal of the car's coachwork came off next. The half-dozen or so bolts fastening the body to the chassis were removed in moments. Two of us lifted the body enough for the other helpers to slide planks between the body and chassis. Then the four of us just lifted the planks and carried the body over to a pair of sawhorses prepared nearby.

The chassis, evil-looking with its coating of fifty years of filth, now stood nakedly on jacks. The wheels came off; the radiator was quickly detached from its water lines, unfastened from the chassis, and leaned against a wall. The engine, disconnected from the gearbox and from the chassis, took a bit of muscle to lift out, but by a judicious use of ropes from the garage's rafters and some planks, we soon had it sitting on the floor near the radiator. The rest—transmission, rear end, front axle—came away with only small expected difficulties due to a few immovable nuts and these we split with a cold chisel. I don't think it took more than six hours to reduce that car to a pile of greasy parts (and the four of us to equally greasy objects).

The ease and rapidity of our labors, helped by the simplicity of the Pope, had caused us to make a bad mistake. In our haste we had neglected to carefully note where each bolt and nut had come from and had merely thrown them indiscriminately into boxes. When my friend came to reassemble his car, it was almost a life's work.

It is well-nigh impossible to completely dismantle a modern, assembly-line-generated (it is hard to say "built") "Special-Interest Car." Their bodies, interiors, and chassis are so put together that it is hard to tell where one ends and the other begins. Their coachwork, welded from large sheets of thin pressed steel, can be taken apart only with cutting torches and air chisels, and can be put back together only by welding. Their crude and filthy mechanisms (and I include the innards of those giant Chevrolets and Cadillacs and those even bigger Fords, the Lincolns, built since World War II)—hanging on flaccid rubber and buried in impenetrable jungles of tubing, wiring, and whatnot—are almost impossible to remove from their foul nests. Nothing fits quite right; holes for bolts are not round, but slotted to allow for inevitable misalignment. Plastic parts, pot-metal parts like carburetors, are warped, rotted, and irreparable. I could continue.

There are some people who don't believe in coddling their old cars. These are the members of the Vintage Sports Car Club of Great Britain, and its American counterpart, the Vintage Sports Car Club of America. They not only drive their old sports cars, they flog them unmercifully in races and hill climbs, seemingly not worried overmuch about what terrible damage they might be doing to almost irreplaceable engines and transmissions. The British VSCC, which for some years admitted only pre-1931 machines to its events, relented and formed a classification for "post-vintage thoroughbreds." The Americans have looser qualifications, and quite-late Ferraris and Maseratis of the nineteen-forties and fifties go charging around in races against Type 55 Bugattis and chain-drive Frazer Nashes. (I suppose that any Ferrari seems recent to me. It's hard to realize that some Ferraris have been around for a quarter of a century.)

There are, among devotees of automobilia, many kinds of hobbyists. One group couldn't care less about owning and caring for cars. These people covet brass. Acetylene headlights, kerosene sidelights, horns, speedometers. The shine of polished brass is as a vision of Paradise to them. Big collectors line their homes with cases of the stuff. They have perfected means of removing dents. Some send the more convoluted horns to musical instrument repairers. They know all the formulas for cleaners, brass polishes, protective lacquers (which they mostly disdain). They build weirdly complex motor-driven brass-polishing machinery. They could have drawn and quartered the rich car collector I know who had the brasswork on his cars gold-plated to avoid polishing the stuff. They're crazy.

Then there are the catalogue collectors. They have filing cabinets filled with every possible car catalogue they can buy or trade from other catalogue freaks. Such collections can be worth a small fortune. Imagine what a brochure (if such a thing ever existed) in pristine condition for Karl Benz's first model might be worth. There are similar enthusiasts who love early car advertising. Seventy-year-old (and younger) copies of *Harper's, Leslie's Weekly, Collier's*, and the rest are in grave danger of being knifed to pieces by these boys.

The gentlemen who frighten me are the one-make experts. They become attracted to one kind of car, usually because they own one. They cannot rest until they collect and know *everything* about it. Let's say it's an Ostaczinski Two-Stroke built in Lwow in 1911.

The proud owner of the Ostaczinski Two-Stroke digs into the life story of Rodolfo Ostaczinski, its builder. He exhumes the history of the Ostaczinski clan right back to the first Ostaczinski, who fought the Teutonic Knights in A.D. 1241. He digs into patent-office archives in Vienna, Prague, and Madrid, as well as Warsaw. He finds ancient magazine articles about his beloved marque in Czech, Polish, Rumanian, etc., and has them translated. Within a few years he knows more about Ostaczinski Two-Strokes than any man on earth. He forms an Ostaczinski Owner's Club with himself as president (he has found another Ostaczinski Two-Stroke owner in Buffalo, New York). Then he lies in wait for an innocent automotive journalist to write something foolish about Ostaczinski Two-Strokes, say, that the 1911 Ostaczinski had a thirteen-plate clutch. Then he pounces. He proves that the journalist is an idiot for not knowing that *all* Ostaczinski Two-Strokes had *eleven*-plate clutches.

The typical old-car collector, however, owns a few cars upon which he and his family lavish an unbelievable amount of time, money, and energy. The machines are kept warm, dry, polished. Before being transported to meets they are meticulously cleaned, but the word clean means CLEAN to these types. Every crevice, every invisible cranny is explored with toothbrushes, pipe cleaners, Q-Tips. Mufflers and the nether parts of crankcases are anointed with wax. Brass is made to glitter like the sun. Cleaning a car can take a whole family a week.

Richer collectors keep their cars in specially built, air-conditioned buildings. (A few years ago I saw a building where the cars stood on Oriental rugs.) Hired hands spend their days flicking dust off the machines and looking for nonexistent finger marks on the brasswork. Before a meet they again clean the already spotless cars. Then they load them into closed trailers and transport them to Hershey, or wherever. A well-heeled collector will have several cars entered, necessitating a caravan of trailers. Only after the cars have been set in place at the meet does the owner fly out for the judging. Sometimes the owner avoids the meet entirely, and only deigns to show up at the prize-giving banquet if one of his cars has won an award.

Then, there's the pack-rat collector. He cares not at all about the condition of the cars he owns. His interest is quantity. Mention a type of car and he's happy to tell you, "I own six of those." There is such a fellow who lives near me. He must own a hundred cars which he has stashed away in leaking sheds, chicken houses, and a tumble-down barn. The cars are all rusting ruins, some without bodies, some sans engines, some even lacking wheels. He loves them all and keeps trying to buy more. One such character, lacking space, stored his cars vertically and hadn't seen the cars behind the edges of his collection for years. But he was happy in the knowledge that he owned some very rare, if invisible, machines.

There are, in many countries, collections grown so huge, so expensive to maintain, that it has become necessary for their owners to turn them into commercial enterprises, to open

Lord Montagu of Beaulieu
contemplates his National
Motor Museum in
Beaulieu, England. In
foreground is a corner of
exhibit of World's
Land Speed Record cars. In
middle distance, 1907
Napier, 1930 Bentley, and 1933
Alfa Romeo are visible.
Early London bus can be seen
behind Alfa Romeo.
Large collection of motorcycles
is also displayed.

them to the public and charge admission.

The biggest of these great museums is the Harrah Automobile Collection in Sparks, Nevada, near Reno. Mr. William Harrah, who started with a 1911 Maxwell and a 1911 Ford in 1948, now has 1,100 cars on display in his ten-acre, thirteen-building fiefdom (allied to his other interests which include huge gambling complexes and hotels in Reno and Lake Tahoe). To say that about 150 people are involved with the cars (rebuilding, painting, striping, researching, running a big automotive library, selling tickets), or that more than 250,000 people pay to see the cars each year, conveys little. Certainly the numbers are impressive. But what impresses most is the sheer quality of the whole operation.

The spaces in which Harrah's cars are restored are as clean as operating rooms. When a car is being assembled each part is almost surgically sanitary. Before this stage is reached there is no doubt whatever that the parts, the paint, the upholstery, and top are absolutely correct. For as soon as it is decided that a car is to receive the full Harrah treatment, a program of intensive research is started. The results of this research, plus any and all documents relating to the particular car, are bound into a book which stays with the machine while it is being operated on by the mechanics in their white coats. Books I've seen even had chips of the car's original paint bound into them. And great care was taken to insure that the chip came from hidden crevices where later repaintings or fading had had no effect. No detail escapes the scrutiny of the Harrah's restorers.

Mr. Harrah's aim is historical. He wishes to preserve the history of the motor car by actually preserving the cars themselves (the museum is also a fine way of promoting the gambling casinos). The emphasis is on American cars; there are hundreds of Fords, Packards, and Franklins. Only about ten percent are foreign, but ten percent of 1,100 cars means that there are quite a few Bugattis, Rolls-Royces, Alfa Romeos, and the rest of Europe's cream.

There are, of course, other notable museums in the United States. One that particularly delights me, not only because of its remarkably good although not huge collection, is that organized by Josiah Lilly III at his Heritage Plantation in Sandwich, Massachusetts, on Cape Cod. Set in an exquisitely land-scaped park, the cars are housed in a stone-by-stone reproduction of a drum-shaped nineteenth-century Shaker barn.

There is no shortage of car museums abroad. But there is no doubt about which one is, by far, the most important. This is the National Motor Museum in Beaulieu (pronounced Bewley), Hampshire, about ninety miles from London, not far from Southampton. The National Motor Museum was originally called the Montagu Motor Museum after the supercharged young Lord Montagu who organized it in 1952 and installed its exhibits in a building near the stately home he both lives in and opens to paying visitors.

Today's Motor Museum is a joint venture of Lord Montagu and British industry, which forked up millions of pounds to build the complex of stunning new buildings, parking areas, library, research center, and other projects dreamed up by the fertile brain of his young Lordship. (The monorail which is to run through the grounds and past the ruined thirteenth-century Cisterian abbey and then through the main exhibition hall is not yet complete.)

The cars are, however, the main attraction. A Hall of Fame exhibits the cars of the great pioneers: an 1899 Daimler, a 1909 Rolls-Royce Silver Ghost, a 1913 Prince Henry Vauxhall, and other nobility of motordom. I don't intend to list the phalanxes of other automobilia on display, but notable cars are an 1898 Cannstatt Daimler, a 1906 Renault, a 1920 Stanley Steamer, a 1937 Chrysler Airflow. World-land-speed-record cars are there, too. Among these are the 350-hp Sunbeam driven by Sir Malcolm Campbell, Sir Henry Segrave's "Golden Arrow," Donald Campbell's "Bluebird." Further, there are thirty-four sports and racing cars, early Bugattis, Alfa Romeos. Fifty-five historic motorcycles, plus early buses, trucks, and even horse-drawn equipages add to the wheeled glitter of this very discriminating collection.

Car collectors are not really much crazier than the people who collect other artifacts. They only seem so because the objects they collect are bigger and showier and usually noisier (if they're running) than stamps or coins or Picassos. Are the hoarders of inoperable Victorian cameras, early American barbed wire, and glass telephone-pole insulators any less nutty?

AFTERWORD

The entire history of the automobile, from Gottlieb Daimler's and Karl Benz's feeble and faltering gas buggies, to the sure, sleek, and speedy road expresses of today, spans but a lifetime. Many a man now alive clearly remembers the days when the air was pure, and the roar of the expressway was not heard in the land.

But that hardy octogenarian can tell us about other less felicitous things. About the crash and rattle of iron-shod wagon wheels on city cobblestones, about the horse-generated effluvium which slimed streets and bred disease-carrying flies. Above all, he can tell us about his dependence on trolley cars—or, if he lived beyond the range of the tracks, about his frustrating feeling of imprisonment in a narrow and backward rural world.

At the turn of the century, young men like him happily, albeit very cautiously, entered the new world which was opened to them by the automobile. And now a new breed of men, the designers and builders of cars, fought each other in the drawing office and in the factory for preeminent success in supplying that new boon to mankind—the automobile.

Some turned toward building cars for the millions and succeeded beyond their imaginations. Others, perfectionists, saw the automobile not only as a means of making stupendous amounts of money, but also as a way of satisfying their instincts for building fine mechanisms. Artists in metal, like Ettore Bugatti or Henry Royce, were most certainly interested in money, but not at the expense of their aspirations toward constructing cars which pleased them as much (or more) than they pleased their customers.

In the preceding pages I have tried to concern myself not only with the fascinating evolution of the automobile, but also with those areas of our society which have been so strongly influenced by it. Obviously, the automobile is inextricably entwined with our lives. Today it is under attack—for polluting, for crowding our cities—and radical changes in engineering can be expected. What will the car be like, say, ten years hence?

The automobile will certainly become smaller, lighter. Thus, it will require a smaller and less powerful engine, which will contribute a lesser amount of polluting residues to the atmosphere. This engine will, in one way or another, burn hydrocarbon fuel, but new ways will be found to burn it more cleanly. Perhaps it will be a gas turbine, which thus far does that job best.

The engine may be neither in the front nor in the rear, but may end up as a flat package beneath the car's floor. The car's body may no longer be of metal; new, undentable, springy plastics are already in use for some body components. New, more positive means of steering—the Citroën SM points the way—will inevitably supplement the vague and flaccid systems that steer most of today's cars.

But this is not the kind of machine I foresee as being ideal in cities. There, I think, the future lies with the quiet, odorless electric car.

The average speed in cities is hardly more than 20 mph. The average day's run *inside* a city is barely over fifty miles. Why not, then, stop the hydrocarbon car at the city's edge and rent a tiny, nonpolluting electric car for town use? Taxis, too, could be electric, as could delivery trucks. (Some electric trucks, fifty years old, are still in use in New York.) Even the old-time lead-acid batteries, which propelled a car at no more than 25 mph for fifty-odd miles, would still work fine. New types of batteries already in existence are still expensive, but mass use would make them economically viable.

As for me, what kind of car would I like to drive ten years hence? I'd still want a fairly old-fashioned type, say, a 2.3-litre, twin-cam, supercharged Alfa Romeo of about 1933.

Unless they make me pedal my tricycle.

PICTURE CREDITS

DPL   Detroit Public Library, Automotive History Collection
NMM   National Motor Museum, Beaulieu, England
RS   Ralph Stein

Cover & page 2: RS, courtesy of Ed Bond. 5: DPL. 6: RS.

Chapter 1

10-11: RS. 14-15: Zumbach Motor Repair Co. 16: RS Collection. 18-19: RS. 20-21: RS Collection. 22, 23: RS. 24: RS Collection.

Chapter 2

26-27: Charles Dollfus. 30-31: (1) RS Collection; (2, 3, 4) Museo Nazionale della Scienza Tecnica Leonardo da Vinci, Milan; (5) Charles Dollfus. 32: Charles Dollfus. 34-35: (1, 3) Charles Dollfus; (2) Radio Times Hulton Library. 36: Radio Times Hulton Library. 37: RS Collection. 38-39: (1, 2) RS; (3) *Autocar*.

Chapter 3

42-43: RS. 45: Rolls-Royce Ltd. 46-47: RS, courtesy NMM. 48-49: Rolls-Royce Ltd. 50-51: RS. 53: (1, 2, 3) Rolls-Royce Ltd.; (4) RS. 54: (top) NMM; (bottom) RS. 56: Rolls-Royce Ltd. 57: RS. 58-59: RS, courtesy NMM. 60: *Autocar*. 63: RS, courtesy NMM. 64-65: (1, 2) NMM; (3) *Autocar*; (4) British Leyland Motor Corp. Ltd. 66-67: RS; (2) courtesy NMM. 68: (1, 2) NMM; (3) *Autocar*. 70-71: RS. 73: (1, 2) DPL; (3) RS Collection. 74-75: RS. 76: NMM.

Chapter 4

78-79: RS. 81: (top) S. Smith & Sons Ltd; (bottom) RS Collection. 82: RS, (1, 2) courtesy NMM. 83: RS Collection. 84-85: S. Smith & Sons Ltd. 86-87: RS, (3, 4) courtesy NMM. 88-89: S. Smith & Sons Ltd.

Chapter 5

90-91: RS. 94-95: RS, courtesy NMM; (poster) NMM. 96: (1, 4) RS Collection; (2, 3) NMM; (5) *Autocar*. 99: (1) NMM; (2, 3, 4) RS Collection; (4) RS. 102-103: RS. 105: (1, 2) *Autocar*; (3) Mercedes-Benz of North America. 106: RS. 108: (1, 3) Jacques Rousseau; (2) RS Collection. 110-111: RS. 112-113: (1, 2) NMM; (3) RS Collection. 114-115: (1, 3, 4) RS; (2) *Autocar*. 118-119: (1, 2, 3) Citroën S.A.; (4) RS.

Chapter 6

122-123: NMM. 124-125: Brown Bros. 126-127: (1, 2) RS Collection; (3) Culver Pictures; (4) *Autocar*. 128: New York Public Library. 129: Culver Photos.

Chapter 7

130-131, 133, 134-135: DPL. 135: (top) DPL; (bottom) New York Public Library. 136: Long Island Automotive Museum. 137: DPL. 138: Exxon Corp. 139: RS Collection. 140: (top) Exxon Corp.; (bottom) Long Island Automotive Museum.

Chapter 8

142-143: RS. 145: Jacques Rousseau. 146: RS. 148-149: British Leyland Motor Corp. Ltd. 150-151: (1, 2) British Leyland Motor Corp. Ltd.; (3) Group Lotus Car Companies Ltd.; (4) RS Collection; (5) RS; (6) Aston Martin Lagonda Ltd. 153: (top) *Autocar*; (bottom) RS Collection. 154-155: RS, courtesy NMM. 158-159: RS. 160-161: British Leyland Motor Corp. Ltd. 162: RS, courtesy NMM. 163: RS. 164-165: (1) RS; (2) AC Cars Ltd.; (3) Jacques Rousseau. 166-167: RS. 170: (top & middle) RS; (bottom) NMM. 174-175: RS, (4) courtesy NMM. 178-179, 180, 182-183: RS. 184: Carrozzeria Pininfarina. 186-187, 191, 193, 194: RS. 196: Porsche-Audi.

Chapter 9

198-199, 202: RS. 205: (1, 4) NMM; (2) Régie Nationale des Usines Renault; (3, 5) DPL. 207: RS. 208: (top) NMM; (bottom) Mercedes-Benz of North America. 210-211: (1, 5) RS; (6) RS Collection. 212: M. F. Schoenhofen. 213: British Leyland Motor Corp. Ltd. 214-215: (top) UPI; (bottom) Michael R. Sesit. 216: UPI.

Chapter 10

218-219: *Autocar*. 221: DPL. 222-223: (1, 4) Albert Squillace; (2) RS Collection; (3) RS. 224-225: RS.

Chapter 11

226-227: RS. 229: UPI. 230-231: RS. 232: RS. 234-235, 237: Ron Nelson. 238: Heritage Plantation of Sandwich, Massachusetts. 239, 242-243: RS.

INDEX